"My father, Ted Williams, firmly believed, 'Perfection is attainable if you dare to work hard enough.' I applaud Anne Keene for capturing the untold historical facts of the first group of men who were sent to Chapel Hill for this pathbreaking naval aviation training program. Coupled with fantastic photos (many of my father, which I had never seen), the stories come to life with amazement in *The Cloudbuster Nine*."

—CLAUDIA WILLIAMS, author, *Ted Williams, My Father*

"Anne Keene's remarkable *The Cloudbuster Nine* is a terrific piece of research into a forgotten corner of American history—a place where the myths of major-league baseball intersect with the myths of the Second World War. It is also a place inhabited by her own father, who becomes the myth that ties it all together. An excellent read!"

—S. C. GWYNNE, author of *New York Times* bestsellers *Rebel Yell* and *Empire of the Summer Moon*, finalist for the Pulitzer Prize

"*The Cloudbuster Nine* is a captivating look at a fascinating piece of baseball—and American history. Hats off to Anne Keene for unearthing this story, and writing it down for us all!"

—SCOTT ELLSWORTH, *New York Times* bestselling author of *The Secret Game*

"Just when you think you've read quite enough about baseball and WWII the Big One—thank you!—along comes Anne Keene, and you realize there will always be one more great story, lovingly told."

—ROB NEYER, author of *Powerball: Anatomy of a Modern Baseball Game*, 2018 Casey Award Winner

"*The Cloudbuster Nine* is a superb historic read that will inspire athletically gifted young men to also Patriotically Fly in Naval Aviation."

—DAN PEDERSEN, author of *Topgun: An American Story*

"An important story enriched by solid research and authorial commitment."

"Nearly two decades after his death, we are still discovering how remarkable Ted Williams was—yes, as a ballplayer, but also as a man. *The Cloudbuster Nine* not only adds to that story, but reminds us how essential baseball was and still is to America, especially in a time of crisis. Teddy Ballgame was one of millions who deeply loved baseball and that passion, played out on thousands of dusty fields around the country, helped us win a war."

—TOM CLAVIN, *New York Times* bestselling
author and co-author of *Being Ted Williams*

"In the 14 years I knew Ted, I was one of the few who constantly asked about his military service. Keene did an outstanding job researching and writing about it. Her information was right on the money!"

—DAVID McCARTHY, Executive Director of
The Ted Williams Museum and Hitters Hall of Fame

"Finally, there is a book about the only time North Carolina was No. 1 in professional baseball in *The Cloudbuster Nine*."
—D.G. MARTIN, author and host of "North Carolina Bookwatch"

Among 12 authors nominated for the CASEY Award for the *"Best Baseball Book* of 2018."

—*Spitball Magazine*

Named among top "12 Titles for the New Baseball Season."
—*Newsday magazine*

"If you like history and baseball, this is a solid read."
—*New York Post*

Featured on *FOX and Friends* as a Father's Day gift idea

"A great read wrapped around two of my loves—aviation and baseball."
　　—Lt. Gen. ROBERT "BOOMER" MILSTEAD JR., USMC (RET.)

"This is a wonderful book for all baseball fans: a warm, rich personal story of America in the WWII era, a tale of boyhood, heroes, war, respect, and remembrance. I loved it."
　　　　　　　　　　　　—NOEL HYND, author of *The Final Game at Ebbets Field* and *The Giants of the Polo Grounds*

"As a cultural, documentary photographer I can appreciate Anne Keene's account of America's greatest sport and its connection to America's greatest generation. Her book 'illustrates' in meticulously researched prose how major-league baseball's best players chose to wear the Jersey of the Navy, as they trained to become elite fighter pilots. These athletes approached their new mission in the same manner as they trained as athletes—with their body and soul. I gained not only new knowledge but a deep respect for these brave heroes."
　　　　　　　　　　　—IRA BLOCK, author of *Cuba Loves: A Photographic Journey*

"Well-written and impeccably researched, this captivating book offers new insights into the training that forged some of the most fabled members of the 'Greatest Generation.' *The Cloudbuster Nine* opens a new window into baseball that would appeal to any military buff, and to readers looking for a compelling family memoir."
　　　　　　　　　　　—BILL NOWLIN, author or editor of more than 70 books on baseball including *Ted Williams at War*

# THE
# CLOUDBUSTER NINE

## THE UNTOLD STORY OF TED WILLIAMS AND THE BASEBALL TEAM THAT HELPED WIN WORLD WAR II

### ANNE R. KEENE

**FOREWORD BY CLAUDIA WILLIAMS**

SPORTS PUBLISHING

Sports Publishing books may be purchased in bulk at special discounts for sales promotion, corporate gifts, fund-raising, or educational purposes. Special editions can also be created to specifications. For details, contact the Special Sales Department, Sports Publishing, 307 West 36th Street, 11th Floor, New York, NY 10018 or sportspubbooks@skyhorsepublishing.com.

Sports Publishing® is a registered trademark of Skyhorse Publishing, Inc.®, a Delaware corporation.

Visit our website at www.sportspubbooks.com.

10 9 8 7

Library of Congress Cataloging-in-Publication Data is available on file.

Cover design by Brian Peterson
Cover photo of Cloudbusters team and all photos in insert courtesy of The United States Navy Pre-Flight School (University of North Carolina) Photographic Collection #P0027, North Carolina Collection Photographic Archives, The Wilson Library, University of North Carolina at Chapel Hill, unless otherwise noted.

ISBN: 978-1-68358-362-2
Ebook ISBN: 978-1-68358-208-3

Printed in China

*To every man and woman who has served our nation in uniform and to the members of the Cloudbusters baseball team.*

# CONTENTS

# PROLOGUE

### Babe's Yanklands versus the Navy Pilots
### July 28, 1943

In mid-July 1943, the United Press wire service carried a report about a doubleheader like no other at Yankee Stadium. The story was about a team of budding fighter pilots from a North Carolina Navy base, scheduled to face a hodge-podge team of players culled from the New York Yankees and Cleveland Indians to raise funds for the Red Cross. This hand-picked major-league team was called the "Yanklands," and they were going to be managed by the greatest baseball star in the galaxy, Babe Ruth.[1]

The July 28 game was the second major War Relief game of the season organized by professional baseball to swell contributions to the war effort. After dismal attendance at a recent exhibition, Yankees president Ed Barrow turned to the one and only man who could pack the stadium to the rafters. The Bambino had hungered to manage a team for well over a decade, and he viewed his Yanklands as a job audition, longing to return as the boss of everything, if only for one day.[2]

The Navy pilots wore generic wool jerseys, with NAVY stitched across the chests in blue letters and North Carolina patches on the

---

[1] United Press, July 17, 1943.
[2] Associated Press, July 24, 1943.

sleeves. They played for a team with a quirky, weather-inspired name known as the "Cloudbusters," earning a reputation as one of the best service-league teams to step between the lines.

During the war, nearly 25 major-league players, including a few future Hall of Famers, found themselves in classrooms and on training fields at this naval base for pilots at the University of North Carolina at Chapel Hill.

In the season of 1943, the Cloudbusters played a grand total of 45 games, picked up in sports columns making their way to the South Pacific. By the end of the war, the team's name had vanished from the headlines.[3]

Cloudbusters players scheduled to face Babe's Yanklands included Red Sox stars Ted Williams and Johnny Pesky; pitcher Johnny Sain and his Boston Braves teammate Lewis "Buddy" Gremp, an infielder; and Joe Coleman, a hurler from the Philadelphia Athletics. The captain of the team was Yankees first baseman and hometown favorite Buddy Hassett. Harry Craft, who won a 1940 World Series title with the Cincinnati Reds, played center field. Other Cloudbusters included former Red Sox, Yankees, and Reds outfielder Dusty Cooke; Ray Stoviak, who had played for the Phillies; Ed Moriarty, who had played for the Boston Braves; and former Senator Alex Sabo, who was scheduled to catch. Eddie Rommel, a contemporary of Ruth's who was father of the modern knuckleball, was called in to umpire.[4]

Without earning an extra dime, the flyboys defied gas and tire rationing, logging thousands of miles on cramped tin-can buses to play colleges and military teams. The 'Busters also played rag-tag collections of no-name shipbuilders and even factory workers who built the planes fighting in the war, and they played some of the best professional outfits in North Carolina, including the darling of the Piedmont League, the Durham Bulls.

Near the end of the season, the Cloudbusters were thrilled to

---

[3] A *Daily Tar Heel* story notes that team won 32, lost 13 games in the 1943 season, October 9, 1943, p. 3.

[4] *New York Times,* July 25, 1943, p. S3.

play at the "House that Ruth Built," yet as the team barreled up the highway toward New York, its players could not help but wonder if they survived the war, would the Yanklands game be their swan song in a major-league park?

As soon as the Yankees organization announced the game, the media focused on two left-handed hitters—Babe Ruth and Ted Williams.[5]

Two of the world's greatest hitters met in person for the very first time at Fenway Park on July 12, when Ted was cleared by the Bureau of Naval Personnel to appear at a special All-Star benefit with Ruth to raise funds for underprivileged kids.[6] The mayor of Boston, Maurice Tobin, had personally lobbied to lure Ted back to town. The media blitz was tremendous. Back on his home turf at Fenway, Ted stepped out in his baggy 1942 Red Sox traveling uniform and knocked the hide off the ball. He smacked three home runs in a pregame contest against Ruth and then belted a tie-breaking home run into the center-field stands in the exhibition game that followed as the All-Stars beat Casey Stengel's Braves, 9–8. His bespectacled Red Sox teammate Dom "The Little Professor" DiMaggio, another Navy trainee, also thrilled the crowd with a two-run triple, but poor old Babe showed his age at the plate, and he felt like a fool.[7]

When Babe's trick knee acted up, he chopped at the ball like a bloated old codger, stomping off the field in a fit of frustration. In typical bulldog fashion, Babe snorted around the locker room with a black cigar. With a hoarse voice, he swore to *Boston Globe* reporters Fred Barry and Mel Webb that his appearance at the All-Star Game would be his last.[8]

---

[5] Associated Press wire story, July 13, 1943.

[6] Bill Nowlin, *Ted Williams at War*, Rounder Books, 1997, p. 42. BUPERS telegram from Chief of Navy Personnel to Lieutenant Commander C. S. Appleby, Aide to BUPERS, Chapel Hill, 1943.

[7] *The Sporting News*, July 22, 1943, p. 18.

[8] Fred Barry, *Boston Globe*, July 13, 1943. (Also swore he'd never wear uniform again to Mel Webb, *Boston Globe*.)

Babe's temper thawed after he threw back a few drinks that night at the Hotel Kenmore when he serenaded the crowd with "Let Me Call You Sweetheart," bragging that his team was going to whip the Navy pilots at the end of the month.[9]

To gin up ticket sales, the Yankees' press office trumpeted Babe's role as the "pilot for his Yanklands." The *St. Louis Post-Dispatch*'s Short Waves sports columnist hailed the retired home run king's patriotic return as a manager.[10] *New York Sun* sportswriter Frank Graham, who had covered New York baseball since 1915, pumped out teasers about Cloudbusters who had worn the Yankees jersey, like Buddy Hassett, a hometown boy returning as a Navy lieutenant, and Dusty Cooke, coming back as a pharmacist's mate third class.

But in times of war, military games could be canceled for no specific reason and players could be detained on base at the last minute for training. Celebrity players faced the greatest scrutiny, and fans' hearts sank when Williams's commanding officer announced that he would *not* make the trip to New York for reasons beyond his control.[11]

As Yanklands gossip lit up the sports pages, the Cloudbusters stayed busy in North Carolina, training all day in a heat wave, taking classes, then loading up on the bus with aching bones to play double duty baseball at night. On July 24, the pilots rallied for five runs in the last two innings of a game against the Burlington Mills Weavers factory team, 9–4, before a crowd of 3,000 fans for their 22nd victory in 26 games.

On July 27, UP posted another news flash, confirming the names of 22 Yankees and Indians players chosen by Babe to man his Yanklands. When the Sultan of Swat announced that he *might* step in as player number 23, papers blasted the news from the shores of Honolulu to the steel mills of Sandusky, Ohio.

---

[9] *Boston Daily Record, Boston Globe,* and *Boston Traveler,* July 13, 1943, and poet laureate Dick Flavin's article, "The Day Ted and Babe Squared Off," which ran in Red Sox program in the summer of 2000.

[10] "Shortwaves," *St. Louis Post-Dispatch,* July 24, 1943, p. 6.

[11] *The Harris Telegraph,* July 20, 1943, p. 13.

During the war, Babe Ruth was the ultimate patriotic symbol, joining the bald eagle and the American flag. He knocked on doors to raise Red Cross funds, sold war bonds over the radio, donated baseball films to the Navy, and knew how to make an audience root for team U.S.A.[12] Barrow and Ruth made sure the patriotic War Relief benefit had all the bells and whistles to build a crowd. Captain Sutherland's Seventh Regiment band, with its plumed hats and military uniforms, was booked to perform before the first regularly scheduled Yankees-Indians game at 1 p.m. Relay races and a fun-go-bat hitting contest were organized to raise funds for war bonds before the Yanklands exhibition that afternoon. A collectable red, white, and blue souvenir scorecard was produced for ten cents a copy by the company founded by concessionaire extraordinaire Harry M. Stevens, who introduced the hotdog to ballparks.[13] Centered on the cover was an image of a Yankees slugger, bannered by an American eagle and a band of stars. A stable of companies promoting ballpark delights such as Gulden's mustard, Schrafft's chocolates, and Beech-Nut gum purchased advertisements. The Yankees' preferred hotels, such as The Hotel Astor and The Commodore, advertised rooms at special rates for the game, and Benny Goodman, "The King of Swing," promoted his rooftop orchestra beside Uncle Sam's callouts to buy war bonds.

With cars running on fumes and restricted train service, there were no luxury Pullmans or dining cars with fancy china for the Navy coaches and their cadets. Faced with a 48-hour window to return to base, the pilots took an overnight bus to the city, cranking up the highway at a breakneck "victory speed" of 35 miles per hour.[14] Players were beaten down, bruised, and exhausted from the constant

---

[12] Marshal Smelser, *The Life That Ruth Built: A Biography*, University of Nebraska Press, 1975, p. 526.

[13] Marty Appel, *Pinstripe Empire: The New York Yankees from Before Babe to After the Boss*, Bloomsbury USA, 2012, p. 20.

[14] Regarding "48-hour time limit" to return to base. Official U.S. Navy Press Release, August 7, 1942, Physical Fitness Correspondence, Command File.

grind of drills and training. Combat boots rubbed their feet raw with blisters and blackened their toenails; their hands were calloused from climbing cargo nets and swinging axes to cut timber for the base; and scratches webbed their arms from bug bites and poison ivy from overnight hikes. Some players' faces stung so badly from sunburn that it hurt to smile, but as soon as they laid eyes on Yankee Stadium, standing like a concrete mountain over the Bronx, the pain melted away like a dime ice cream cone.[15]

The gates opened at 11 a.m. for the doubleheader festivities, and the Indians easily defeated the Yankees, 6–2, in the first game. When Babe Ruth and Lieutenant Donald Kepler, the coach of the Cloudbusters, stepped out on the field to exchange the lineups for the Yanklands and the Busters, they were swarmed by 100 photographers and reporters. With flashbulbs exploding around them, some of the reporters were unaware of the biggest surprise, who awaited in the clubhouse.

That day temperatures hit 91 degrees. It was still perfect ballpark weather with clear blue skies as 27,281 fans clicked through turnstiles at Yankee Stadium, where a soft breeze stirred American flags and red, white, and blue bunting. Defense workers fresh off afternoon shifts were in the grandstands wearing canvas jumpers from shipyards and munitions plants where they pumped out shell casings. Kids were ecstatic as they sang "Anchors Aweigh" with Captain Sutherland's band, as lines of cabbies wrapped around the ballpark to listen to a play-by-play account of one of the most anticipated games of the season.

No one noticed that they were drenched in sweat and sunburned when they took the roof down with cheers as the Navy fliers barreled out of the concrete chute, with Ted Williams, who was on the overnight bus after all.

Ruth added an artistic touch to the game to make it his own. That day, he replaced Joe McCarthy of the Yankees and Lou Boudreau of the Indians with Coaches Art Fletcher and Del Baker.

---

[15] *Dime ice cream cone* term used commonly by Babe Ruth, Associated Press, July 29, 1943.

Feeling bold, Babe had another trick up his sleeve as he surveyed the crowd, pondering his promise to step up to the plate for an at-bat.

The Yanklands game did not break records at the box office. It fell short of the attendance goal of 70,000, but for other reasons that exhibit was prominently mentioned in biographies of Babe Ruth and Ted Williams, as well as every famous ballplayer who wore the Cloudbusters jersey.[16]

Seventy-five years after that game, Ivan Fleser, the sole survivor of that 1943 Cloudbusters team, described the Yanklands exhibit as an All-American "homecoming," reminding baseball fans of the way of life the pilots were fighting for.

When I journeyed back to one of baseball's most elegant eras, this 96-year-old pitcher explained why the Cloudbusters were glorified one day in the *New York Times*, then rarely mentioned again. Ivan knew why military games were canceled at the last minute. He also explained why cadets like Ted were often kept on base and knew why the Navy baseball team was rarely captured in civilian photographs and never mentioned in diaries.[17]

At the Yanklands game, Ted Williams and the Navy pilots shined, and the rafters trembled when Babe Ruth trundled up to the plate with a big chew in his mouth, twirling a bat.

Though Babe did not realize it at the time, that game was his swan song, and it would go down in history as his last at-bat appearance in his number 3 pinstriped jersey at Yankee Stadium. Patriotic collectables from that game pop up at auction houses to this day. Unusual lore about the Yanklands benefit also lives on, including a tale about a sportswriter who bronzed one of the most bizarre souvenirs ever passed down from Babe Ruth at a game. Young sportswriters like Arthur Daley, who would win a Pulitzer Prize for the *New York Times*, wrote emotional columns about that charity game with

---

[16] Marshall Smelser, *The Life That Ruth Built: A Biography*, University of Nebraska Press, 1975, pp. 525–526.

[17] The Navy strictly prohibited diaries. Personal photography was banned in many areas of bases, even sports fields.

great affection because they knew the Yanklands game, with its suspense and unfilled seats, symbolized the generosity of the human spirit, when everyone (kids, factory workers, professional baseball management, the Babe, Navy pilots, and the press who paid their way into the park) banded together and sacrificed to win the war.[18]

---

[18] Arthur Daley, "The Babe Comes Home," Sports of the Times, *New York Times*, July 28, 1943, p. 20.

# INTRODUCTION

This book was born on a cold winter evening, a few days after Christmas in 2013, when I opened a metal trunk holding the keys to one of baseball's greatest untold stories. It harks back to the golden age of baseball when minor- and major-league players sacrificed the best years of their careers to serve Uncle Sam, and they served willingly, by the thousands. When I searched through the battered old trunk for clues to write my father's eulogy, I knew two things about him— he loved baseball, but he was haunted by his decision to leave the game he loved for reasons he never explained.

The trunk had been sealed since the early 1960s, when he threw his last pitch. Buried under a mountain of newspaper clippings and collectable baseball cards was a tattered scrapbook from World War II, displaying pictures of the immortals of baseball, staring back at me from another century. For the next two hours, I sat on a cold concrete floor in the basement, using a flashlight to study images of the Navy flier team called the "Cloudbuster Nine" and their batboy, who happened to be my father.

When I headed upstairs after midnight, the house was silent for the first time in a decade without my father's gurgling oxygen machine and his television blaring with laugh tracks of sitcoms and nonstop sports. If baseball was not rolling across the television screen, it could be heard in the sound of box scores being torn from the morning newspaper, which my father collected in a drawer and memorized like Bible verses.

Growing up, baseball was a double-edged sword in our house: it flooded my father's heart with tremendous happiness, but it drowned him in greater swells of sorrow, which he hid from the world and left for his family to see every single day of his life. Until I discovered that trunk, I never wanted to see another baseball game or be annoyed by the roar of the crowd blaring from a television set for as long as I lived.

Later that night, when I Googled my father's professional baseball career for the first time, I came to realize how a failure to make it to the major-leagues and one trade in a manager's windowless office could make a man feel like he was walking on a broken leg for the rest of his life.

But it was the Cloudbuster Nine that grabbed my attention when I realized how the game of baseball was repurposed and toughened up to train a new generation of fighter pilots during World War II. When Pearl Harbor was bombed, there were 16 major-league teams across America, with roughly 500 players during any given season. The number of minor-league players exceeded 5,000. Ninety percent of those men served in uniform during the war in some capacity, and many of them chose the most dangerous path of all—fighter pilots, the Top Guns of their generation.

Baseball aficionados might recall as many as nine big-league players who wore the Cloudbusters jersey.

In reality, that number tripled.

During the war, nearly 25 major-league baseball players, including future Hall of Famers such as Ted Williams and Charlie Gehringer, trained at this small Navy base stationed at the University of North Carolina at Chapel Hill. Ballplayers cycled through training at varying ages in different phases of their career, and I grew to revere and love them all as I read about their exploits.

The Cloudbuster Nine barnstormed the East Coast, playing baseball in county ballparks with chicken-wire fences and the most iconic stadiums on American soil to boost morale. When players were not on the road or training, they were in classrooms, where cadets including Ted Williams mastered the Theory of Flight, which likely influenced his Science of Hitting.[1]

Approaching the 50th anniversary of the Korean War, Williams admitted in an interview with a fellow Marine that even though he invested in a fine Leica camera, he lost all of his pictures from the war in a hurricane in Florida. Ted did not save letters either, so it is likely that he never saved a photograph or a memento from his time in Chapel Hill.[2]

There are other reasons why this story about Ted and the Navy pilot baseball team is missing from bookshelves.

Proof of this grand Pre-Flight sporting experiment lives on tattered documents, sadly losing a battle with time—yellowed telegrams with fading ink, decaying housing logs for cadets handwritten by WAVES, and baseball players' autographs fading away like ghosts on antique baseballs. Because the Cloudbusters' baseball games were covered by a bare bones press with so many reporters swept into the service, game scores were sometimes inconsistent, and ink and paper shortages put an end to printed game programs. The Cloudbusters did not always get the copy they deserved, but certain players made a lifelong impression on the people who saw them, and that memory, sometimes stained with tears of joy and a yearning for heroes, endures from generation to generation.

The U.S. Navy was never disillusioned by death. Faced with the reality that any pilot might perish, the Pre-Flight schools took extra care to provide every officer, cadet, and base worker with a special scrapbook, marking this time when they served Uncle Sam.

---

[1] This statement is not made lightly; it is supported by specific naval aviation courses in physics and the Theory of Flight taught in Pre-Flight classrooms, where, after preliminary courses at Amherst, pilot trainees had to master the finer points of flight before they advanced to the next level training, when they actually flew and accrued significant solo hours.

[2] Major General Larry Taylor, (USMCR) Ret., *The Retired Officer Magazine*, November 1999.

Had I not found that World War II scrapbook picturing that little-remembered team of pilots, my father would have taken the story of the Cloudbuster Nine to his grave. But on that cold December night a few days after Christmas, I went on a journey to understand what happened to that lost kid under the dark-blue ball cap, and my father's pain and disappointment led me to one of the greatest untold stories of wartime baseball.

# FOREWORD

My father, Ted Williams, never did *anything* "half-assed." He was bold and courageous and did not apologize for being completely authentic and brutally honest. Anything he approached in life was with passion and determination to achieve perfection. He firmly believed that *"Perfection is attainable if you dare to work hard enough."*

I would like to applaud Anne Keene for telling the untold historical facts of the first group of men who were sent to Chapel Hill for this pathbreaking Naval Pre-Flight pilot training program. Ted Williams was among the few who volunteered and were selected for this rigorous training. He is not only the greatest hitter who ever lived, but he was also among the highest caliber of men who completed training to be the best at defending our country. Coupled with fantastic photos (many of which I had never seen of my father), the stories come to life with amazement in *The Cloudbuster Nine*.

Anne has taken the time to discover the elements of what were then-secret Navy training methods, including rigorous physical training regimes, character-building challenges, and land and sea survival skills that even today few men could accomplish. Her time and diligence in seeking out the former cadets and pilots who are still living is reflected in these incredible stories told by our heroes and elite athletes. She has captured what it means to have great character, principles, and integrity. She redefines what it means to have a strong work ethic and perseverance. Perhaps most important, she honors our men and women in uniform who sacrificed so much to protect our country and leave behind what is truly important to our younger generations—*how to be a proud American.*

*Claudia Williams is the last surviving child of Marine Ted Williams. She penned a loving and forthright memoir,* Ted Williams, My Father, *about his life after the Hall of Famer hung up his spikes. As the daughter of a World War II and Korean Conflict combat pilot and one of the greatest athletes who ever lived, Claudia strives to inspire future generations with examples of the courage and principles that her father exhibited his entire life.*

# PART I

# MAY 11, 1943

# Chapter 1

## THE "BASEBALL SQUAD"

The wartime baseball diamond was skinned down to dirt and clover, bordered by a threadbare carpet of Bermuda grass. On game day, fans could smell the rain as storm clouds rumbled over pastures bordering the campus. Still, thousands of baseball fans dripping with sweat elbowed their way through security to grab a seat for one of the most unusual games ever to take place at the University of North Carolina at Chapel Hill.

Even though the ballpark was a crow's flight from Durham Athletic Park, the historic ballpark featured decades later in the film *Bull Durham*, there were no giant Chesterfield packs bolted to railings at Emerson Field. The concession stand closed during games, and the little ballpark didn't have an outfield fence, just a canvas railing bordered by privet hedges that blended into the woods.[1]

In the spring of 1943, the grand old game of baseball was the most popular sport in America for civilians and millions of men and women

---

[1] *Greensboro Daily News*, April 2, 1916, p. 7. (Article based on special Star correspondence filed on April 1; also Nicholas Graham, "History on the Hill," and another web story, "A Brief History of the Pit," filed January 12, 2016.)

in uniform. But the best players didn't wear jerseys for the New York Yankees or the St. Louis Cardinals, champions of the 1942 World Series. As war raged in Europe and the Pacific, some of the most famous players in America were drawn to the Navy, where they took the most dangerous path of all, aiming to become fighter pilots.

The May 11 game between the Cloudbuster Nine and the home team Tar Heels was the talk of the base for weeks, thanks to sportswriters who built up the newest lineup of players as a "Homecoming Day in the Major-Leagues."[2] Never before had Chapel Hill experienced such suspense on the baseball field, stemming from a decision made by one of the most beloved and controversial figures of baseball a year earlier.

Wearing a baggy trench coat and high-waisted trousers, Ted Williams made headlines worldwide when he enlisted in the United States Navy at 150 Causeway Street in Boston on May 22, 1942. One day after Ted Williams hit his 100th career home run for the Red Sox, he was photographed by a military publicist, holding up his right hand to take the Navy oath. He stood in front of a wall of recruiting posters with a self-satisfied grin on his face, sending a message to the world that the Triple Crown winner was pleased with his choice to become a pilot.

Long before Pearl Harbor was attacked, the Army and Navy lobbied to secure Williams, whose draft status zigzagged between I-A and III-A as the sole supporter of his mother, a divorcée living in a run-down cottage under a water tank in San Diego. The press made it appear that Williams was destined to carry a rifle in the Army. The public and even his manager, Joe Cronin, went along with the prediction until Ted made an unexpected trip to an air base without alerting the Red Sox. That day, sitting in the cockpit of a hornet-yellow training plane, Ted put on a pair of aviator goggles for the first time. The Piper Cub smelled like metal, fuel, and sun-cured leather. Running his hands over instruments he did not recognize, he gripped the control stick and set his mind on becoming a pilot.

---

[2] *Daily Times-News*, Burlington, N.C., June 1, 1943, p. 7.

Ted chose the V-5 Naval Aviation program for reasons that had little to do with baseball. The V-5 had recently lowered its education requirements from college to high school, opening up a huge pool of candidates who never dreamed of flying. After he finished out the '42 season, Ted reported to ground training at Amherst College in mid-November, when the Berkshire Mountains were lit by a blaze of red foliage. The first snow had fallen when Ted moved into Genung House dorm with Red Sox teammate and best friend Johnny Pesky, along with three major-league cadets, including Boston Braves pitcher Johnny Sain and his teammate, infielder Buddy Gremp, and Philadelphia Athletics hurler Joe Coleman.

The naval cadets were known as the "baseball squad." They were joined by Alex MacLean, a Boston sports reporter who filled in for columnist Dave "The Colonel" Egan when he went on benders. It was no secret that Ted despised Egan, especially when he hit the sauce and his mean streak was brought out by his typewriter. But during those months, MacLean never published a negative word about Ted or any of the players because they were all on the same team of trainees aiming to win the war.[3]

Ted wanted to become a pilot long before he ever touched a baseball. His childhood idol was Charles Lindbergh, who in 1927 crossed the Atlantic in a single-engine, 223-horsepower plane—an antique Christmas tree ornament compared to the torpedo bombers landing on carriers in the Pacific during the Second World War. Before V-5 cadets could even think about grasping the stick of a Grumman, they had to pass through six months of ground training and academics that weeded out thousands of cadets. Amherst's Civilian Pilot Training Course was the first phase of officer-candidate training, where players were mixed in with about 60 Army and Navy cadets. Cadets took navigation, aerology, mathematics, Morse code, and theoretical work, and they learned to behave like officers. For the first time in his

---

[3] Leigh Montville, *Ted Williams: The Biography of an American Hero,* Doubleday, 2004, p. 99; Ed Linn, *Hitter: The Life and Turmoils of Ted Williams,* Harcourt, 1993, p. 131.

life, Ted was an excellent student, earning a 3.85 on his transcript.[4] Taking off on frozen runways, students also flew Cubs, Wacos, and Kitty Hawks with wire struts between the wings for about 35 hours a week at the Turners Falls Airport.[5] If Ted passed muster and did not pop off to his superiors, he was scheduled to ship out to the Eastern Seaboard Navy Pre-Flight School in Chapel Hill, North Carolina, on April 15, around the start of the 1943 baseball season.[6]

As a student who scraped by with Ds at Herbert Hoover High, Ted had good reason to be anxious about the Navy's academics, especially the math and physics so crucial to pilots. Just because the Splendid Splinter could knock the hide off a baseball didn't mean he could calculate angles for takeoff and landing. In fact, Ted nearly killed himself in a Piper Cub, barely missing a powerline straddling the Connecticut River.

It was not grades or flying that almost derailed Ted's naval career. Since grammar school, he had pushed his body like a freight train— always first, faster, and harder than his peers. Amherst's physical drills were no different. Ted saddled himself with extra pull-ups and attacked commando drills with a mock ten-pound rifle. He added extra miles around the track and laps in the pool with his usual degree of self-induced, gut-busting strain. Then one day a twinge of pain landed him on the operating room table with a bulging hernia. The media caught wind of his operation at Chelsea Naval Hospital, staking out the hospital with cameras. Reporters then followed Ted back to Amherst's infirmary, where he was confined to a month's bedrest in a hospital gown, wondering if he would be cleared to go to North Carolina.

---

[4] Naval Aviation Records obtained by author from the National Archives and Records Administration NARA listing grades for Amherst.

[5] Bill Nowlin, *Ted Williams: A Tribute*, Masters Press, 1997, p. 78. Commentary from aviation pilots, about Amherst being a blend of officer candidate school and scientific training.

[6] Ted Williams, *My Turn at Bat: The Story of My Life*, Simon & Schuster, 1988, p. 100.

# Chapter 2

## THE COMEBACK KID

Ted Williams and "Joltin' Joe" DiMaggio were America's biggest baseball stars at the dawn of the war. If they were lucky enough to get a muddy copy of the *Stars and Stripes*, soldiers read updates on Ted and Joe by the glow of cannon fire in foxholes. Sailors and airmen read about them on board battleships and airplanes, and the rest of America followed the players in the papers and on the radio.

Some of their neediest fans were exhausted factory workers like the "Rosie the Riveters" on production lines, mechanics and shipbuilders living on rations. They were farmers struggling to put food on the table, teachers, and nurses working for the Red Cross. They were housewives volunteering for war bond drives and frightened kids wishing upon a star for heroes.

Joe joined the Army Air Force and Ted enlisted in the U.S. Navy, where his destiny was changed at a small training base in Chapel Hill, North Carolina.

During the war, more men were being trained for battle and other wartime jobs in North Carolina than any other state. Highways were empty. Weekend trips to Myrtle Beach and the mountains were canceled, as people adhered to orders to stay off roads. Blackout drills were occurring on a weekly basis from Tennessee to the Outer Banks, as German submarines crisscrossed the Atlantic. When the air raid sirens wailed, people across the state kept buckets of sand on their porches to put out fires. Butter and milk were restricted, women applied for sugar rations at town halls, and "victory gardens" supplied half of the state's vegetables.

War bond and Red Cross posters blanketed storefronts along Franklin Street, as Boy Scouts and 4-H clubs pulled Radio Flyer wagons through neighborhoods, gathering scrap metal, newspaper, and old string. Women joined the War Relief Society, where meetings were held on Monday mornings at the home of Mrs. C. T. Woollen.[1]

They also organized the "Gray Ladies" for the base's Naval Pre-Flight hospital, where Red Cross volunteers rolled bandages and trained to entertain injured men in hospitals. American flags were raised on every corner, where homes and businesses displayed banners with blue and gold stars. People scoured the casualty list every day in the newspaper to see if they knew any of the dead, wounded, and missing in action; and that palpable tension never disappeared for families, praying that they would not get that dreaded telegram or a knock on the door.[2]

Through it all, one of the best remedies to salve fears was baseball, and that season a team of Navy fliers electrified Chapel Hill.

In the early months of 1942, the University of North Carolina at Chapel Hill took in the V-5 Navy Pre-Flight School. The Pre-Flight schools were but five of over 200 military institutions in operation during the war, and they functioned like mini naval academies, dropped in the middle of campuses.[3] During the war, four other

---

[1] "War Relief Society Meeting," *Chapel Hill Weekly,* May 7, 1943, p. 1.

[2] "The 'Gray Ladies,'" *Chapel Hill Weekly,* May 14, 1943, p. 2.

[3] Original Plan for Pre-Flight Training Syllabus presented by Tom Hamilton to Captain Radford, December 1941. Memo from Head of Physical Training Department to Director of Aviation Training; subject: Tentative Proposed Physical Training Program for Naval Aviation, p. 1 (handwritten cover, no date noting the territory of the South).

Pre-Flight schools would be housed at the Universities of Iowa and Georgia, along with St. Mary's College in Moraga, California, with a fifth station established at the Del Monte Hotel on the Monterrey Peninsula. The aim was to train 30,000 pilots a year—the most ambitious pilot training program ever attempted by the modern Navy.[4]

When the Navy marched into Chapel Hill, no one knew if the Pre-Flight School would be open for nine weeks or nine years—no one knew how long the war would continue or if it would ever end.

This elite 90-day ground training program was created by Naval Academy graduates for one purpose: to get pilots in the best physical and mental shape of their lives. With a reputation similar to modern-day SEAL training, these schools earned blood-soaked headlines with the most difficult and dangerous training in the world.

Security barriers around these schools held secrets and an extraordinary amount of pain.

There was truth to rumors about the dangers of Pre-Flight training, where several cadets died and black eyes were a badge of honor. Broken bones, scratches, and deep-yellow bruises were all part of the culture. One cadet broke his back on a trampoline. Another drowned in Chapel Hill, and the *Raleigh News & Observer* reported that base's mascot dog, Ensign Brown, dropped dead from a heatstroke after a 14-mile hike on the "hottest day of the year."

Every parent feared the worst when they put their boys on those troop trains to Pre-Flight bases. Professional athletes knew they might never play baseball again if they got hurt, but that risk and sense of sacrifice was the *thing* that changed them.

Ted was assuredly lonelier than many of his peers who felt the love and support of their families back home when they entered the service. He did not wait for any packages from his parents and relied on his instincts to bond with guys like roommates who wanted him to succeed.[5] Ted knew he might look like a meathead in the classroom.

---

[4] *Cloudbuster*, December 19, 1942, p. 1.

[5] "Ted had an ability, actually a gift, to align with the right people who would be loyal." Interview with Sarah Pletts, January 8, 2018.

He expected a lot of cuts and bruises on the training field, too, but the hard-headed hitter would have it no other way. Even though Ted dreaded the heat and mosquitoes that came with living in the South, his mind was set on perfection in Chapel Hill, and he would not settle for anything less.

By May of 1943, the Pre-Flight School dominated the campus. During the war more than 20,000 servicemen would live and train in Chapel Hill, turning the university into the largest naval base in the state.[6] That year, the Navy expanded its V-12 and its ROTC programs. Troops of Marines arrived along with foreign language specialists and interpreters, and Army Air Corps meteorologists who marched through campus chanting, "Sing . . . drill . . . study . . . kill." During the war, hundreds of French aviation cadets trained at Chapel Hill, too, including General Charles de Gaulle's son, Philippe H. X. de Gaulle, who shipped in with cadets from French Morocco and West Africa. The French thought the girls were better kissers back home, but they swore that Pre-Flight was the hardest training they'd ever seen, working "more in one day" than in a week at home.[7]

During the war, Navy flags were hoisted every morning at 8 a.m. alongside North Carolina and American flags and the Tricolour of France. The entire town converted to military time, and Navy planes literally busted through the clouds, skimming tree lines as they roared in and out of the campus airfield.

During baseball season the campus was in full bloom: coral honeysuckle tumbled down rock walls, azaleas exploded with fuchsia petals, and the smell of fresh-cut grass and wisteria spidered through the air. Spring also brought bursts of rain that could shut down a ballgame in seconds, but on May 11, the distant rumble of thunder and the smell of rain only worked to intensify the rush into the park.

---

[6] William D. Snider, *Light on the Hill: A History of the University of North Carolina at Chapel Hill*, The University of North Carolina Press, 1992, pp. 228–229. *Raleigh News & Observer*, May 16, 1943, p. 2. Note population estimates varied as the civilian, military, and student population shifted from 1942 to 1945.

[7] *Daily Tar Heel*, August 1, 1944, p. 1.

# Chapter 3

## RATION-LEAGUE BASEBALL

With strict rationing for gas and tires, college teams organized a new wartime circuit of baseball in the Raleigh-Durham area called the "Ration-League." Charter member teams included Carolina, Duke, N.C. State, and Navy Pre-Flight. The Ration Loop was designed to reduce travel, keeping players within a 40-mile radius. Teams were scheduled to meet each other four times, for a total of 16 games, and Ration Loop games only included the cadets, while Pre-Flight coaches gathered in the dugout and the sidelines.[1] Other college teams were added outside the Ration Loop, but in times of war, nothing was certain, and games could be rescheduled or canceled at a moment's notice for no official reason.

Before the major-leaguers arrived, the Cloudbuster varsity squad had a lackluster season, cobbling together only 20 or so baseball

---

[1] There was a mention that Ration-League collegiate games were only played with "cadets," according to Smith Barrier, *Greensboro Daily Record*, July 16, 1943. Therefore, it appears that coaches such as Hassett would be on sidelines, playing in other non–Ration-League games, but game coverage does not track with this statement about cadets versus inclusion of coaches. Family lore mentioned 40-mile Ration Loop.

games in 1942.[2] Team members did, however, have a hand in building a new concrete dugout for the baseball diamond in early 1943,
framing benches and a roof to shelter teams in the future.[3]

About 100 Pre-Flight cadets tried out for varsity baseball in March
1943, including a few college scrubs, high school players, and cadets
who'd never thrown a baseball. Roughly 30 made the team, and
about 18 played in those first games in ballparks with practically
empty stands.

Notable naval officers such as Jack Dempsey and war heroes like
Eddie Rickenbacker were constants in Chapel Hill, where dignitaries attended Pre-Flight sporting events, from boxing to baseball.

On April 10, former Connecticut Senator Hiram Bingham, who
as an explorer had discovered the lost city of Machu Picchu in 1911,
threw out the first pitch at the ball game, where the pilots beat the
Duke Blue Devils, 4–0. On April 19, the Cloudbusters beat David-
son's Wildcats, 14–7, with about 1,000 cadets roaring in Emerson's
stands. Then, the Navy fliers went on a dismal losing streak, getting
annihilated by Duke, 7–0. At the end of the month, the fliers lost,
13–5, to the University of Virginia's Diamond Cavaliers, leaving them
demoralized and wishing more than ever that the major-leaguers
would save them.

On May 11, their wish came true when a *revamped* Cloudbuster
Nine came in as underdogs to face the home team Tar Heels, defending Southern Conference and Big Five champs.

A record crowd poured into the park that afternoon. Some 2,000
cadets and officers on base came in the first wave of watchers—
young thickly muscled men, dressed in long-sleeved khaki, and men
in white uniforms with gold braid. Girlfriends dressed to the nines
and wives towed passels of kids in bowl cuts and pigtails into the
stands. The university's president, Frank Porter Graham, the brother
of one-game major-leaguer Archibald "Moonlight" Graham,
attended every game in his staw hat, sitting behind the first-base

---

[2] *Raleigh News & Observer,* May 23, 1943, p. 2.

[3] *Cloudbuster,* January 23, 1943, p. 4.

line.[4] Students followed in droves, emptying classrooms, dorms, and soda shops downtown. Every base employee who could clock out headed down rock paths to the game: this meant doctors, nurses, postal workers, and commissary clerks; dishwashers, cooks, and the servers at Lenoir Hall, who left aprons in the kitchen, to see their first baseball game featuring major-leaguers. Flocks of secretaries and telephone operators poured into bathrooms to primp for the players in low heels and sun hats. The mood was infectious, and giggles echoed against tiled walls of bathrooms as the "lovelies," as women were then dubbed, gathered around sinks to apply lipstick and a dabble of Evening in Paris cologne. The main drag along Franklin Street evaporated into a ghost town: store clerks closed up pharmacies, haberdasheries, and grocery markets; bankers locked vaults and pulled down the shades; gas station attendants tucked in their shirttails and washed up to see if they could get into the game. People came from outside of the village by foot and bicycle—some even hitched a ride from apple orchards around Hillsborough and cotton farms near Durham to see if the rumor was true about the best baseball team ever to hit North Carolina.

If factory workers could get off work, they nudged through the gates with a security pass. Men and women, whose backs ached from double shifts at the munitions plant up the road in Carrboro, grabbed seats on Coca-Cola bottle crates. Others sat on rooftops of utility sheds, and everyone craned their necks to get a glimpse of the great Ted Williams, who supposedly shipped into base with the 25th Battalion.

As fans filled up the park, a nine-year-old boy with freckles, big ears, and buck teeth stumbled across the sidelines with an armful of bats. He was dressed in a baggy uniform handed down from a player and a dark-blue ball cap, covering a fringe of blond bangs. The boy's name was Jimmy, and he was the official batboy and mascot for the Pre-Flight base. Jimmy's parents, seated in the front row of the

---

[4] Ray Jeffries, assistant dean of students, recalled seeing Graham with various deans and professors from the university at games, interview, July 8, 2017.

stands, were formal buttoned-up types who beamed at their only child, never imagining that his role as the team mascot would be the high point of his life.

Jimmy's father, Lieutenant Commander James P. Raugh Sr., moved his family to Chapel Hill from the outskirts of Philadelphia in the spring of 1942. He was the second-in-command at the station and would go on to become the commandant the following year until the end of the war. His wife, Eleanor, known as "Dolly," was an urbane woman who claimed that she was not terribly excited about the move to the shabby little town but enjoyed a good old-fashioned baseball game.

People who knew little Jimmy described him as a spirited kid who could not be corralled. He was the kind of boy who jumped up from his desk as soon as the school bell rang, and he rode his bicycle to the baseball field every afternoon, peddling through guard posts without identification because everyone knew him.

Since the beginning of baseball season, Jimmy had grown accustomed to hearing the boatswain pipe when the bigwigs shipped into base. And he knew how to work the Navy photographers when they prompted him to smile for the cameras. That day, reporters from the base newspaper and the *Daily Tar Heel* kneeled on the sidelines to capture the biggest story of the year. For the remainder of the season, the Cloudbusters' games would attract fleet admirals, senators, governors, diplomats, and war heroes. As North Carolina was one of the first states to house prisoners of war, German and Italian POWs who worked in the Pre-Flight dining hall were escorted to baseball games by security guards to catch a glimpse of the democratic, All-American way of life.[5]

---

[5] "North Carolina was one of the first states to take in prisoners of war, with two of the largest camps based at Fort Bragg and Camp Butner. Thousands of prisoners worked tobacco fields, picked cotton and cut pulpwood on farms." *Chapel Hill Weekly*, June 30, 1944, p. 1. An unidentified source remembered that German POWs accompanied security guards to Pre-Flight baseball games for a lesson on the All-American democratic way of life. They were not there in 1942 or 1943. See Arnold Krammer, *Nazi Prisoners of War in America, Stein & Day,* 1979; and Dr. Robert D. Billinger Jr., Prisoner of War in North

The advertising mascot from Big Tobacco was there, too. During the war, the bright leaf industry thrived. Companies like R. J. Reynolds Tobacco supplied free cigarettes to troops and sailors around the world, and Philip Morris's "Little Johnny" Roventini, the four-foot-tall mascot dressed in a red bellhop suit, was a constant at Pre-Flight games. That day, he wheeled up to the base in his custom MG coupe with "Call for Philip Morris" written on the door, razzing from the dugout with Jimmy and a troupe of the world's most famous major-league players.[6]

## What They Didn't Have

After Pearl Harbor, professional baseball came under fire. Critics thought the game was a waste of resources with its distracting publicity and gas-guzzling travel. The harshest protestors thought the major-league parks should be padlocked, but one of the most powerful men on the planet disagreed. On January 15, 1942, President Roosevelt penned his famous "Green Light" letter, keeping major-league baseball alive for the sake of the nation. Roosevelt had been a mildly talented outfielder at the Groton School, where he managed the baseball team.[7] He played recreational baseball at Harvard; and, of course, he and his wife, Eleanor, loved nothing better than sitting in the sun, munching on peanuts at games. Though Roosevelt could scarcely throw out the first pitch from the stands of Washington's Griffith Stadium, he pushed for games to be scheduled in the evenings so factory workers could attend after their shifts. He rallied to raise dollars for the Bat and Ball Fund, supplying equipment for troops to play baseball on battleships, carriers, and camps behind barbed wire fences in Europe. He also made sure he and his boys got

---

Carolina, "Enemies and Friends," *Tar Heel Junior Historian Association*, NC Museum of History, Spring 2008.

[6] Roventini captured in Images from Louis Round Wilson Library Collection; also pictured in family scrapbook and many *Cloudbuster* issues in 1943.

[7] Alex Coffey, *Memories and Dreams*, "The Game Must Go On," Opening Day 2017, pp. 38–40.

complimentary copies of *The Sporting News*, the Bible of baseball, and access to baseball games on shortwave radio overseas.[8]

At the beginning of the 1942 season, professional baseball was definitely feeling the pinch of the draft, and sportswriters predicted that America's pastime would be played in a scaled-back, no-frill setting with a different mental attitude—what that attitude was they did not know. As the military siphoned hundreds of professional players from major- and minor-league rosters, Americans got by with a comical lineup of "has-been" and "never-wuz" players. There was St. Louis Browns outfielder Pete Gray, who lost his arm as a child in a trucking accident. Skinny, knobby-kneed youngsters took to the diamond with 4-F rejects too decrepit or drunk for the draft. All along, fans' hearts remained with players such as Hank Greenberg, who had joined up with the Army, or Navy cadets like Ted Williams as they learned to fly planes on American bases.

Jack Troy, a young writer from the *Atlanta Constitution*, reported on a game that cast a new light on wartime baseball. In April 1942, Troy watched the commander of Naval Air Station Jacksonville throw out the first pitch of a game inaugurating the base's new ballpark. Half a dozen pilots screamed overhead in flying boats when Atlanta's minor-league Crackers met Jacksonville's home-team Fliers. Six thousand uniformed officers, cadets, and sailors packed the park. When the announcer shouted, "Now, let's have the Old Navy Spirit," the stands were in bedlam. After the Fliers rallied to edge out the Crackers, Troy urged military bases to schedule more contests against professional teams. In bold letters, Troy made this plea to the naysayers of baseball: "AND I KNOW NOW, FOR CERTAIN, THAT THOSE WHO CRITICIZE BASEBALL JUST DON'T KNOW WHAT THEY ARE TALKING ABOUT."[9]

---

[8] Daniel M. Daniel, *Baseball Magazine*, June 1945, LXXV. pp. 227, 228, and 249.

[9] Chet Webb, "In the Realm of Sports," *Call-Leader* (Elwood, Indiana), April 6, 1942, p. 2.

By May of 1943, military baseball thrived on a shoestring budget. Fans didn't miss the swanky programs or the felt pennants. In fact, they cinched up their belts and welcomed simpler trimmings.

When the Cloudbusters shot out of the dugout for that May 11 game, the scrappy little ballpark showed that "Old Navy Spirit" that Jack Troy described: whistles, cheers, and waves of hand clapping and foot stomping grew louder and louder. There were some tears, too, as major-league fighter pilots, going to bat for Uncle Sam, lined up with their heads bowed and ball caps pressed to their hearts for the national anthem.

Two days earlier, the Associated Press hailed Joe Coleman as a star who would convert the Cloudbusters into "the strongest service league team in the nation."[10] Coleman, property of the Philadelphia Athletics, started on the mound with the Boston Braves' Johnny Sain as his relief. The Red Sox' Johnny "Needle Nose" Pesky was at shortstop with Buddy Hassett, a coach and a former Yankee on first. Buddy Gremp from the Boston Braves was at second and George "Bonny" Bonifant, a future semipro player, at third, with the St. Louis Browns' Pete "The Polish Wizard" Appleton and Washington Senator Al "Giz" Sabo as the umpire and catcher, respectively.

Even though the *Daily Tar Heel*'s Bended Knee columnist confirmed that "His Majesty," Ted Williams, had indeed shipped into Chapel Hill, the King was not in the outfield. Jimmy knew exactly where he was that day, and Ted's absence built on the anticipation for his comeback at Emerson Field.

As the sky rumbled, Whitey Black, a lanky tow-headed freshman from Norfolk, Virginia, loped up to the plate first, knocking mud and grass out of his cleats with the bat. Whitey did not play high school baseball before he came to Carolina, playing instead for American Legion teams, whose pitchers could not whip a ball over the plate at warp speed like Coleman. After a few swings, Whitey kicked off the contest by reaching first base on an error, and he never forgot the view of the major-league talent on the field. For

---

[10] Associated Press story in the *Philadelphia Inquirer*, May 9, 1943, p. 42.

Black, the memory was all too short when he was erased on a double play and Coleman struck out Lew Hayworth to end the inning.

When Johnny Pesky stepped up to the plate with Frenchy Marchand on first after a leadoff walk in the bottom of the first, the highstrung shortstop set the tone for the rest of the season. He pounded out a ground-rule double into the right-center-field hedges. Buddy Gremp marched out to the plate next, putting on a show that would have thrilled his former manager, Casey Stengel. Buddy's home run seemed like it was a mile long that day, ringing in three runs as Carolina struggled to get a decent hit.

When the sky broke open in the fourth inning, soaking the campus with a good hard cry, the game was called at 3–0. It was announced the next day that the rainout would not be made up since exams were approaching and the Carolina players needed time to study.[11] The Tar Heels finished with the best record in the RationLeague, and though the Cloudbusters trailed behind in the rankings, they were just getting started.

## A Ballpark with a Story

It was a time when everyone lived by the slogan "Use it Up . . . Wear it Out . . . Make it Do . . . Or Do Without." Despite bare bones rationing, Emerson Field experienced its most glorious era during WWII—and the season of 1943 stayed with people for the rest of their lives. Long before that magical season, the ballpark had a story of its own to tell, starting with a Navy seadog who built the stadium.

In the fall of 1915, Emerson Field was completed with a $30,000 donation from Captain Isaac Edward Emerson, a chemist, naval officer, and baseball-loving alum who invented the world-famous headache and digestive remedy Bromo-Seltzer.[12] That same year, when his daughter's husband, Alfred Vanderbilt, lost his life when the RMS *Lusitania* was torpedoed by a German submarine, the stadium would be one of the few things that brought him lasting joy.

---

[11] Associated Press story in *Asheville Citizen-Times,* May 13, 1943, p. 12

[12] *Greensboro Daily News,* April 2, 1916, p. 7.

It was in 1888 when the inquisitive young chemist mixed up a batch of the fizzy effervescent salt behind the counter of a pharmacy on East Pratt Street in Baltimore. Emerson's friends and customers were the first to sample the bubbly concoction, and they encouraged him to abandon his business to market Bromo-Seltzer full-time. Packaged in iconic cobalt-blue bottles manufactured by Cumberland Glass Company on the Jersey shore, Bromo-Seltzer allowed Emerson to become one of the first entrepreneurs to harness the power of mass-market advertising. The chemist blanketed newspaper and drugstores with in store sales campaigns in multiple languages. He bolstered sales with jingly *chug-chug-chug* radio commercials, peddling his remedy to millions around the world. When his blue glass bottles became collectors' items, Emerson arranged tours of the factory for 30 cents, sending tourists home with samples of the bottles that were displayed in pharmacy windows from downtown Baltimore to London.[13]

Emerson's roots were planted in North Carolina, where he grew up on a farm near Chapel Hill. When his mother died prematurely, Isaac was sent to live with an aunt and uncle. During a tough and lonely childhood, one of his greatest joys was baseball. To allow others to enjoy the game, he funneled a big chunk of his fortune into the construction of one of the South's most impressive sports parks by the old bell tower. He modeled Emerson Park after Homewood Field at Johns Hopkins University, building raised concrete bleachers seating more than 3,000 spectators for baseball, football, and track events. There was a concession stand and locker rooms with polished marble sinks and modern, hot-water plumbing—real luxuries for athletes and fans.

A six-year supply of cinders from the local power plant was hauled in on Model T flatbeds to lay the foundation for a track that wrapped around the field like a band of taffy. For the next ten years, Emerson Field, with its moon tower–style lighting, hosted homecomings and

---

[13] Engraved advertisement certificate 1930 of Bromo Building in downtown Baltimore.

sporting events day and night. But its glory was short-lived. By 1927, at the peak of a peacetime America, the university's football team vacated the field for a much grander stadium about a quarter mile across campus, where railroad tycoons built a palatial Mediterranean-style clubhouse for Kenan Stadium. From then on, the baseball field received stepchild treatment, never receiving funds to build a decent fence or professional below-ground dugouts for visiting teams.

After Pearl Harbor was bombed, Emerson Field got a second chance. With its superior training facilities and forward-thinking leadership, the University of North Carolina was selected from among 80 institutions to host one of only five regional V-5 Navy Pre-Flight schools. The university received millions of dollars to convert the campus into a wartime training center, and Emerson Field was center stage for the toughest combat training known to man.[14]

The baseball field also served as a hub for one of the most critical training labs in the war. After Pearl Harbor, 75 percent of all pilots shot or forced to land came down alive. Yet, out of that group, barely 5 percent survived if they could not find food, shelter, or water. The Navy learned that the experienced outdoorsmen, including country boys with a background in hunting, fishing, and camping, had a better chance of survival, so they set up schools to teach cadets how to live off the land and sea. Unbeknownst to the fans, cages of poisonous snakes were around the corner from the diamond, where the head of the survival school was the baseball coach who taught cadets how to distinguish harmless rat snakes from deadly rattlers.

Before Lieutenant Don Kepler formalized the Navy's survival methods, he was a baseball player. He spent more than ten years in the minor-leagues, playing for several teams, including farm units of

---

[14] Report on work done to make the UNC-Chapel Hill campus ready for the Navy Pre-Flight School. From the Office of the Vice President for Finance of the University of North Carolina (System) Records, 1923–1972, #40011, University Archives.

the White Sox and the Washington Senators. Fresh out of Penn State, he made baseball history pitching the first semiprofessional game on a lighted diamond.[15] Ever since that night, Kepler became known as a man of firsts, establishing a lifelong bond with guys like Ted Williams, who viewed themselves as boys who liked to fish and hunt.

## More Than a Little Baseball

Winning baseball teams were seldom put together by accident, and the Cloudbusters were no exception to the rule. From that afternoon on, the rejuvenated nine expected to take on a few college and military squads now that the Ration-League season was over. But players did not know they would hit the road several times a week in hot, tin-can buses, facing teams they had never heard of. They also did not expect to be criticized for trying to do something good for people when Americans needed baseball the most.

As Pre-Flight schools opened their doors, critics voiced concerns that cadets should stay off the roads and focus on drills at home. Most Pre-Flight cadets left the base two or three times on forced hikes in 90 days if they were lucky. Baseball players lived in the middle of the road, and they took the heat for following orders.[16] Even though it was a thrill to see America's diamond heroes reeling in the War Relief dollars, some parents felt like their sons were being shipped to the Pacific and used as cannon fodder in Europe while celebrities such as Ted Williams got the star treatment at home. Certain high-ranking officers also disputed the selection of men they labeled as "fat, drunken football coaches" who were training the pilots. Even coaching legends such as Jim Crowley and Bernie Bier-

---

[15] Interview with Richard Kepler, December 6, 2017. (Kepler was playing for a minor-league team in Indianapolis when the Cincinnati Reds came to town, and he pitched in an exhibition game to help them test out the new lights at the ballpark in 1930.)

[16] Diary entry from cadet K. Ray Marrs, who rarely left campus, *I Was There When the Earth Stood Still*, 1st Book Library, 2003, p. 55. Frank Selwyn Johnson also indicated in September 17, 2015, that he rarely left campus.

man were not immune to the critics, who threw a wrench in the Pre-Flight game schedules.[17]

By design, Pre-Flight bases had well-staffed public relations offices that managed relationships with carefully vetted reporters and state legislators who followed the embryonic fliers. Publicity officers came from bustling operations such as the *Chicago Tribune* and powerful college athletic departments, wielding influence over the national press corps.

The Chapel Hill station was different.

The man in charge of base communications was a pile-driving politician in the making and a former football star who built a reputation on diving headfirst into the fight. Pierce Oliver "Kidd" Brewer was one of the most storied athletes born on Tar Heel soil, and a full-blown eccentric. When Pearl Harbor was bombed, Kidd wanted to become a fighter pilot, but he was too old to fly, so he applied for a desk job "where the fighting was the thickest."[18] Kidd had hosted a weekly sports program for a radio station that started with a receiver in a chicken coop. In addition to broadcasting *Amos & Andy* and *The Lone Ranger*, WBT aired Pentecostal holy roller church services, followed by Captain Kidd's folksy show that electrified sports fans from Miami to Maine.

While Brewer may have lacked cosmopolitan appeal, he was a brilliant pitchman, who put a sporty spin on every newspaper, pamphlet, postcard, matchbook, cartoon, and photograph that came out of his Pre-Flight station.

Growing up dirt-poor on a tenant farm in Winston-Salem, North Carolina, with seven hard-handed older brothers and two younger sisters, Kidd was used to turning scraps into movable feasts. With no secretary and a bare bones staff, Kidd hired his kid

---

[17] This was the case with Ted Williams being pulled from Yanklands game, then reinserted; former heavyweight boxing champion Gene Tunney complained to the press about "fat, drunken football coaches," enraging Commander Tom Hamilton.

[18] Kidd Brewer's personal application, U.S. Naval Reserves, 1942.

sister, Faith, to write copy and built his publicity department from scratch.[19]

He launched a logo-branding contest for any cadet who could draw a stick figure and a plane. The winner was a Yale fine arts student who drew the Cloudbuster emblem—an amphibious PBY Catalina seaplane busting through the clouds.[20]

Like the top Pre-Flight brass, Kidd was a natural-born athlete with a rare gift of complete ambidexterity. Growing up, Kidd was not only the fastest boy on two legs in Forsyth County, he could beat most kids to the finish line running upside down on his hands.[21] Kidd was one of the first members of his family to finish high school, and he placed third in the state track meet as the sole representative of Reynolds High School. He earned his laurels as an All-American football player at Duke in the 1920s, earning 12 athletic letters in baseball, basketball, wrestling, and boxing, and even serving as captain of the track team. When he was not on a sports field, he was doing handstands on the wing of an airplane, running a limousine service and a boarding house, or selling insurance. Kidd used his scrappy brand of magic as the football coach at Appalachian State Teacher's College, where he built a wonder team out of farmboys and rough-and-tumble players in 1937. That year, the Mountaineers achieved a perfect, unscored-upon regular season, and Kidd Brewer's name graces that college stadium to this day.

---

[19] Family letters, written memorial honoring Pierce Oliver Brewer by sister Faith Brewer Laursen, November 28, 1991. Materials provided by Brewer's daughter, Betty Brewer Pettersen.

[20] The Cloudbuster nameplate designed by cadet Malcolm L. McGuckin Jr., a Yale fine arts student, was chosen among 12 entries offered by competing cadets. He apprenticed for a New York illustrator and commercial artist. In the U.S. Marine Corps, he was awarded the Distinguished Flying Cross for extraordinary achievement while participating in aerial flight, in actions against enemy Japanese forces in the Pacific Theater of Operations during World War II.

[21] Family letters, written memorial honoring Pierce Oliver Brewer by sister Faith Brewer Laursen, November 28, 1991. Materials provided by Brewer's daughter, Betty Brewer Pettersen.

He never forgot his hardscrabble beginnings, and he believed in the magic of sports. As soon as the major-league posse shipped into base, Kidd aimed to trail them with cameras, pairing Ted with the little people he got along with—kids.[22]

---

[22] Wade Rawlings, *Raleigh News & Observer*, November 26, 1991, 1B. (Note: Observations about Kidd being first in family to graduate high school vary; in the eulogy previously footnoted, his sister, Faith, mentioned handstands on wing of a plane and Kidd's claim that he was listed in *Ripley's Believe It or Not!* for being elected captain of nine athletic teams through high school and Duke.)

# Part II

# THE TRUNK

# Chapter 4

## A TRUNK HOLDING SECRETS

*"Baseball grips a man down to his soul like a love for the sea, until he will make any sacrifice to follow it."*
—*Harold C. Burr*, Baseball Magazine, *April 1939*

On New Year's Day 2014, my father, James Plummer Raugh Jr., died of emphysema at age 79. He had fallen ill three days earlier when his lungs closed. As a former professional athlete, his body was in good shape, but his lungs were ravaged from a 40-year, three-pack-a-day smoking habit. For his last decade, Jimmy did not smoke, but he was tethered to a plastic oxygen line attached to a machine that gurgled like a fish tank in the middle of the mid-70s ranch house with a distant view of the Blue Ridge Mountains where he lived with my mother.

My father had been in palliative hospice care for three years before he died. On the worst days, he was literally starved for air, hunched over the kitchen counter, resting on his knuckles as he struggled to breathe. Sometimes this fight went on for hours. Dad rarely complained. Although he had a stash of liquid morphine hidden behind a ragged row of encyclopedias, I only saw him use it once or twice.

Dad loathed going to the doctor. "Doctors are all quacks . . . they just want ya money," he yammered, but boy, did he look forward to those Wednesday afternoon visits with his two nurses, who sat in the living room with highball glasses of iced tea, laughing at his jokes from the 1960s and stories about the long-gone days of baseball.

My father was a man from another era. When we gave him a cell phone, he couldn't turn it on, so he threw it in the drawer. He never once used a computer and struck up long, personal conversations about baseball with telemarketers as if they were long-lost friends. He was the kind of guy who still thought women wanted corsages for anniversaries, and when I explained that the custom fizzled out in the 1950s, he reluctantly sent my mother a vase of roses.

My sister, Carson, and I went away to college and never moved back home. I lived in Austin, Texas, almost 1,500 miles from my hometown of Hickory, North Carolina, where miles of kudzu-covered furniture mills had seen better days. I had not been home since the summer when I arrived on that Christmas evening in 2013.

I was told that my father was his regular self at the annual Christmas Eve party, where he held court at the kitchen table with a fistful of peanuts, telling jokes and talking baseball with neighbors.

But on the evening I arrived, a cold draft blew through the house from an ice storm, and Dad was slumped over in a chair in the den wearing a loose cotton robe. The expression on his face was blank. His hair was a shock of white and it was as if he had shrunk an inch or two since July.

Dad had managed his own medicine for a decade, which he took at the exact same time every morning from a plastic days-of-the-week pill case. The routine never changed. He nebulized three or four times a day, cursing as he struggled to assemble the plastic inhalers like Lego pieces. Though he never complained once, Dad got by day to day literally starved for air.

The morning after Christmas, he did not get up at his usual time around 7 a.m. Instead, he dozed until three in the afternoon. For the first time ever, he misplaced his plastic pill case and barely knew his name but refused to go to the hospital.

With his nurses away for the holidays, a substitute nurse drove up to the house the next day in a little red car. From the second-floor window, I watched her tiptoe to the front door, crunching across a layer of ice on the lawn.

Dad had cycled in and out of the hospital that year. He miraculously pulled through illnesses like double pneumonia because his body was conditioned from years of athletics. A few minutes after the nurse listened to my father's lungs, she summoned me into the hallway. In a soft yet authoritative voice, her eyes locked on mine, she said, "Ma'am, his lungs are closed. There is no mooove-ment whatso-ever. He needs to go to hospice house right away. They have a room. He needs to take it."

Mother knew that Dad would pitch a fit if an ambulance roared up to the house with sirens and flashing lights. "It's a waste of taxpayer dollars," he'd rant, swatting at paramedics from a gurney, calling them "sons-a-bitches." Initially, Mother argued with the nurse, assuring her that my father would rebound like always, but the girl shook her head, insisting that he would suffocate right in front of us if he did not to go to the hospital or hospice, where he belonged.

When I walked upstairs to the room where Dad slept for three decades, it amazed me how compactly he lived. The privileged guy who grew up in the stately Tudor house on Pine Road on Philadelphia's Main Line, as he routinely reminded us, slept on a mattress without a headboard beside a purple plastic table that had been picked up off the side of the road. All of his toiletries were stored in a freebie Tupperware bin from a hospital stay. There were no family pictures in his room, just a few crumpled *ESPN* magazines and a General Electric fan from the 1930s with a gnarled fire-hazard cord.

My father had not traveled beyond the county line in several years, and the fine leather luggage he inherited from his parents had rotted in the attic. As I placed his plaid bathrobe and slippers into a plastic bag from the pharmacy, I thought about the night before, when he sat on his bed scratching at his face, looking confused, with his feet dangling off the mattress in loose slippers like a child. He was never a physical man requiring any kind of affection. That night, he asked me to scratch his back with a wire hairbrush because his entire body itched. As I pulled the brush across his back, he hummed like a dog, digging his fingernails into his scalp. Anyone with a hint of medical knowledge would have known that his body was toxic and he was dying.

I knew that the hospice house was located on some winding backwoods rural route behind the shopping mall, a no-man's-land of feed lots and high-grassed pastures with rusted-out tractors. Too many years had passed for me to form a mental picture of the site of the facility. Fearing that my father would turn blue in the backseat when we got hopelessly lost in the country, way out of the range of Google maps, I called a friend to drive him to the place where he was summoned to die. That friend was a good Samaritan neighbor—a man who had taken my father to lunch five days a week, year after year—rain, sleet, or drivable snow. Bill was a newly retired neighbor who loved baseball as much as my father, and I would come to understand their connection based on amends. As calm and steady as a smooth-watered stream, Bill sailed into the driveway within minutes, as if he knew the call was coming. That morning we followed his shiny red Buick, watching my father's head bob as they laughed, twisting around newly paved backroads, deep in the country.

The spokes of Dad's wheelchair glimmered in the afternoon sun as he was wheeled into the hospice house. He was checked in by a pleasant, middle-aged nurse named Vickie who wore a silver pin on her lapel. The pin was shaped like an angel, displaying a picture of her son, a blond boy dressed in a baseball uniform. When I asked about the boy, she told me that he was a left-handed side-arm pitcher who died a month before his 25th birthday. I told the nurse that many moons ago my father had been a professional baseball pitcher and she might want to visit with him for some stories about the good old days.

I did not know that nurse Vickie was a whiz at baseball trivia. Later, I heard that he asked her his token riddle, "What are the nine ways a hitter gets on base?" Their exchange ended with an unusual—some might say prophetic—twist that we would come to appreciate three days later, when he died.

# Chapter 5

## THE SIZE OF A DREAM

*"Of three million kids a year who play Little League baseball only 45 will see the light of day in the major-leagues and only 15 will last five years."*

*—Dale Petroskey, former president of the National Baseball Hall of Fame and Museum*

Jimmy Raugh was a creature of baseball. It defined the narrative of his life. He talked about the sport nonstop—and boy could he talk about the good old days with the Detroit Tigers, about striking out Mickey Mantle in spring training in 1960, about that glorious moment on the mound when the pitcher controls the energy of the game and carries the team on his back. But to me, it was not as if he had lightning pouring from his fingers—he was more of a baseball folklorist, with a photographic memory for stats that spilled out of him like shiny coins from a slot machine. Though he did something extraordinary on the diamond, he hung up his cleats for good long before I was born.

So, I never knew that part of him—just the memories he repeated ad nauseam. And those memories made me sad.

Instead of becoming a professional scout or a coach, he became an armchair devotee with a cocktail in one hand and a burning cigarette in the other. For as long as I knew him, he was one of those guys who lived for the baseball that left him long ago.

Whether it's obvious or not, the super fans of baseball are amongst us—always. In shopping malls, airports, bars and churches, and, of course, at the ballpark. My father was that guy with the fringe of gray at the temples scouring *Sports Illustrated* in the crook of his arm at a wedding. He was the guy in the pew with the hidden earpiece listening to a ballgame on a free bright-yellow ESPN transistor radio at a funeral. Occasionally, I'd hear him react to a hit with a grunt or his favorite phrase, "What in the Sam Hill?" People glared from pews as Mother ribbed him with her elbow . . . *the nerve of that man*, people think . . . *in the house of the Lord, listening to a ballgame*. But at that moment, he was with his Lord: baseball.

When he retired, some people gravitated toward the old stories and the trivia—others were repelled by him, avoiding the has-been who could not let go of the past. As his daughter, I was stuck somewhere in the middle—longing to find some way to relieve him of his pain.

## Famous Last Words

Before my father died, we had a few minutes of one-on-one time with wordless pauses that felt like the Grand Canyon. As he leaned back on the pillow in his hospice gown staring out the window, I told him that he was a good father.

At a loss for words, I told him that I'd see him in about 30 years. He didn't respond. Rather, he shrugged his shoulders, and said two final words, "Oh, well," like he just lost a hand of cards.

After struggling to tell his nurses one final joke, he slipped into a coma that afternoon and never woke up.

Two days later, he was the first person I ever watched die. When he exhaled his final breath, his body began to curl up into a ball with his head rising off his pillow, freezing into position like a hydraulic crane.

My sister put his stainless-steel Timex watch on her wrist, and she swore that she felt his spirit lift from his body. The only feeling I had upon his death was relief, and I was grateful that Dad did not gasp for air for several weeks in an oxygen tent like so many victims of cardiopulmonary disease. Though my sister and I did not admit it, we were glad that he could let go of the sadness stemming from his failed baseball career that weighted him down like an anchor for decades.

Within minutes, our family gathered in a bereavement room across the hall—a nondescript taupe-colored room with dimmed lights, plastic ferns, and taupe-colored furniture. When we discussed his obituary, it was the first time in my life that I heard the word "baseball" without my father there to gleefully fill in the gaps with a story. This time, I was tasked to tell the story—his story—all by myself, a story about a man who lived to talk about a sport he lost, and I was speechless.

That night I sketched out a few conciliatory lines about my father's less-than-exciting sales career in textiles, with blank spaces about his life in professional baseball. Scouring the house for details about his pitching years, I asked my sister if she knew where or for how long he played major-league baseball. She shrugged her shoulders and replied, "Detroit." My mother, who was married to him for 55 years, was consumed with the business of funeral arrangements. When I pressed for details she said, "I don't remember. Just write something. You know the story."

But I didn't.

Evidence of his career was displayed on the bookshelf in the den, lined with copper-plated trophy mugs from the 1950s containing dozens of autographed balls. As kids, my sister and I played catch with those baseballs autographed by legends such as Johnny Pesky and Ted Williams, letting them roll in the creek where many were lost and never recovered. Dogs chewed up his mitts and he mowed the grass in his cleats until the leather rotted off the soles.

That night, I looked at my father's memorabilia through different eyes. Dust and cobwebs covered his trophies, and some were beginning to rust and rot. I knew his favorite trophy was the Wish Egan Most Improved Player award from spring training in 1959, when life was good. For the first time, I examined the two-foot-tall trophy crowned with a bronze player who seemed emblematic of his life, with a broken arm and paint peeling from his face. More telling was the unblemished white square of paint underneath the base of the trophy, outlined by the decades-old stain of the smoke that killed him.

An All-American baseball certificate from college marbled with cigarette smoke was framed on the shelf beside a varnished wooden fraternity paddle from the Delta Kappa Epsilon house in Chapel Hill. Stacks of yearbooks from high school and college featured him on scores of varsity teams and even president of his class at The Haverford School for four years running. The quote under his senior year picture at Haverford made my stomach hurt as I read this passage: *"He continually has a smile for others, a laugh for every joke, and a sincere interest in all the school's activities. The implication of Jim's future is one of complete security."* In a college yearbook, as senior class president, my father was pictured with the folk entertainer Andy Griffith before he gave a graduation speech to his classmates in 1957. As I studied that image, with him smiling in his tasseled graduation cap, I marveled at his success, feeling guilty about the priceless memorabilia we had desecrated, as questions raced through my mind.

*What went wrong?*

*How does a man go from being such a happy-go-lucky big man on campus to a guy selling twine?*

Oddly, all evidence of Dad's major-league history was missing, making me question if he even tried out for the big leagues, as he claimed.

*Was he telling the truth?* I wondered.

*What if my understanding of him was completely wrong?*

Late into the night, I sat in front of the computer in Mother's laundry room-office reading his minor-league statistics for the very first time in my life: 6-foot-2, weight 185, pitcher, bats right, throws right. He last played Triple-A ball in 1961 for the Syracuse Chiefs, a farm club of the Minnesota Twins. There was no mention of the major-league Detroit Tigers, and I calculated that my father was 26 years old when he retired from the sport he loved.

The rest of his career was a question mark.

For decades, he bellowed about how he threw out his arm. He said his parents didn't approve of the sport, where he lived on a bus with uneducated, rough-around-the-edges players. But until that night I never really knew or cared why he quit baseball.

We were exhausted with his stories.

At his funeral, I felt like it was sacrilege to spit out a few compulsory lines about the one true thing that mattered to him. Raised by a man who *almost* got a sip of the proverbial cup of coffee, I knew just enough about my father's sporting days to understand that baseball was sacred territory for fans, especially former players with broken dreams. Dad had his faults; he chain-smoked until his fingers turned yellow. He often soaked his pain with cocktails in front of the television in the basement, ossified and removed from his family in a windowless room that resembled a fallout shelter from the Cold War. But my father was a good, honest man with a pure heart. He was just broken by something I did not understand.

I also knew that baseball fans would surely read his obituary, so I was determined not to screw up the one true thing that gave him dignity. And that thing was baseball.

Somewhere in the basement, I thought I might find missing clues to his baseball career in a footlocker that I had seen years before but never bothered to open. It was around ten at night when I padded down an outdoor metal stairwell to his fallout shelter with sleet clicking against the windows. The light had long burned out in the storage room draped with spiderwebs. Using a flashlight, I found his baseball trunk in a closet under a pile of rusty lawn tools. The trunk was not a fancy Hartman piece with brass hinges that famous players took on the road. It was a crude metal container, tied shut with a vinyl cord since John F. Kennedy was president. With frozen fingers, I jiggled the lid open, meeting, for the first time, the father I never knew.

Sitting Indian-style on an oil-stained floor beside a mower, I rummaged through ten pounds of newspaper clippings until well past midnight with tears in my eyes.

The flashlight illuminated calling cards from baseball scouts from the Brooklyn Dodgers, Baltimore Orioles, and even the New York Yankees. There was an orange-paneled roster from the Detroit Tigers, too, featuring his name with a paragraph about his potential as a pitcher. There were stacks of technicolored Topps baseball cards mixed in with news clippings, along with a taped-up photograph of Ted Williams with an endearing personal inscription to his good friend "Jimmie."

In a black-and-yellow Kodak film case, my father was pictured at the height of his youth, clear-eyed and alive with his teammates from the farm leagues in the late 1950s and early 1960s. One picture stood out from the rest: Dad posed in front of the batting cage, with his arm slung around the neck of a scruffy teenage clubhouse boy with small ears and close-set eyes. My father's jersey read "Cardinals" in cursive letters, and he and the handicapped boy both beamed with an exultant smile.

Until that moment, I had never seen such a pure expression of content on my father's face, and from that night on, I longed to find that lost baseball player under the dark-blue ball cap.

At the bottom of the trunk was a blue-and-gold broadcloth scrapbook from the U.S. Navy from World War II, when my grandfather, James P. Raugh Sr., commanded a school for pilots in Chapel Hill, North Carolina. Over the years, my sister and I heard stories about my father's batboy days at the Navy base, which we sadly dismissed, rolling our eyes. For the first time, I studied the glossy black-and-white publicity stills of him at age nine, getting private batting lessons from the great "Splendid Splinter" and his sidekick "Needle Nose" Pesky.

When I first laid eyes on those images of the Navy baseball team, I did not know the difference between a curveball and a knuckleball. My father never bothered to take me to a professional baseball game—not even a high school game, though we had a fine stadium down the road, so I thought Class AAA and Class D ball were one and the same. I assumed the name of his favorite team, the Red Sox, was spelled Red Socks, and I never knew if he really even met his alleged friend Ted Williams.

The only baseball connection I had with my father was the one year that I played softball in the fifth grade. Our team was terrible, and we played on a crummy little field behind a furniture plant. My father went to two or three games, chain-smoking on the edge of the bleachers, then he never came back.

It was after he died that Mother told me that it frustrated him too much to watch "amateurs," as he called them, "desecrate the game." He could not bear to watch the uncalled balls, and pigeon-toed little girls with sunburned cheeks, standing on the field in a daze with our mouths gaping open. Lackadaisical scorekeepers who forgot to tally a score or added a run for the wrong team drove him crazy. But the one thing that frustrated him most of all were the players who crossed over home plate, never bothering to put their foot on the plate itself. He watched obsessively and counted every time the plate was missed. "Jesus, Mary, and Joseph," he'd rant, storming over to the plate in polished penny loafers, "are you people blind?" When the umpire did nothing to correct the mistake, my father realized that no one cared or even noticed the error, not even the coach. He felt like the "amateurs" of my era had lost respect for the rules of the game, so he never returned to that ball park again.

After my lackluster softball season, I avoided the subject of baseball altogether because the game seemed to bring him so much pain. But on the night my father died, sitting on that cold floor near his Cold War bunker, my impression of baseball changed when his childhood pictures grabbed my heart.

What I discovered was both heartbreaking and awe-inspiring.

A five-minute Google search on the Navy's Cloudbuster baseball team dredged up headlines and Hollywood-style pictures from the golden age of baseball. At one time, the team was entirely manned by major-league coaches and fighter pilots in the making who became darlings of the press in 1943. Though I could not find any one book that explored the history of the team, every single player would write about that impactful training school in their autobiographies. Memories were not just about baseball, either—players were moved by something of a Titanic nature, when they faced failure on a daily basis, got beaten to a pulp, and truly mastered the art of teamwork.

As a daughter of the base mascot, I knew that Dad's batboy duty rivaled an encounter with Captain Marvel—an otherworldly experience that lit the fuse that sparked his obsession with the sport that had broken so many hearts. The battered old trunk not only gave me information to deliver a respectable eulogy, but I was also able to honor the Cloudbuster Nine baseball team, whose story inspired a love of country and a love of sport, and I found clues to understand my father's greatest regret, when he allowed a *time clock* to end his career in baseball.

# Chapter 6

## MY NEW FRIEND TED

As it was, the legend of the Cloudbuster Nine almost went from the hospice house to the bank vault, where it could have been lost forever amongst crumpled land deeds and Civil War letters. The morning after my father died, we drove to the Wells Fargo branch on Highway 127 to set up an account for the burial. For safekeeping, I brought an envelope stuffed with baseball memorabilia for the safety deposit box, never intending to share the pictures with anyone outside the family.

As we walked through the front door of the bank, someone remarked, "Here comes the spitfire," as Mother beelined toward the back office, where an advisor managed her affairs. When I told the staff that my father had died, the tellers all stopped counting cash. Even the lady servicing a customer at the drive-in window turned off the intercom, straightened her skirt, and walked toward me to express her condolences.

"The candy man has died," announced a young man in a black suit, with a grin concealing some kind of joke I did not understand.

When the staff broke out into laughter, the man said, "Let me show you something." Near the teller window he opened a drawer filled with mismatched pieces of candy. For years, my father drove his silver Buick through the drive-in, dispensing miniature candy bars, half-melted in his pockets, along with free butterscotch and Starlight mints from the local pizza joint. With my mother engaged behind closed doors down the hall, I told the staff that I had something they might want to see. Spreading the contents of the envelope on the counter, the tellers and a security guard were in awe of one picture. The black-and-white glossy photograph of Ted Williams with its long personal message to his friend "Jimmie."

The staff put their hands over their mouths when they noticed that someone had run a yellowed piece of Scotch tape over Ted's face to hold the picture together.

When I asked, "What's the big deal about Ted Williams?" I got a cockeyed look and no reply.

That morning I learned that the tellers and half of the waiters, grocers, and dry cleaners in town knew more about my father's days with Ted and the Cloudbusters than his own family, because they had listened, yearning for a connection to a hero we had ignored.

When we left the bank, carrying a complimentary stuffed Wells Fargo horse, a teller grinned and remarked, "There goes the spitfire." In the parking lot, my mother, who was always the responsible one, looked at me hard and said, "Well, I'd rather be known as the 'spitfire' than the 'candy lady' any day."

## The Eulogy

With sunlight streaming in bright-colored rays though stained-glass windows of the old stone church, the Presbyterian minister opened his service with this line: "There are Easter and Christmas Christians. Jim was neither, but he was a good man." With that cue, I approached the pulpit to retell my father's prized story about his batboy days in the ragged, hand-me-down Cloudbuster jersey. In the parish hall, we arranged a display of pictures and baseball memorabilia, taking people back to simpler times. There were baskets of autographed baseballs, caked with mud from ballfields past. There were letters from scouts and the glossy orange-and-black Detroit Tigers roster, listing a profile of my father as a pitcher.

I thought about adding an audio component to the display with a boombox to play his old radio interviews from the local station from the 1970s and the '80s, when he offered thoughts on the World Series. We even had an interview from the College Baseball Hall of Fame, which he recorded six months before he died, but when I listened to the tapes, I thought the salty ballpark profanity might get us excommunicated from the church.

With the Navy scrapbook on exhibit, a fascination was reawakened about the star-studded baseball team with a name that no one remembered.

I was pleased that we could redeem my father with proof of his playing days, and how close he came to realizing his big-league dream. At the service, one old friend mourned the memorabilia, enlightening me to an agonizing truth about the pain men who "almost made it" carry with them. With a hardened expression, he held out his hands, as if he were holding a bowl, and said, "Your father had *it* all right here, in his hands—that major-league audition that no one ever touches and that dream were all taken away from him."

My father's friend wondered if I ever knew what happened to him. "Why did he quit?" he asked.

I had no answers, and, at that moment, I felt my father's anguish running through my bones.

For the next few days, the house swelled with parishioners and friends bearing casseroles, pound cakes, and jugs of iced tea. The Haverford contingent was missing. Most of his former teammates from the Carolina baseball team were dead, and fraternity pals were few and far between.

It took about 15 minutes to clear out the belongings and the breathing machines in my father's bedroom.

After his body was cremated, his clothes were donated to Goodwill, and literally all that was left of him were the memorabilia from the trunk and his stories from the old days of baseball.

He was buried in a plot beside the neighborhood elementary school (and we illegally dumped the ashes of his faithful dog in his grave). With a headstone not much larger than a pancake, it's difficult to spot when the grass grows tall, but as the years go by his grave glistens with the shine of Lincoln pennies.

I've always heard that when a person passes away, they go back to the happiest, healthiest, most peaceful time in their lives. I am convinced that my father did not go back to those hard, uncertain months of spring training at Tigertown. Rather, he raced back to the season of 1943, to that hot and hackneyed ballfield in Chapel Hill, where he walked among the gods of baseball.

# Chapter 7

## A DREAM TEAM

Pick up any photograph of Ted Williams in 1943 and there's a good chance you'll see him seated on a footlocker beside Babe Ruth or perched on a chipped cement wall wearing a jersey stitched with dark-blue Navy insignia. Many of those photographs were taken while he was training in Chapel Hill, and they tell a story about the summer Ted changed.

Ted's disdain for attention is apparent in every team photograph, where he is wincing in the back row, with a forced smile. But as time goes by, there are moments, like sunbursts cracking through clouds, when he comes alive for the cameras and actually grins.

As winter thawed and buds pressed through the campus grounds, visions for a Navy baseball dream team took shape around March of 1943. Officers with a hand in the fliers' schedule included the base's Commander John Packard "Packy" Graff; Pre-Flight's athletic director Harvey Harman, a salt block of a man who had served as head football coach at the University of Pennsylvania and Rutgers University; and the varsity baseball coach, Don Kepler. The university's athletic director, Robert Fetzer, who was always angling to stage competitions between the home-team Tar Heels and the "Pre-Mighters," as he called the cadets, was in those meetings, along with the base's publicist, Kidd Brewer.

The powers on the base were keeping close tabs on Ted Williams, who was performing better than expected at Amherst, especially in the classroom. If all went well and Ted did not shoot off his mouth or wreck a training plane, he would ship into Chapel Hill right on the nose of baseball season.

With gas rationing kicked into high gear and tires sold on the black market, officers knew it would be like moving heaven and earth to take the Pre-Flight baseball team on the road to Chicago to face squads like Naval Station at Great Lakes or the Commodores at Bainbridge Air Station in Maryland.

Aside from colleges, North Carolina had some fierce factory squads such as Cameo Hosiery and Burlington Mills Weavers. There were shipbuilder outfits, and teams that built the planes, and, of course, the base's next-door neighbor, the minor-league Durham Bulls. Military teams were always in flux, and North Carolina had some good ones, such as Camp Lejeune's New River Mariner Bombers. There was the Wake Forest Army Finance School near Raleigh, and the paratroopers who leaped from planes at Camp Mackall near the golfing resort at Southern Pines.

By far the most exciting competition was a few hours up the road in Norfolk, Virginia. During the war, Norfolk morphed into the ultimate baseball recruiting machine, landing the most talented players in the service. Recent additions that season included Phil Rizzuto, Dom DiMaggio, Pee Wee Reese, Hugh Casey, and Walt Masterson— just a drop in the bucket of the talent they would recruit that year.[1]

During those meetings in Chapel Hill, the men broke into laughter like little boys. For a few moments, they even forgot about the pressures of the war when they imagined the level of players who were going to slam into the Pre-Flight school like a hurricane.

As the 1943 Pre-Flight baseball schedule was being sketched out, Hall of Famer Rogers Hornsby described what people in America

---

[1] Hugh Fullerton, Associated Press, February 8, 1943.

really wanted in an interview that ran in *The Mediterranean Algiers Stars and Stripes*. In an interview, Hornsby asked Harry Salsinger of the *Detroit News*, "What good is them one-base knockers? Three of them guys have got to hit safe to get one run. Give me the guy that can slap the ball against them outfield walls."[2]

With Ted Williams wrapping up his training at Amherst, that is precisely what baseball fans across America were dying to see when he returned to the game in a Navy jersey that spring.

## The Untold Legend of the Cloudbuster Nine

*"I would not go through Pre-Flight again for a million dollars, but I would not trade the experience for ten million."*
—*Television personality and entertainer Ed McMahon,*
*who trained at Georgia Pre-Flight in 1943 and become*
*a Marine Corps pilot, serving in World War II and Korea.*[3]

When I found myself in the middle of one of the war's greatest untold baseball stories, I had been a ghostwriter for 25 years, hiding behind clients' words with speeches and opinion editorials. My career was built on public relations—impersonal and shallow; certainly not work imbued with family lore about naval gladiators who helped win a war.

Nothing I'd ever seen or written about came close to the allure of this team. And it wasn't just a story about baseball—though the 'Busters' magical season certainly was a tale worth telling—it was a personal story about my father's brush with the greatest ballplayers on Earth; it was a story about how he trained his heart out in the

---

[2] Harry Salsinger, *Detroit News* story in *Stars and Stripes*, February 17, 1943, p. 6.

[3] Ed McMahon, Hollywood, California, telephone interview by H. Michael Gelfand, April 8, 1994. Appeared in Gelfand's master's thesis, *Tomorrow We Fly: A History of the United States Navy Pre-Flight School on the Campus of the University of Georgia*, University of Georgia, 1994, p. 99.

minor-leagues to follow in the footsteps of his idols who morphed into the Navy's most powerful symbols for recruiting.

To understand the sport that has made and broken so many men, I headed to the archives at the University of North Carolina at Chapel Hill, ground zero for Cloudbuster history, with more than 6,000 items and images. Since I was a baseball novice struggling to find my father, archivists at the Wilson Library initially felt sorry for me, the tall, disheveled blonde with thick eyeglasses, scouring through images of a long-disbanded team. Using my family's World War II scrapbook as a show-and-tell guide, I found that librarians from different departments were instantly captivated by the sheer number of professional players who streamed through Chapel Hill.

Box by box, slide by slide, and clip by clip, the archivists handed me the keys to a largely untold story about a hero factory that had literally been gathering dust since the war. Because cadets' letters were censored and photography was restricted at athletic events on base, much of the personal history of this story was never recorded, or so we thought.

Good fortune, however, would have it that the story was beautifully preserved by something I did understand—publicity.

Thanks to Kidd Brewer and the *Cloudbuster*'s newspaper editors, the gritty Pre-Flight culture was captured 24–7 in an artistry of light and shadow, film and scribe. Teams of photographers, writers, illustrators from New York, and filmmakers camped out on the sidelines to capture the wartime campus in motion. After the war, thousands of *LIFE* magazine–quality images were stored in stacks of boxes under the dome of UNC's Wilson Library, where fabled photographers like Hugh Morton preserved a little-remembered story for seven decades.

It didn't take long to hit the jackpot on the baseball team.

When the spotlight was put on Ted, almost 25 major-league players emerged. They were officers and famous coaches and cadets in different phases of their careers. They ranged in age from their early 20s to their late 40s, and they all trained in Chapel Hill during the war.

## No Regrets

For Ted, the door to the V-5 program came out of the blue, in the spring of 1942, when he met a Navy recruiter who took him on a spur-of-the-moment ride to Quincy.

After an unexciting loss to the Tigers at Fenway Park, Williams's Red Sox publicist, Ed Doherty, introduced him to a young recruiter named Robert P. "Whitey" Fuller. The handsome, tow-headed lieutenant from Beverly, Massachusetts, was a former track star and sports publicist at Dartmouth who reported on the school's Big Green teams. Dressed in Navy blues with a polished line of brass buttons, Fuller carried himself like a college athlete and guy's guy who walked the talk, which Williams respected.

Squantum Naval Air Station, located on a sandy boot-tip point of Quincy, Massachusetts, was about an hour's drive south of Boston. On May 6, Ted had the day off before he had to play at Philadelphia. That morning, Fuller approached Ted with a curious prospect. If he was interested in seeing some aviation training exercises, he was welcome to pop down to Squantum Point, a base with runways for airplanes, harbors for seaplanes, and marshes for amphibious crafts. Without alerting the press, they drove down the coast with Doherty in a beach wagon for a secret tour of the base. It was a cool day with foamy waves churning in the Atlantic as red-winged blackbirds darted through salt-water marshes, ushering the dawn of spring. Thousands of miles away from the Boston coastline, the Battle of the Coral Sea roared in the Pacific Theater, proving that the war had moved from the sea to the skies as allied pilots bombed Japanese carriers.[4]

Squantum Point had captivated the world since the beginning of the air age. In 1910, the hooked point, with its beaches and giant pink-and-golden blocks of granite from Quincy's quarries, hosted one of the world's largest air meets, just seven years after the Wright

---

[4] James M. Scott, *The War Below: The Story of Three Submarines That Battled Japan*, Simon & Schuster, 2014, p, 61. (reference the first battle fought solely in the skies); multiple references, U.S. Department of Navy and Naval Historical Information Center.

Brothers made their historic flight over the dunes of Kitty Hawk, North Carolina. Over 11 days, nearly one million spectators gathered on the high meadows and boats in the harbor. They pushed into Squantum's narrow dirt streets by train, automobile, carriage, trolley, bicycle, and foot to see the world's most fantastic flying machines piloted by Wilbur Wright, Glenn Curtiss, and Britain's most dashing pilot, Claude Grahame-White, who won the highly publicized over-water race to the Boston Light in a Blériot monoplane. President William Howard Taft stood on a raised platform to watch the theatrics with Boston mayor John F. Fitzgerald (grandfather of John F. Kennedy) as 28-year-old Franklin D. Roosevelt milled through the crowd in a straw boater. Spectators were in awe of the aerobatics as flying machines danced over the peninsula, but the most popular attraction at the meet was a bomb-dropping contest that foreshadowed the use of airplanes as weapons. As Secretary of the Navy George von Lengerke Meyer watched plaster of paris-and-flour dummy bombs make direct hits on model battleships on the ground, he realized that he was witnessing the airplane's future role in the military.[5]

Originally called Dennison Base, Squantum Air Station was built after the First World War as a naval reserve station. When Ted toured the base, Squantum was a full-fledged air station with pilots living in the barracks and the wood-frame cottages near the marshes. The smell of aviation fuel hung in the air, and throughout the war Quincy rumbled, day and night, with the roar of Corsair and Hellcat engines blasting off in pairs over the Atlantic.[6]

During the three-hour tour, taking in a gunnery class and eating lunch at the officer's mess, Fuller elaborated on the Navy's decision to lower its education requirement to high school, opening up spaces

---

[5] Gordon Nelson, *Quincy Historic Society*, Spring 1981, Issue 4. John Lenger, "Conquests of the Air" *Harvard Magazine*, May–June 2003. Images, Quincy Historical Society.

[6] Interview with Ted Spencer, former historian, National Baseball Hall of Fame and Museum (who grew up in Quincy, remembering the war).

for a hungry pool of pilots. Ted knew that the V-5 Naval Aviation Cadet Training Program was gaining the reputation as the ultimate fraternity for fighter pilots. He knew the training was fierce and admission was not guaranteed—detractors that worked to whet his interest.

When Ted toured the base, he had barely flown in an airplane, let alone piloted one, so he did not know what it was like to sit in the cockpit.[7]

Commander John Voight, like Ted, was from San Diego. Although the two had never met, they hit it off as Voight put Williams in the cockpit of a hornet-yellow training Cub. Like a child, he pulled on goggles, running his hands over instruments and gauges. Looking through the windshield of the plane, taking in the smell of gasoline on metal, he felt a commanding sense of power similar to the charge he felt when he stood in the batter's box before thousands of fans. Though shy, Ted liked being the center of attention on his own terms, and that little yellow training Cub put him in the driver's seat of the war.

On the drive back to Boston, Ted signed the papers to apply for the Naval Aviation Cadet Training Program. It was just the first step in a four-year commitment; there were physicals to pass, insurance forms, publicity negotiations, letters of recommendation, and transcripts to gather with dismal grades, but Ted knew that he had found his calling.

The most common grade on Ted's Hoover High report card was a D. In fact, he earned Ds in 15 classes, including English and Spanish, a second language that his mother still spoke in San Diego. He earned a couple of Cs in geography and history, Bs in wood shop and typing, and the only A on his transcript was in physical education, where he earned a C in the second semesters of three out of four years of high school.

---

[7] Leigh Montville, *Ted Williams: The Biography of an American Hero*, p. 103. (Montville reported that Ted "flew" to tour Great Lakes Naval Training Station before Squantum, but I have read sources indicating that he had *never* flown in a plane when he toured Squantum.)

Ted may have barely passed core subjects for aviators, like science and arithmetic, but he was one of the most supremely focused athletes in the major-leagues. That will to win and sheer refusal to accept loss or the slightest imperfection was exactly what the Navy wanted and America sorely needed.

When Ted returned to the Shelton Hotel, he wrote a letter requesting consideration for the V-5 in thick black ink, mirroring the intensity of his booming voice.[8] He immediately reached out for letters of recommendation from the Red Sox management and former administrators at Hoover High School who could verify his graduation. On May 17, Ted officially requested reclassification to 1-A status, putting to an end the 3-A controversy that reporters hung around his neck. On the morning of May 22, he passed through the heavy wooden doors at the recruiting office at 150 Causeway Street in Boston, joining the Navy Reserves for four years as a seaman second class.

In a rare move, Ted tipped off Dave Egan about his secret enlistment, and he rewarded the slugger by reporting, "Ted Williams, without the benefit of a bat, hit the longest and hardest and loudest home run of his career yesterday, when he enlisted in the aviation branch of the United States Navy."[9]

Two weeks later, Ed Doherty wrote a glowing recommendation letter for Williams that read as if it had come straight out of the Pre-Flight recruiting book. On Red Sox stationery, he described Ted as a candidate with "perseverance, determination and the will to win." As much as Doherty hated to lose his star hitter, he said of Ted, "despite the fact that he is the champion batsman of the Major-Leagues, he has never let himself be carried away by thoughts of his own greatness."[10] That was the legacy that Ted carried into the war. For any reporter who secured a copy of his grades, the principal of Hoover High School, Floyd Johnson, rose to his defense, describing

---

[8] Bill Nowlin, *Ted Williams at War*, p. 31.

[9] Dave Egan, *Boston Record*, May 23, 1942, p. 1.

[10] Correspondence, June 5, 1942, recommendation letter for USN Aviation Training Selection Board.

Ted, who graduated in February 1937, as an "excellent school citi-zen."[11]

Little did he know he was about the get the best education of his life in the Navy.

## Ted and the Hero Factory

One might think that no stone has been unturned when it comes to Ted Williams, one of the most analyzed and profiled athletes of all time. Not so.

From May through August 1943, the curtain on his life closes during Ted's aviation training in Chapel Hill. And it was during this time that he played the majority of his World War II service-league baseball games wearing a jersey for the Cloudbuster Nine.[12]

Thanks to the Navy's meticulous record-keeping methods, the Pre-Flight archives opened up this thinly explored dimension of Williams's life when the UNC campus was transformed into a Camelot for elite athletes. With the exception of the Olympic Games hosted on the home front, never again would American campuses house so many elite athletes on one site, at one time, with one mission.

Pioneering outdoorsmen, who became the founding fathers of survival training, were there, along with Olympic boxers, members of the U.S. skiing team, world-champion rowers, and an assortment of athletes whose faces graced the iconic orange Wheaties box. Pre-Flight campuses enlisted the support of professional golfers and even circus performers, who taught the art of tumbling. Be it a major-league baseball player, or a professional football coach, world-class athletes were, in the words of Orville Campbell, "a dime a dozen," and reporters beat down their doors to learn the secret to the Pre-Flight formula.[13]

---

[11] Correspondence, June 9, 1942, Hoover High letter of recommendation.

[12] Per Bill Nowlin's records, Ted played a total of 40 service-league games in 1943, only about 20 in 1944, and about a dozen in 1945.

[13] "Dime a dozen," interview conducted by Mary Lane Baker with Orville Campbell, April 24, 1979.

While the war stole the immortality of athletes who missed Olympics and World Series pennants, they won laurels through the press with the Navy's help.

As soon as Pre-Flight sports camps were opened, publicity officers invited select reporters with honorable intentions to put on their sneakers and sweats to participate in the training firsthand. The snarky Dave Egans of the world who preyed on Ted's vulnerabilities were shunned. Crotchety fossils like the *Boston Globe*'s Mel Webb, who got the "Why don't you drop dead, you old bastard?" greeting from Ted when he stopped by his locker at the beginning of spring training, were banned from Pre-Flight bases and team buses. At long last, cadets like Ted Williams were safe to be themselves, leading a patriotic troop of sportswriters to write some of the most dazzling accounts of military baseball.[14]

Grantland Rice, nicknamed the "Matthew, Mark, Luke, and John of American sport," hailed the V-5's 90-day program as the roughest sports training he had ever seen. In Rice's gentlemanly words, Pre-Flight was a "man-making, battering collision that begins with daybreak and ends with darkness." When critics questioned favoritism of celebrity cadets, Grantland was quick to declare that the pilots in the making "drew no outside breaks."[15]

If there was ever a man who recognized sports legends it was Rice, who immortalized Seabiscuit's defeat of War Admiral and lyrically branded Notre Dame's "Four Horsemen" who stormed the field outlined against a blue-gray October sky. Twenty years later, Notre Dame's Jim Crowley came back as a Pre-Flight coach, and Rice assured readers that the Pre-Flight teams could slay any college squad had they not been overworked and lost star players by the week when they were shipped off to other bases.[16]

---

[14] Ed Linn, *Hitter*, p. 142.

[15] Charles Fountain, *Sportswriter: The Life and Times of Grantland Rice*, Oxford University Press, 1993, p. 4, regarding nickname of Matthew, Mark, Luke, and John of American sport.

[16] Grantland Rice, North American Newspaper Alliance, December 6, 1942, and *Valley Morning Star* (Harlingen, Texas), December 10, 1942, p. 9.

Frank O'Gara of the *Philadelphia Inquirer* wrote that the goal of the program was to "win that one big game" that was not played at Chapel Hill or any other Pre-Flight campus. He observed that the competition is "booked for the far reaches of the sky, where you can't lose, settle for a tie, score a moral victory, or wait til next year."[17]

When Dale Stafford, sports editor of the *Detroit Free Press*, watched a few days of training, he felt as if the Navy was hell-bent on ascertaining if its future pilots were "indestructible." He also made another keen observation that characterized the Pre-Flight culture: while there was no rule that bound cadets to stay, and no bell to ring when trainees collapsed, surprisingly few gave up.[18]

At age 80, Amos Alonzo Stagg, who had been named National Coach of the Year in 1943, visited a Pre-Flight campus. In awe of what he observed, he stated, "It's one of the finest things I've seen in all my years. My only regret is that I haven't been able to hold back the calendar," wishing he could have been on the inside of training when the schools were launched.[19]

As if he was gazing at a crystal ball, Francis J. Powers, a *Chicago Daily News* sports reporter and president of the Football Writers Association of America, declared that the Navy had created a training program that would be just as valuable to America after the war was won.[20] Proof of Powers's estimation came from the caliber of leaders produced by the Pre-Flight training lab.

Pre-Flight campuses produced an extraordinary concentration of astronauts, U.S. presidents, athletic coaches, Hollywood entertainers, major-league baseball and football luminaries, and the most decorated combat pilots in history. During the war, some

---

[17] Frank O' Gara, *Philadelphia Inquirer*, November 6, 1942, p. 37.

[18] Dale Stafford, *Detroit Free Press*, November 8, 1942, p. 47.

[19] George Davis, *Los Angeles Evening Herald and Express*, story reprinted in the Camp Lejeune Versus Chapel Hill Pre-Flight program published by Athletic Associations of U.S. Navy Pre-Flight Schools, 1945, p. 48.

[20] Francis J. Powers, *Chicago Daily News*, reprint in the Camp Lejeune Versus Chapel Hill Pre-Flight program published by Athletic Associations of U.S. Navy Pre-Flight Schools, 1945, p. 45.

80,000 cadets cycled through the Pre-Flight training program, representing a mere .5 percent of the 16 million Americans who served in uniform.[21]

Teamwork was the magical ingredient that drove this training experiment. Seventy-five years later, that long-archived formula, written on a kitchen table by two brothers from Ohio, would create a roadmap for success amongst military trainees and kids of the future.

## Descendants

For two years, I reached out to living cadets and players, and people connected to the Chapel Hill base, to understand this formula and how it factored into baseball. There were some embarrassing moments, like the day a pair of former cadets in a retirement community looked at me and howled with laughter when I told them I'd never heard of the famous World War I ace pilot Eddie Rickenbacker.[22]

As I met with descendants of the Pre-Flight coaches and players, they shared a strikingly common narrative. Because the base was cloistered behind guard posts and much of the activity was classified, most of the children were bewildered by their fathers' experiences at Chapel Hill. Descendants of ballplayers such as Johnny Pesky and Ted Williams never realized that at one time their fathers were amongst nearly 25 major-league players who trained at the University of North Carolina. David Pesky knew Pre-Flight training was rough-and-tumble but did not realize how much time his father spent on the road, boosting morale. Ted Williams's daughter Claudia, who advocates for child athletes, did not recognize any of her father's photos with the kids on the base, and she knew virtually nothing about her father's Pre-Flight training in Chapel Hill. She, too, was intrigued by the amount of time her father spent on the

---

[21] Sixteen million Americans did serve in uniform, but BUPERS presents the number of successful naval aviation graduates at 61,658 between 1942 and 1945, accounting for washouts who failed to graduate; thus, about a quarter flunked. BUPERS, The U.S. Navy Bureau of Naval Personnel.

[22] Interview with Charles Howard Kahn and Joseph Warren Mengel, July 20, 2017.

road playing baseball and was touched by the time he made for bat-boys and kids, scared to death that a parent or a loved one might never return from the war.[23] Claudia felt that Ted's time in Chapel Hill captured his truest self, as a highly principled man with a profound loyalty to country who proved that the "impossible is possible." Looking into the window of his Pre-Flight training, she felt that it was a beautiful example of her father's work ethic, when he strived for perfection in everything he set out to achieve.

At Chapel Hill, Ted was placed on a level playing field with like-minded men with "core and character" who put their lives on the line for their country. Whether they pitched for the New York Yankees or worked in a steel mill, he admired each and every one of them, treating his peers with equal admiration and "respect"—a value that is slipping away with the generations. Claudia was delighted to learn more about the humble band of brothers her father stayed in touch with over the years—extraordinary men she never knew whose Pre-Flight stories had never been fully told until now.

All of these encounters led me on a journey to the places where the spirit of Pre-Flight was conjured. My shoes crunched over the remains of a crumbling runway at the naval base where Ted sat in the cockpit of his first airplane; I smelled musty auction houses with crates of trading cards and saddle-soaped mitts; and I heard the roar of baseball fans who make the rafters tremble at games. Heading back to ground zero, I visited Pre-Flight dormitory rooms in Chapel Hill, university cottages tucked away on wooden lots, and used Donald Kepler's original survival map to hike the woods near Carrboro where trainees were tested for final exams. I toured old wooden airport hangars at Horace Williams Field that look just as they did in 1943 and visited what was left of the old ballparks where a secret history of this long-gone baseball team remains.

---

[23] Interviews with Claudia Williams, on November 6, 2016, and December 6, 2017.

# Chapter 8

# A TRAIN TO DURHAM

On the afternoon of Thursday, May 6, 1943, a 6-foot-3, 185-pound pilot in training with dark-blue eyes and a tangle of shiny black curls swaggered off the train into Union Station in Durham, North Carolina, not Chapel Hill, as many have believed after all these years.[1]

Theodore Samuel "Ted" Williams was 24 years and eight months old when he left Boston to report for his junior-level phase of training at the Pre-Flight Naval base. Decades later, he would remark that he pulled into the station at dusk—a time when the sky is the color of peaches that grow wild in orchards across eastern North Carolina.

The Splendid Splinter shipped into Durham train station during a heat wave, with temperatures hitting the 90s.[2] As heat rose from

---

[1] Chapel Hill Naval Aviation Physical Training Record Card indicated Ted weighed 185 pounds at check-in, and 176 pounds when he shipped out in August.

[2] Weather according to the National Ocean and Atmospheric Association for week of May 6, 1943.

the tracks, downtown blurred like a mirage. Crickets whirred from scrubby, knee-knocked trees around the platform, grackles cawed from sagging telegraph wires, and people hunched over on benches outside the station, too hot to notice the famous baseball star stepping off the train. And if they did catch wind of the news that Ted was rolling into town, most locals were too polite, and even a little scared, to ambush the famous slugger for an autograph. It was just the Southern way.

Miles before the Pullman clacked into the station, passengers could smell the sweet scent of freshly cured tobacco, which gave them a buzz. Years later, cadets would associate that smell with their arrival into the Bull City.

That afternoon Ted shipped in as cadet number 46854857485, assigned to the 25th Battalion, Company B, Platoon 1.[5] Instead of being met by the Pre-Flight bus like most cadets, he was picked up by his new baseball coach, Donald Kepler, who was nervous that he might not be up to speed on his facts about baseball. When Ted stepped off the train, shaking Kepler's hand with an extra-firm grip, he wore a wrinkled sports coat without a necktie and high-waisted trousers. He carried a battered Navy-issued suitcase and a duffle bag, and his permanent address was listed on the Navy clipboard as 4121 Utah Street, San Diego, California, with a temporary address as Fenway Park.

As America's greatest hitter crunched across the tarry platform, sweat poured down his back. He squinted in the afternoon sun, with dust gathering in the creases of his eyes from smokestacks belching cinder into the skyline. Though no sentiments have been recorded to describe Williams's specific mood that day, he had a sour expression on his face in those early Pre-Flight pictures. Reporters knew that he dreaded his time in Podunk, North Carolina, with egg-frying heat and the relentless mosquitoes. They knew he wasn't very excited

---

[3] This number was attached to Williams's personnel file in Chapel Hill; his official V-5 service number recorded by the Naval Aviation Cadet Selection Board, Suffolk County, Boston, Massachusetts on May 22, 1942, was 705-53-11.

about playing military baseball either, but what Ted did look forward to was flying, and no one was going to hold him back.

Because Ted wanted to get behind the controls of the most powerful aircraft in the world, he decided to pursue his time at Pre-Flight with absolute perfection. For the next 90 days, he was determined to brave the heat and the bugs; he would do whatever he was told and push himself beyond his limits if it got him in the cockpit of a Grumman fighter.

America sorely needed pilots in the spring of 1943. That week, full-page V-5 aviation advertisements ran in the *Raleigh News & Observer,* sold on racks inside the station. The Traveling Naval Association Selection Board had come up from Atlanta to Raleigh to accept applications from boys graduating from high school. The campaign's recruiting motto was "For attack today, for civilian life tomorrow," attracting hundreds of anxious parents with brave sons who'd never left home before.[4]

Cadets shipping into the Eastern Seaboard Pre-Flight School came from training stations in the Northeast, travelling on noisy troop trains that rolled along like a fraternity on wheels. Many were fast-talking city boys. Some were from coal-mining towns. Some were from the northern reaches of Maine and could not help but notice the still, slow-as-molasses pace of the rural South. For city slickers, it was like going back in time. Mules pulled wagonloads of produce into downtown Durham, where slack-jawed men, dripping in duck-cloth overalls, hovered around tobacco warehouses. The Jim Crow South had "white" and "colored" bathrooms and segregated water fountains, and there wasn't much entertainment either, evidenced by a peeling poster for a bingo game and an advertisement for a movie in downtown Durham.

It is likely that Ted shipped into Durham hours or perhaps a day after Red Sox shortstop Johnny Pesky, Philadelphia Athletics pitcher Joe Coleman, Boston Braves fireballer Johnny Sain, and first

---

[4] *Raleigh News & Observer,* May 6, 1943, p. 8.

baseman Buddy Gremp shipped into base due to medical checks following his surgery.[5]

Expectations upon arrival were the same for every cadet, even if their face had graced the covers of *LIFE* magazine and every major baseball publication in America. All of the Pre-Flight cadets knew that Chapel Hill promised the most brutal phase of physical training in the service. If they were honest with themselves, even the best athletes worried about making the grade. At this training camp, Ted and his friends knew that recreational baseball was a given and prepared to wear a jersey for a team they had barely heard of. The players expected to hit the road to face teams close to base, but they didn't foresee the number of games they would end up playing.

## The Drive to Chapel Hill

It took a few minutes to load up the jeep for the drive to Chapel Hill, a hiccup down the highway. Kepler had heard that Williams was notoriously hard to handle, but they quickly hit it off, talking about hunting and fishing without a word about baseball. Ted was not a smoker, and as Kepler drove through downtown he could not help but notice Big Tobacco's mark on Durham. Colorful hand-painted murals of bulls signifying the Bull Durham brand peeled off red brick walls of warehouses and factories; Chesterfield cigarette advertisements screamed from rooftop billboards; and the Lucky Strike water tower with its target-shaped logo rose like a beacon, welcoming cadets to the land of bright leaf tobacco. When the jeep headed down the two-lane road toward Chapel Hill, the landscape gave way to furrowed, rust-colored fields with scrap-lumber tobacco sheds. Every now and then there was a gas station with a falling-apart vegetable stand, but the rest of the trip felt like wide open country with cattle and goats and tenant shacks in the distance.

As Kepler shifted the gears of the jeep to reach the top of the hill, the oldest state university in America with its arcade of live oaks and

---

[5] Claims that Williams arrived two weeks after Amherst teammates. Leigh Montville, *Ted Williams: The Biography of an American Hero*, p. 109.

grassy lawns was a welcoming sight. Because Ted was not confined to the old tin-can bus that packed in cadets like sardines, he got the quick nickel tour of town, and of the Carolina Inn, which stood on the grounds like a Southern plantation. Main Street resembled Cambridge with rows of two-story colonial-style buildings. Franklin Street abounded with bakeries, pharmacies, barber shops, and sandwich shops and diners. There were campy bookstores and record shops, shaded by pinstriped awnings, along with hardware stores, souvenir shops, and grocers. Military uniforms were displayed in windows of clothiers advertising the return of the "straw hat days of summer." War bond signs were mounted on every window.

That week, *When Johnny Comes Marching Home* was playing at the Village Theater, and *The Fountainhead* was placed on bookshelves that very day.[6] The front page of the *Raleigh News & Observer* on the rack at Sutton's Drugstore reported American and French forces driving toward the Axis stronghold in North Africa. Japanese feared attacks from new bases in Alaska.

Even though the U.S. Navy practically owned the town, attractive coeds strolling sidewalks with books in their arms were a welcome sight to the new cadets. Ted Williams would joke that Chapel Hill was a quiet little burg in the middle of the "country," but with the pretty Southern women, the Hill didn't look so drab after all. In fact, from that moment on, it actually looked downright appealing.[7]

All of the cadets had heard of the torments of Hell's Half-Acre long before they landed on campus. When the jeep rolled through the security entrance toward Alexander Field, where Commander Hamilton's wingless Vought-Sikorsky observation plane was parked on the tarmac for instrument training, it was a greeting Williams never forgot.

---

[6] Jewish Women's Archive, "Ayn Rand's 'The Fountainhead' is Published," https://jwa.org/thisweek/may/06/1943/ayn-rand.

[7] Author's father and family made references to Chapel Hill being located in the "middle of the country," and players like Williams from larger cities did the same, but they found Chapel Hill to be endearing.

Fifty years later, Ted threw his head back and roared with a belly laugh when he remembered cadets with black eyes, leaning on crutches, bandaged up with casts on their arms and legs. Some were half-dressed, hanging out of dorm windows in dungarees, and they chanted, "We know you are out there, Williams. You'll be SOR-RY."

But Ted neither regretted those months at Chapel Hill nor his decision to become a fighter pilot. Not for one minute.[8]

At Carolina, he was glad to disappear into a mixing bowl of 1,875 cadets, listening to the chant "BOOTS, BOOTS, BOOTS" until the next battalion arrived.[9] From the very beginning, Ted insisted on being treated like every other cadet in a dog tag—and the Triple Crown winner got his wish when he stepped onto base like every other rookie.

From dawn until dusk, cadets snapped into formation, marching double time through the quads to class. The pilot stock was tough as nails with trainees from backgrounds so rough they listed their education as the school of "Hard Knocks."[10] The base newspaper described the arrival of the first cadets as "Main Street" youth from different civilian paths. "There was Bill from Boston, who worked in an arms factory. He did manual labor at the plant but also wasn't one to stray away from Stanlies Bar in 'Southie.' Ed came from New York, he had worked in a bank, was slightly underweight, had buried his nose in the books too long, and so was in need of the course. There were men fresh out of high school, men who had worked for years in factories, on the farms, and there were always the athletes."[11]

---

[8] Ted Williams, *My Turn at Bat*, p. 100. In subsequent interviews, Ted laughed about his pilot days in programs like HBO's *Legends and Legacies: Ted Williams*, July 15, 2009.

[9] K. Ray Marrs, *I Was There When the Earth Stood Still*, pp. 27–28.

[10] Cadet Howard Wood from Lansdale, Rhode Island, listed education as "hard knocks," amidst descriptions from Penn State, Boston College, etc. Cited from U.S. Navy Pre-Flight handwritten registration log May 21, 1943. Wilson Library holdings.

[11] *Cloudbuster*, September 19, 1942, page 2.

Ted enlisted in the Navy six months after Pearl Harbor after a long and painful seesaw between his 3A and 1A status. He resented being called yellow and unpatriotic by reporters, and he went into the service with a cloud over his head. But as soon as he shipped into Amherst, Ted surprised his worst critics, taking to the discipline of the military that he craved as a child. Reporters took a crack at him when he wheeled up to his dorm in a hired car after missing the train from Boston. In Ted's mind, his entrance into Chapel Hill would be different. And it was.

## Room 315

From the minute Ted and his teammates stepped foot on Alexander Field, nicknamed "the tarmac," they lost control of their lives. Unlike at Amherst, the baseball players were immediately separated and micromanaged by superiors who kept them busy during every waking minute. When incoming battalions shipped into base, the dorm was a beehive of activity as cadets were settling into their new rooms. Instead of letting buddies room together, the baseball players were split up to enforce studying and much-needed sleep. Ted was sent to Room 315 in Everett Dormitory, where he bunked with a Mainer who dived and swam at Bowdoin named Donald Cole Pletts. His other roommate was Philip Herold Regan from Salem, Massachusetts, who studied at the Massachusetts College of Optometry.

Pesky was assigned to the floor below in Room 206, with Louis Gremp in 207, Joe Coleman in 218, and Johnny Sain in Room 301. Players were so far away they could not even yell at one another from the windows.[12]

The university had taken over 12 dorms for military cadets. At the commander's insistence, Pre-Flighters lived in spartan, monastic quarters with whitewashed walls. Barracks were furnished with government-issued, double-decker metal bunks, a single wooden

---

[12] James E. Wadsworth Papers, 1942–1976, University of North Carolina Archives, Collection Number 05075, Box 1: Folder 3 [1943]. "Tarmac" reference from oral history interview with cadet Edward Deutchman, Del Monte Pre-Flight jargon. May 2, 2011.

dresser, and a desk for four men instead of for two roommates, as it was before the war. Girlie pinups were banned from rooms, while books were shelved military style, in a graduated order. Small luxuries like portable radios and electric fans were permitted during restricted hours, and windows remained open year-round.

That evening, Ted received strict orders for personal hygiene and room maintenance, and the orders never stopped. Buckles polished like mirrors; bed covers stenciled with the U.S. Navy logo made at a 45-degree angle—double fold (four inches) at the head, approximately nine inches from the end. Pillow slips folded neatly with loose end tucked under outboard side; towels centered at front of bed on crossbar; two pairs of shoes beneath bed always cleaned, shined, and squared off with the end of the bed with inboard shoe touching inboard bunk post.[13]

Newcomers visited the Small Ship Store to draw regulation uniforms and sports gear to complete the transformation into naval aviation cadets. The star treatment from the Red Sox was gone. Cadets were responsible for stenciling their own linens with the U.S. Navy logo and initialing their clothing. Sometimes heavy work boots did not fit, high-top tennis shoes had no arch support, and buttons popped off uniforms, but there were no alibis or complaints for blisters or clothing malfunctions. The only special gear Ted did receive was a baseball uniform, with a dark-blue ball cap and a jersey with NAVY stitched across the chest and no name on the back. Cranked out of textile mills by the thousands, Navy baseball uniforms came in small, medium, or large and nothing in between, and they were woven with a blend of cotton and wool. Ted's cleats were size ten and a half, and for the first time in years, he did not always get his lucky number nine.[14]

---

[13] Navy regulation manual for incoming cadets. Wilson Library papers, University of North Carolina at Chapel Hill. June 3, 1942, memo from executive officer, Packwood Graff, noted executive order 16 on identification of clothing.

[14] Ted's number is not visible at games; however, he was referenced in the Yanklands game scorecard as number 39. His clothing Ship Store receipt dated May 7, 1943, lists him with a shoe size of 10 1/2.

At Ted's initial physical, on May 22, 1942, he looked like a normal All-American male: his vision tested at 20/20, and his hearing at 15/15. His chest was 35 and a half inches at expiration and 38 and a half inches at inspiration, and his tonsils had been removed. His pulse was 76 before exercise and 96 with activity, and, like every other young American male, his body was nicked up with small scars: a burn on his forearm, small scars on his temple and his upper lip. Most of his teeth were intact with the exception of three lower molars.[15]

At Pre-Flight, there was another physical and the rough handling began. Cadets stripped down for measurements, with buzzcuts and painful inoculations. Athletic officers pulled out tape measures, and the cadets stepped on scales to determine exact height and weight down to the ounce, repeating the routine every month to measure fitness. Like guinea pigs in a science lab, painful dental work was to be done during Pre-Flight to avoid delays in later training, and Pre-Flight dentists did not hesitate to yank out wisdom teeth before cadets were sent back out on the training field. Even though the baseball players shipped into training in supreme shape, they would be surprised by the quick results of drills that worked muscles they didn't realize they had.

From the very beginning, the Navy did not need Superman, they wanted average All-American boys, with the stuff to make a naval aviator. The prodding and physical torture was a small part of the molding process, where pilots' minds were sharpened with lifelong skills.

When Ted collapsed into bed that night, fingering a newly issued dog tag, his arms itched from the first of the typhoid, smallpox, and tetanus vaccinations.[16] His back ached from the bone-jarring jour-

---

[15] May 22, 1942, Naval Aviation Cadet Selection Board, Boston, Massachusetts. Report of Medical Examination.

[16] Notes, V-5 1943 vaccinations described by John Sain, applied to all cadets, including Williams, who had same vaccinations administered in stages. According to Williams's medical records, he received a smallpox

*(Continued)*

ney from Boston, and though he put on a brave face, consenting to a few autographs, he was still sore from his hernia operation.

Rather than stewing about lucrative contracts he'd left behind, the greatest hitter in the world stared at a pitch-black ceiling as his roommates snored into oblivion. With the windows open, he listened to the rhythm of the woods beside the dorm. The meditative call of the great outdoors would bring him comfort during those long hot summer nights. Away from Boston, and the screeching cab lines and the trains clacking around Fenway Park, Ted Williams, some might venture to say, embraced his inner country boy that summer.

As he drifted off to sleep, Ted was focused on keeping his mouth shut and getting through the next 12 weeks. Even with his .406 batting average in 1941, the Hoover High School graduate understood that he would wash out of the program if he popped off or flunked his classes, and he knew that thousands of guys were dying to take his place as a Navy flier.

The next morning, the "Reveille" bugle trumpeted from intercoms at 5:30 a.m., and as one cadet noted in a diary, "the Navy didn't mean 5:31."[17] Years later, Johnny Pesky confided to a reporter that Pre-Flight life really was "up with the light of the moon . . . Double-time all day . . . Drill 'til tongues bulged," for 90 days straight. Officers were always trying to see if cadets had a cracking point . . . Pre-Flight was the place where they found it.[18]

---

vaccination on May 15, 1943. Dental notes: Taylor Morris, telephone interview by Michael H. Gelfand, June 5, 1994; Robert Rea, interview by Michael H. Gelfand, June 21, 1994; Naval Air Primary Training Command to C.E. Smith Bureau of Naval Personnel Papers, National Archives and Records Administration. Cadets noted that dentists were enthusiastic about pulling teeth, particularly wisdom teeth, so that possibility would have come next when Ted got his dental exam, which may have worried him.

[17] DeWitt Diary, "Diary, I'm Doing Graduate Work in the Navy," by Lieutenant (j.g.) DeWitt A. Portal, USNR, p. 7.

[18] Austen Lake, *Boston Evening American,* January 11, 1952, p. 46.

## Ted's Father Figure

In baseball circles, it is a well-known fact that Ted's father, Samuel Stuart Williams, was an absentee father fond of his drink. He was not a man who took the time to play catch with his son, leaving a void to be filled by other men like his uncle, Saul Venzor, who struck out Babe Ruth, Lou Gehrig, and Joe Gordon at a 1936 exhibition.[19]

In Chapel Hill, Ted forged an unshakable bond with people that stayed with him for life. Decades later, Ted welcomed buddies from Pre-Flight and their families to the dugout. After all those years, reporters missed the story because they did not understand or appreciate the old Navy connection.

Over the decades, these mentors showed up quietly, slipping into the clubhouse without notice to help him through tough times. One of those meetings took place in 1946, during his disastrous 5-for-25 performance at the World Series, when the Splendid Splinter's confidence was badly shaken and he needed someone outside of baseball to lift him up. Unbeknownst to Ted, Johnny Pesky picked up the phone after Game Three and called their old baseball coach from Pre-Flight for moral support. "Can you drop by and talk to him about fishing to get his mind off the game?" Johnny asked, offering to leave a ticket at Will Call with a pass to the clubhouse. "Make it look like a surprise," he said, "Casual, like the good old days . . . he'd love to see you."

It was during Game Five of the World Series when Don Kepler came through the door of the Red Sox clubhouse. Reporters, who lived to invade Ted's private life, did not notice the middle-aged man under a ball cap sitting in the clubhouse talking about fly casting. Though he never complained, Williams's elbow was terribly swollen, and he was stuffed up on antibiotics from the flu.[20] In rare form, he wept after the Series loss, but his mood was lifted by some-

---

[19] Jim Prime and Bill Nowlin, Ted Williams: *The Pursuit of Perfection,* Sports Publishing, 2002, p. 31.

[20] Ed Linn, *Hitter,* p. 214.

one he trusted—a man who cared. According to Kepler's son, Ted never found out that Johnny made that call.[21]

Ted was not a man who worshipped many heroes. But he always took the time to write his friends from Pre-Flight, even if he was exhausted from marathon train rides, living from one hotel to the next, or going through a painful divorce. Unbeknownst to some of his biographers, he wrote long, personal letters to his mentors' families when they died because in his bullishly, discreet way, these men were his heroes. Ted scribbled heartfelt condolences on hotel stationery in his loud and potent penmanship to wives and children. Sometimes, families received personal typewritten letters on Red Sox letterheads, yet Ted made sure they knew that he put loyal, hard-working men like Donald Kepler on a pedestal where they belonged.

This unshakable trust with a rare few was forged by something deeper, and more important, than baseball. Some might call it a brotherhood.

When Pre-Flight cadets came to Chapel Hill, they were trained to risk their lives to protect their fellow man, and they did so gladly with 100 percent effort. Ted had no patience with people who did not strive for perfection. With unfailing loyalty and a shared sense of purpose, Chapel Hill was one of the places where Ted found his tribe, and it did not matter if they grew up on mill hill or had their face on a Wheaties box, he treated every peer and coach with the same level of respect.

He trusted those men with his life, and one of them was still living when I began researching this book, a man who was on the team bus, and the base, watching it all happen in that glorious season of 1943.

---

[21] Phone interview with Rob Kepler, August 14, 2017.

# Chapter 9

## THE LAST LIVING PLAYER

When I searched through the 1943 Cloudbusters lineup, checking the name of every single player from starters to benchwarmers, I never considered that any of the team members were alive. As far as I knew, Johnny Pesky, who died in 2012 at age 93, was the last survivor, passing away a decade after Ted. But when I Googled a pitcher named Ivan Fleser, Betty Fleser's obituary flashed up, saying that she "is survived by her husband, Ivan." In that same small-town paper in Central Michigan, I found a recent story picturing a gentleman named Ivan Fleser, wearing a blue baseball hat with a Navy emblem. He had his arm slung around the shoulder of another former coach when they spoke at an event about America's favorite pastime at a local church.

Thinking the Ivan Fleser who played for the Cloudbusters would be pushing 100 years old, I almost threw the clipping away, but he kept staring back at me with bright-blue eyes. When I telephoned the *Advisor & Chronicle* newspaper, I was in the midst of asking the receptionist about a man named Ivan with the last name F-l-e-s . . . when she interrupted in a clipped Michigan accent, saying, "Oh sure, everyone knows Ivan. He was the baseball coach at the high school . . . lives right down the road."

It was a Monday afternoon in Marshall, Michigan, with two inches of fresh snow on the ground when Ivan answered the telephone. In late March, he was frustrated that he'd missed church that week because he could not drive on the roads. It was on that frosty afternoon that we embarked on the first of many conversations about the players every baseball fan admired, the team that very few people remembered, and the kid in the dugout.

At age 96, Ivan drove, mowed his own grass, and had just given up ice fishing a few years earlier. The former right-handed pitcher from Michigan shipped into Pre-Flight in March of 1943, joining a home state officer known as "Jerry" Ford, who would later become the nation's 38th president.

Ivan described Ted Williams as a quiet, regular Joe kind of guy who did not want any special treatment. He described his sidekick, Johnny Pesky, as a "ball of energy . . . a real talker," and then he told me stories about those long hauls on the bus.[1]

Weeks later, I flew to Grand Rapids, Michigan. Winter clung to the land as I drove toward Battle Creek down farm roads with views of grain silos and red barns set on flat pastures. For much of his life, Ivan lived in Marshall, a Norman Rockwell–type town of 4,000 residents, with a turn-of-the-century town square and outlying farmland dotted with shallow lakes that freeze in the winter. He lived near the historic district in an immaculate one-story wooden cottage, with two small American flags crisscrossed in the window. When I arrived around ten o'clock in the morning, Ivan answered the door wearing a pressed plaid shirt and shined loafers. When he smiled, he appeared to be in his 70s.

That morning, Ivan told me that he had never really been to the doctor and he'd only had one cavity. Then he said, "If I could do anything right now I'd go ice fishing. Best fish you ever had in your

[1] When I first spoke with Ivan Fleser, he was 96 years old. His birthdate is September 19, 1919.

life . . . bet I've cut 1,000 holes in the ice around these parts in my lifetime."

Taking me back to his years in the Navy, Ivan clasped his hands together, going back to the day he could have died. On his wall was an oil painting of a P-29 (PB4Y) Privateer patrol bomber, the Navy version of the B-24 bomber. On the morning of January 12, 1945, Ivan's plane crashed down into the Pacific, 500 miles off the coast of California en route to Hawaii. Ivan was the navigator in the glass bubble mounted on the bottom of the plane, a workhorse for the Navy with huge double-wasp engines. When the first two engines failed, most of the crew scattered toward the hull, where they furiously inflated rafts. When the third and fourth engines died, the Privateer glided toward the ocean in silence. The last sounds Ivan heard were the waves before the plane slammed into the Pacific at five o'clock in the morning. It took about three-and-a-half minutes for the plane to sink, and the crew used Pre-Flight skills to escape the suction of the sinking bomber. The men were in life rafts for 12-and-a-half hours, in swells so high the Navy had to send a special plane for the rescue. Sporting a busted lip, Ivan was the only crew member injured. Four of his friends were still living when we met, and Ivan calls them every Christmas day.

According to Ivan, Pre-Flight school was "definitely" the most difficult phase of aviation training—a real "pressure cooker," he said, both physically and mentally. "Everything had to be done their way, as perfectly as possible," he said. And after all these years, Ivan admitted that he may not have gotten through the course without one diversion—baseball.

Having been raised as a dyed-in-the-wool Cubs fan, Ivan converted to the Detroit Tigers. He had watched the game with neighbors he had known most of their lives, and he felt like the ritual of popcorn and baseball was a part of them.

Ivan was the one of the middle children of eight brothers and sisters, raised in Burnips, Michigan—a town his friends jokingly called "Turnips." His father was a carpenter who made sure all five boys played baseball. In 1940, Ivan arrived at Western Michigan University with $65 in his pocket—his life savings. College cost $37.50 a semester, so he lived in a boarding house with two of his brothers and worked as a carpenter, repairing broken chairs for housing and meals. He played baseball, too, mostly as an outfielder, leaving school his junior year to join the Navy. When Ivan shipped into Chapel Hill on March 25, 1943, he was assigned to the 22nd Battalion, Company H-2, and was the only member of his battalion with significant college baseball experience. Ivan lived in Grimes Dormitory, Room 311.

Ivan told me that baseball tryouts for Pre-Flight were posted on the bulletin board in the rec hall. In the third week of March, about 100 cadets rambled out to the field. Since baseball was a varsity-only sport, not open to all of the cadets, there were only about 30 spots on the team, so only one in three cadets made the squad.[2] Of those players, only 18 or so were really involved. Some of the cadets had never seen a real live professional baseball game, let alone met a player, and they pinched themselves for the chance to audition before the big-league coaches. Coaches included Buddy Hassett, who scouted talent for infielders and hitters, while Pete Appleton and Robert "Ace" Williams took a look at the pitchers. Alex Sabo eyed a dismal display of potential catchers, while Coach Kepler did his darnedest to give every boy a chance to make the team.[3]

At 5-foot-9, Ivan was one of the shortest and, in his words, "chunkiest" baseball players on the squad. He recalled another left-handed pitcher from NYU, but he had trouble getting the ball over the plate, so Ivan pitched nonstop as soon as the season began. That month, there were about a dozen games scheduled against nearby colleges. Manned with high school players and a few college scrubs, the 'Busters lost half of the games against NC State, Duke, and UNC, making comical errors in ballparks with practically empty stands.

Ivan's best and worst Pre-Flight game was against NC State. He laughingly described how he was pitching a no-hitter. "I was doing so well until the eighth [actually, sixth] inning—we were leading 8 to 0

---

[2] The 1942–1943 Pre-Flight yearbook details baseball as varsity-only sport.

[3] *Cloudbuster*, March 13, 1943, p. 4.

when my arm went limp from overuse," he said. "Could not even get the ball over the plate for the rest of the game. It was devastating to me—a killer."

After NC State came from behind to beat the Cloudbusters, 9–8, a coach assured Ivan that "help was on the way" next week. Little did he know his relief pitchers would come in the form of professional pitchers of some renown—Joe Coleman and Johnny Sain.

According to Ivan, the naval base was cloaked in secrecy about the arrival of professional athletes. Officers were especially on the q.t. about Ted Williams, not wanting to disrupt training. He explained that diaries were banned to protect classified interests on the base. If cadets had time to write letters, the content was advisedly banal. Even the base's postcards featuring cadets in training controlled the image of the Pre-Flight training, and Ivan knew that a slip of the tongue about Ted's arrival might earn him a demerit, so he sealed the secret with a smile.

The Boston press would have killed for the news Ivan received. Weeks before Williams arrived, sportswriters scratched away at the story. With unconfirmed intelligence, reporters fueled anticipation about the Cloudbusters' fantasy lineup. Betting on Ted's arrival, they banged out headlines about the strongest service team in the nation that would give Norfolk's teams a run for their money.

Ivan knew that Norfolk's Naval Air Station and Naval Training Station were two of the best service teams in the country. He knew the reporters were on the right track with the headlines, and he longed to play in at least one of those games before he shipped out.

## Competition in Norfolk

At the beginning of the war, the Naval Training Station's commander, Captain Henry A. McClure, was lukewarm about baseball, but when he saw how the game electrified morale, he decided to build the very best team in the Navy.[4]

---

[4] Rich Radford, *Virginia Pilot,* July 24, 2011, p. 1.

Norfolk dwarfed the Chapel Hill base with 16,000 active duty officers and sailors, and a revolving cast of professional athletes who moved around like pinballs from battleships to bases. The station's chief warrant officer, and coach of the Bluejackets baseball team, was Gary Bodie, who spent much of his time cherry-picking the best players from new arrivals. Norfolk spared no expense to accommodate its players with the best equipment and uniforms that Uncle Sam could buy. Bodie was notorious for shipping players out to sea if they did not perform, and his boss, Captain McClure, was even more aggressive, throwing entertainer Bing Crosby out of the dugout at a war bond benefit in Washington, D.C., when he was talking to Norfolk's players before a game.[5]

To upgrade the infield to major-league standards, Bodie summoned the Washington Senators' groundskeeper to his training stadium, later known as McClure Field. Padded seats with tilted backs and armrests were installed in the dugouts, and officers laid sheets over the seats so they could sit with the team in their white uniforms.[6] In 1942, Bob Feller shipped into Norfolk, which set up a schedule with over 30 games, including 11 professional teams. By the spring of 1943, the station had two equally strong teams known as the Airmen and the Bluejackets.

Bodie wrangled former teammates and friends of the Cloudbusters, setting up a beautiful rivalry that became the talk of the Navy. Before the Amherst Five shipped into Chapel Hill, seven games were slated against Norfolk from May through July.

## A Bus to Annapolis

Ted and the players from Amherst barely got a chance to see the base before they were on a bus bound for Annapolis on May 7. At least nine professional players were on the bus that Friday afternoon

---

[5] Clay Shampoe and Thomas R. Garrett, *Baseball in Norforlk, Virginia,* Arcadia, 2003, p. 61.

[6] Eddie Robinson with Paul Rogers, *Lucky Me,* Southern Methodist University Press, 2011, pp. 25–27.

including Yankees first baseman Buddy Hassett and St. Louis Cardinals minor-league catcher Joe Cusick. Alex Sabo from the Washington Senators was there, too, with Dusty Cooke, a veteran with the Red Sox and the Yankees, and Coach Kepler, who bounced on board with a clipboard, wearing his Navy-blue ball cap.

Ted's best friend and constant companion had been by his side since he enlisted, so it was a treat to spend time with Johnny on the drive to Maryland. Johnny "Pesky" Paveskovich had bushy eyebrows, deep-set, dark-brown eyes, and a sharp nose that earned him the nickname "The Needle." But Johnny's most endearing feature was his moonbeam smile.[7]

Pesky was described by one of the *Boston Herald*'s most poetic scribes as a Rockwellian baseball guy weaned on the game in a baggy baseball uniform with the sun on his shoulders, digging his cleats into real grass.[8] In high school, Johnny worked as a dockman, loading and unloading logs for Silverfalls Timber Company. After breaking into professional ball, Johnny passed on offers from the Yankees and Detroit. Instead, he signed with Red Sox scout Ernie Johnson, because Ernie was the nicest to his family. Johnny never forgot those easy conversations at the kitchen table in the Slabtown cottage, where Ernie brought his mother flowers and a fine bottle of bourbon to his father.

Representing the United States of America was an honor Johnny never took for granted, and his father, who served as a cook in the Austria-Hungary Navy before the Great War, was never prouder of his son than the day he wore his dress whites to church in Portland, Oregon.

Johnny's father worked in the lumber mills. As a kid, Johnny hung out at the old Vaughn Street ballpark, just a few blocks from home, where his love of baseball was forged. He worked his way up as the clubhouse boy where players tipped him a quarter to shine their shoes. He even washed their jockstraps and thought he had the

---

[7] Interview with David and Alison Pesky, June 14, 2017.
[8] David Cantaneo, *Boston Herald*, April 14, 1986, p. 82.

greatest job of any kid in the whole state of Oregon. As a batboy, Johnny came up as the little brother Williams never had. Johnny brought that same innocent, easy-going spirit to Hell's Half-Acre, where he tried to keep his friend Ted in good spirits. When Ted snarled, Johnny smiled, setting the scene for those brotherly photos taken by Navy photographers at Chapel Hill.

In an interview with the National World War II Museum in New Orleans, Johnny said that one of the reasons he was so close to Ted and other players in the Army like Bobby Doerr was because they were from the West. When he came to Chapel Hill that May, Johnny was the only player in the Amherst group who lived near the peanut and tobacco fields of eastern North Carolina, where he got his start a few years earlier with a Rocky Mount Red Sox team of the Pied-mont League.[9] Knowing that people from the South were kind and gracious, Johnny drew on the positive memories of his days in North Carolina to help players adjust to the down-home culture.

Boston Braves pitcher John Franklin Sain was the only Southern-born player of the five. Born in Yell County, Arkansas, Johnny was the son of an auto mechanic. He prided himself on being a self-taught observer, operating his own garage during the off-season, and could fix just about anything with a socket wrench or a screw-driver. Raised between a sea of cotton fields and the Ozark Moun-tains, he had a country boy streak, too, loving nothing more than a day in the woods with a shotgun, hunting deer. The 6-foot-2, tobacco-chewing fireballer came up in the Northeast Arkansas League and pitched there from 1936 to 1939. In 1942, Johnny made it to the majors, where he was managed by Casey Stengel. The cheeky hurler had a decent curveball with solid control. His speed would come in the Navy, where he got his best pitching experience at Pre-Flight.

Johnny had been known to watch airplanes, studying their flight path, from the tower atop Corey Hill in Brookline, Massachusetts.

---

[9] National World War II Museum oral history interview with Johnny Pesky, New Orleans, Louisiana, November 9, 2007.

On the ballfield, he was the guy standing in the corner stroking his chin as he studied players with that same intensity. Though he was not in a hurry to get in the cockpit, Johnny enlisted in the Navy in August of 1942. He went about his application in a steady, calculating manner, gathering recommendations from people who described him as a clean-living, patriotic kid, not as a ballplayer.

Johnny's high school burned down in 1937. With no transcript, the superintendent of the Havana public school system wrote a letter to the Navy Recruiting Station, vouching for his degree. The commander of the American Legion Post 147 in Belleville, Arkansas, portrayed Johnny as a straitlaced American who never smoked or drank intoxicating liquor; and Buford Compton, the local sheriff, said he was an upright citizen who never belonged to any un-American organizations.[10]

Johnny came in claiming that he was a slow learner who liked to mull "over things again and again." Decades later, *Ball Four* author and major-league pitcher Jim Bouton credited Sain for teaching him everything he knew about professional baseball, from wearing his socks inside out to prevent blisters from lint to negotiating contracts. Bouton, who felt that Johnny belonged in the Hall of Fame, observed that "Johnny sees very deeply into things." At Pre-Flight, Johnny applied that Machiavellian approach to learn from the best players in the league, using those afternoon practices and games to improve his skills as a pitcher.[11] Playing on a sports squad known as the "Buffalos," Sain not only lost ten pounds at Pre-Flight, he scored 4.0 marks in engineering, football, hand-to-hand, and military track.[12]

Joseph Patrick Coleman shipped in from Amherst with the reputation of learning to pitch from the priest who discovered a bull-

---

[10] John Sain Naval Aviation Cadet letters of recommendation from G. N. Bryan, John R. Harkness, Buford Compton, O. J. Fergeson of Arkansas, 1942.

[11] Matt Schudel, obituary writer, *Washington Post*, November 9, 2006. Pat Jordan, *Sports Illustrated*, May 8, 1972, p. 34.

[12] Naval Aviation Physical Training Record, Chapel Hill Pre-Flight, May 6, 1943, through September 8, 1943.

headed youngster named George Ruth.[13] As a principal and coach at Malden Catholic High School, Brother Gilbert Mathias could be spotted on the field in a long black cassock during batting practice. In three years, Joe became his star right-hander who lost only two games, pitching his team to the state title. In 1940, Brother Gilbert pulled Joe out of class to meet his old student, Babe Ruth, who swung by the school for a visit. Ruth said, "The kid looks good, but he doesn't know how to throw a curve." Using blackboard erasers instead of a ball, Ruth took Coleman out into the hall and taught him the proper wrist action to throw a curve. After Joe was passed over by the Red Sox, Brother Gilbert gave his name to his old friend Connie Mack, who gave him a leg up to the big league with the Athletics.[14]

Coleman's father was a tailor who came from a good Catholic family. He saw to it that his son attended Mass and got an education. Coleman, who came to Pre-Flight School with a degree from Boston College, was one of the few players with a college education. He enlisted in the Navy in November 1942, immediately heading to Amherst.

In 1942, Lewis Edward "Buddy" Gremp considered the Army but decided to enlist in the Navy to follow his friends. The first baseman from Pine Lawn, Missouri, began his professional career with Albany in the Georgia League in 1936 as a shortstop. He was 16 years old, earning a whopping $60 a month for the Club D team, and Buddy never forgot those days.

Toward the end of his life, his favorite memory centered on the day he put on a major-league uniform for the first time and stepped into Sportsman's Park in St. Louis. "I had sat in those stands as a ten-year-old member of the Knothole Gang, and dreamt I would one day play there," he wrote in a questionnaire submitted by a fan.

---

[13] Brother Gilbert, edited by Harry Rothgerber, *Young Babe Ruth, His Early Life and Baseball Career, from the Memoirs of Xaverian Brother*, McFarland, 1999, pp. 20–22.

[14] Norman Macht, *The Grand Old Man of Baseball: Connie Mack in his Final Years, 1932–1956*, University of Nebraska Press, 2015, p. 271.

"It was a dream come true."[15] In September 1942, he was the second Braves player to make military headlines, enlisting in the Navy a few weeks after Johnny Sain.[16] From Boston, the pair shipped into Amherst, where they forged a lifelong bond with Ted Williams, Johnny Pesky, and Joe Coleman.

## The Nine

Third baseman Pete Appleton (born Peter William Jablonowski) spoke with a Polish accent when he arrived at Pre-Flight in 1943. "Jabby" enrolled at the University of Michigan in 1922, wearing ragged clothes with hardly a penny to his name. With speed and an unstoppable work ethic, Jabby could have led the Wolverines in football or basketball. It was Dr. Ray Fisher, a former pitcher with the New York Yankees, who talked him into playing baseball, and he became one of the best pitchers in the Big Ten. In Jabby's senior year, the team won the conference title.

After a stint with Waterbury in the Eastern League, he landed a contract with the Reds. When Jabby came to Chapel Hill, he was 38 years old and had played for seven major-league teams. He was also known as a musician: it was his talent as a classical pianist that made him stand out at Pre-Flight. When he wasn't on the ballfield, he could be found in Memorial Hall, rendering ragtime, jazz, and classical selections to cadets on a grand piano. On the bus, Jabby would chime in with Yankee Buddy Hassett, known throughout baseball for his beautiful tenor voice.

John Aloysius "Buddy" Hassett, nicknamed the "Brooklyn Thrush," was the son of a plumber and grew up in Hell's Kitchen. As he made his way up to the majors, Buddy worked as a plumber, carrying a lucky sixpence in his pocket that paid off big in 1942. That season he realized the dream of every youngster in New York, filling Lou Gehrig's shoes at first base, as *The Pride of the Yankees* played in theaters. Little did Buddy or the rest of the Cloudbusters realize, this

---

[15] Tom Burlin Player Questionnaire Collection, Baseball Hall of Fame.

[16] *Portsmouth Herald*, September 12, 1942, p. 5.

fabled prologue of *The Pride of the Yankees* would apply to hundreds of professional, college, and amateur players who died in the war:

> *This is the story of a hero of the peaceful paths of everyday life. It is the story of a gentle young man who, in the full flower of great fame, was a lesson in simplicity and modesty to the youth of America. He faced death with the same valor and fortitude that is now being displayed by thousands of young Americans on far-flung fields of battle. He left behind him a memory of courage and devotion that will ever be an inspiration to all men.*

When Buddy joined the Yankees, he became the darling of the press, serenading fans with his beautiful tenor voice. One week before the World Series, he was a featured player in the Wheaties "Breakfast of Champions" campaign.[17] When he was written up as the hardest-hitting first baseman in the majors, Buddy did not attribute his performance to a special bat or a new stance; rather, he claimed that confidence came from the Yankees jersey he wore. The feeling was short-lived. On November 5, 1942, Ed Barrow, president of the Yankees, wrote Buddy's naval recommendation letter. His first baseman shipped into Pre-Flight school a few days after Christmas and received a generic jersey for a no-name team no one recognized.[18]

At Chapel Hill, Buddy, who was down to 180 pounds in early 1943, kept his chin up and made himself useful in every way possible. Not only did he coach baseball, he lectured on seamanship, damage control, projectiles, guns, torpedoes, ship drill, and first aid, and even told *The Sporting News* that he looked forward to heading overseas.[19]

---

[17] Wheaties "Breakfast of Champions" ad copy states that ad ran a week before the World Series.

[18] *Morning Call* (Allentown, Pennsylvania), June 7, 1942, p. 12.

[19] *The Sporting News*, "In the Service," February 18, 1943, p. 6.

Vic Bradford shipped into Chapel Hill on May 25, 1943, with the 11th V-5 indoctrination program. Six-foot-2 and packed with solid muscle, Vic worked as a laborer in steel mills, earning accolades for his Superman physique. His reputation as a multisport prodigy began at the University of Alabama, where he was a blocking back for the Crimson Tide's 1938 Rose Bowl team.[20] Despite failing eyesight, he earned a spot as a utility outfielder with the New York Giants in 1943. After surgery corrected his vision, he shifted from 3-A to 1-A status, shipping into Pre-Flight wearing eyeglasses that became his trademark on the field.

Appropriately nicknamed "Wildfire," Harry Francis Craft was born in Ellisville, Mississippi. His father worked as a timekeeper at a local shipbuilding company and passed away when Harry was ten years old. Harry was raised by his mother and an uncle, who owned a grocery store in Throckmorton, Texas, a dusty cotton town where half of the locals were sharecroppers.

Harry was a quiet, handsome guy with a boyish Cheshire Cat grin. Like the other coaches, he was a sports prodigy, playing football, basketball, and track before he landed on the baseball field by chance. At Mississippi College, he was a star halfback. When the coach sent him over to the baseball field for some wind sprints, he was by far the fastest runner on the field. When Harry put on a glove and learned to play baseball, he became one of the most versatile outfielders in college sports. In 1935, Craft signed with the Cincinnati Reds organization for $75 a month. He cut his teeth with the Monessen Class-D ball club, sinking half of his salary into room and board in a dreary Pennsylvania town, where workers rolled steel for Chryslers and cables for the Golden Gate Bridge. In 1937, Harry got the late-season major-league call-up to the Reds, where he stayed put, playing in two World Series. On July 14, 1942, Craft played his last major-league game for the Reds before he enlisted to serve Uncle Sam.[21]

---

[20] *Call-Leader*, (Elwood, Indiana), June 2, 1943, p. 4.

[21] Colt Stadium press release, January 20, 1962.

Allen Lindsey "Dusty" Cooke was one of baseball's all-time fastest runners, earning his nickname for the dust he kicked up stealing bases. Dusty was the son of a Confederate soldier and the youngest of ten children. He grew up in the mill town of Swepsonville, about 20 miles up the road from Chapel Hill, working six months a year picking cotton. Growing up on mill hill, there were two things to do—fight and play baseball. When the Yankees scouts looked at Dusty, some said he was talented enough to "replace Babe Ruth in the outfield." After he graduated from high school, the farmboy clutched a $15,000 contract with the Yankees in 1927, an unheard-of pile of money in his day. In 1931, Dusty debuted with his first widely publicized crash, slamming face-first into a brick wall to make a diving catch against the Washington Senators. By the time he shipped into Chapel Hill, Dusty had undergone several surgeries to repair his knees and shoulders from a decade of reckless injuries. Appropriately, he became a pharmacist's mate in the Navy, toting around a black medic case to treat teammates' injuries on the sidelines of Cloudbusters games.[22]

Joe Cusick shipped into Chapel Hill a few days after Christmas in 1942. He had served as a catcher for Holy Cross in Massachusetts before he became a catcher for the Albany Cardinals and a manager within the St. Louis Cardinals system. When Joe transferred to Chapel Hill, he and Hassett and Appleton were among the first professional players to light up the star power of the Navy flier team.

Alex Sabo, from New Jersey, had played college baseball and football at Fordham University in New York City. He played a career total of five major-league games as a catcher for the Washington Senators in 1936 and 1937 and was one of the first big-leaguers to ship into Pre-Flight on July 21, 1942.

Ed Moriarty was an Irish Catholic who considered becoming a priest before he became a second baseman for the Boston Braves when its name was temporarily changed to Boston Bees from 1936 to 1940. Moriarty was another Massachusetts native who shipped into

---

[22] *Cloudbuster*, March 13, 1943, p. 4.

Pre-Flight on March 25, 1943, to become an athletic coach along with Joe Gonzales, who pitched for the Red Sox in 1937.

## The New Baseball Coach

The team bus, with its eggbeater engine and rattling windows, would become the players' second home over the next three months. According to Ivan Fleser, players would run to the bus with bagged lunches, hoping for some shut-eye on its hard, lumpy seats. If they weren't sleeping, members of the team tutored one another through academic rough spots to keep pace with their studies.

On the bus, Coach Kepler warned newcomers that it would be three months of sober, spit-shine clean living with absolutely no drinking on base, no chewing tobacco or cigarettes, and strict rules with female coeds who were outnumbered by males by a six-to-one ratio. There were mandatory hikes every Wednesday and Saturday in blistering heat. There would be no breaks or perks, but plenty of ditch digging and extra work on the ballfield where the 'Busters were expected to win, and win big, every time.

During the eight-hour trip to Annapolis, the team musician Buddy Hassett led sing-alongs of his Tin Pan Alley favorite, *In the Good Old Summertime*. Ivan Fleser said Johnny Sain chimed in with a beautiful tenor voice as Ted Williams drew into himself, in deep thought.

Still benched while he recovered from surgery, Ted was not permitted to play in the game, but he often traveled with the team to boost morale. He could be a gruff guy, but Ivan claimed he was a true team player who always supported his teammates, regardless of their level of talent or rank.

One of the men Ted talked to on those bus rides was Coach Kepler, who fashioned himself as a Pennsylvania farmboy who was good with a fishing pole and a shotgun. Though Kepler was a head shorter than his star hitter, there was a raw intensity about him. Ted certainly respected his marksmanship, knowing that he hunted bears, a feat hunters do not live to brag about if they miss a shot or make a mistake. But the interest that truly connected them was not baseball—it was fly fishing, which Kepler had mastered in the cool rivers of Pennsylvania. Fly fishing was as technical as the science of hitting, and that sport launched the beginning of a lifelong friendship.[23]

When the team pulled into the gates of the Naval Academy, the moon was high in the sky. That night, players bunked in campus dorms where officers who launched Pre-Flight had lived 20 years earlier. Command staff missed most of the out-of-town games, but not this one, and officers like my grandfather drove up in separate cars to see if the Cloudbusters could beat their alma mater. On May 5, Annapolis's Middle Nine crushed Georgetown, 6–1, so the fliers definitely had their work cut out for them.[24]

On Saturday morning, the 'Busters marched out on Navy field with an unbeatable team: Sain was on the mound, with Pesky at short, Cusick behind the plate, Hassett on first, Gremp on second, and cadet Gunner Hagstrom at the hot corner. The 'Busters went on a hitting spree that day, scoring four runs in the first inning to take the lead they never relinquished. Coleman and Sain handled the pitching, and Pesky knocked out a home run, a triple, and a single. It was also a chance for non-major-leaguers to shine, and that day George Bonifant hit a home run on the second ball pitched in the game.

The *Baltimore Sun* was one of the first papers to announce the arrival of the major-league flyboys. The final score between the Cloudbusters and Annapolis was 15–5—a sampling of the plate power for the rest of the season.[25]

## Inside Intelligence

Jimmy Raugh knew when the big-gun players were coming, weeks before media got the bulletin. His sources were coaches and newspa-

---

[23] Conversations with Ivan Fleser, who claimed Ted loved talking about fly fishing with players. *Carolina Alumni Review*, "It Was Wartime," Fall issue, 1987, pp. 43–47.

[24] *The Evening Capital* (Annapolis, Maryland), May 6, 1943, p. 8.

[25] *Baltimore Sun*, May 9, 1943, p. 98.

per editors who were regulars at his parents' house, located at 224 Vance Street, a few blocks away from the Carolina Inn. Guests included Harvey Harman, the athletic director from Pennsylvania who lived next door; across-the-street neighbor Donald Kepler at 218 Vance; and Gerald Ford, who rented a one-room cabin from a pharmacy professor in the Hidden Hills neighborhood.[26] Kidd Brewer was also a guest at their house, with his deputy, Orville Campbell, the 23-year-old editor at the *Cloudbuster*, who occasionally got tapped to fill in as a sitter.

During the tryouts, Jimmy was there, smacking on gum behind the fence with a glove on his hand. Just as he expected, the initial team was OK—not "first-class caliber," as the *Daily Tar Heel* remarked. But he did not worry because he knew some of the kings of baseball were on their way.

In March, a slew of famous major-league officers went through indoctrination training at Chapel Hill, giving the publicity office fodder for one of its first and all-time-best publicity photos. *Baseball Magazine* featured four major-league players pulling spikes and jerseys out of a lucky bag stamped "U.S. Navy Pre-Flight School." Players included Lieutenant (j.g.) Buddy Hassett and Lieutenant (j.g.) Pete Appleton; former New York Giants pitcher, Lieutenant (j.g.) Hal Schumacher; and future Hall of Famer Lieutenant (j.g.) Charlie Gehringer, a Detroit Tigers coach and former second baseman who left base to serve as the head baseball coach at St. Mary's.[27]

As a warm-up, the Cloudbusters played three scrimmages that first month against UNC's Tar Heels, losing, 4–1, winning, 3–2, and

---

[26] Address and details on Gerald R. Ford, *Carolina Alumni Review*, January Issue, 1974, pp. 14–16. V-5 Indoctrination Reporting and Departure, Detachment of Stationed Officers: *The Cloudbuster* (U.S. Navy Pre-Flight School, published in Chapel Hill 1942–1945 in the North Carolina Collection, Call Number: FFC378 UXC1), Chapel Hill telephone directory (1942–1944 issues), and word of mouth from memory based on family stories and cadet interviews.

[27] *Baseball Magazine*, Press Association wire photo with caption, April, 1943, p. 488.

tying, 7–7, at Emerson Field. Based on those games, the *Daily Tar Heel* labeled the Cloudbusters as "dark horses" while the home-team Tar Heels were coming in as the Ration-League favorites. Tar Heels coach Bunn Hearn looked forward to beginning his 34th season on campus as a manager, a coach, and a player when his team faced Pre-Flight. He started his career as a manager on the Chapel Hill campus during the First World War from 1917 to 1918. Twenty-five years later, Bunn's hair was graying. His face was full and leathered by several decades in the sun when he led the Heels during another worldwide conflict. Like every other person in Chapel Hill, Bunn and his wife, Edith, pitched in to contribute to the cause. She rolled bandages and supported the Red Cross, and he sold insurance on the side to make ends meet when he was not coaching baseball.[28]

---

[28] *Raleigh News & Observer*, April 1, 1943, p. 11.

# Chapter 10

## A BATBOY'S PERSPECTIVE

*"Is there anything that can tell more about an American summer than, say, the smell of wooden bleachers in a small-town baseball park, that resinous, sultry, and exciting smell of old dry wood?"*
—*Thomas Wolfe, 1939*

The first time my father laid eyes on Ted Williams, the hitter was strolling across Emerson Field, dressed in dungarees, a saggy T-shirt and black high-top tennis shoes. He had seen his idol on the cover of *LIFE* magazine and on the stack of baseball cards he kept on his bedside table. In person, Williams was as skinny as ever, pacing back and forth in the dirt with his hands on his hips.

That day, dozens of kids raced over to the ballfield like bloodhounds, comparing trading cards with real players just a few feet away at practice. Ted stuck close to his Red Sox teammate, Johnny Pesky, and my dad said they looked like regular Joes, tugging at their ball caps and pacing around the field in the Carolina heat.

My father was nine years old—around the same age as Ted when he declared that he wanted to become the *"greatest hitter in the world."* When my father got a little closer to the team and met Williams, he sensed that the future Hall of Famer liked kids, even if they were brats. Officers' sons were automatic recruits for the top batboy job, and the Navy put them to work all season hauling bats and carrying water to the players. I will never know how my father got the top job as the base mascot and head batboy, but I'd guess that it had something to do with his father's seniority and the family's friendships with the coaches.

Regardless, from that day on a buck-toothed, big-eared, freckled-faced brand for Navy recruiting was born, and my father never realized how far his image traveled during the war. As soon as the big-name cadets arrived on campus, the publicity department suited him up in a hand-me-down baseball uniform that ballooned off his frame and adult-sized cleats with newspapers stuffed in the toes. For two years, he served as a prop to illustrate the soft underbelly of cadets with kids. The photo sessions were hot and dusty, and sometimes players were not excited about the posed pictures, but they always warmed up to the kids, especially Johnny and Ted.

There was no clubhouse at Emerson Field, so my father and the other kids spent their time in the dugout with "Little Johnny" Roventini, the Philip Morris mascot, mugging poses with players and traveling to games in the back of the bus.

Some of those iconic photographs made their way to baseball fans in the Pacific, where even the Japanese soldiers were awed by Ted Williams's .406 season in 1941. Of course, Ted's and Johnny Pesky's were the only faces people noticed in posed photographs with batboys that ran in the service section of *The Sporting News* in the summer of 1943. But for the kids gazing up at the players, time stood still, and they remembered those photo sessions for the rest of their lives.

In the mythological world of baseball, Dad always said that superstitious players called batboys their "good luck charms." The job was officially recognized around 1910, when kids who worked around the ballpark took on the official title as batboys. Before the job became glamorous, some of the most famous mascots were characterized by hardship and physical deformities. There was "Smiling Eddie" Bennett, Babe Ruth's hunchbacked assistant whose incantations helped bring six American League pennants and three world championships to the Yankees.[1]

Lil' Rastus Cobb was a homeless ten-year-old black orphan who was discovered sleeping in the stadium's stands by Ty Cobb. Though Ty Cobb was a prickly figure, he fed and clothed Rastus, and eventually he packed him up and took him home to Georgia.[2] Louis Van Zelst was another hunchbacked talisman for the Philadelphia Athletics. From 1910 to 1914, he was in the dugout when the team won four American League pennants and three World Series titles.[3] There was Charles "Victory" Faust, who got a job after telling New York Giants manager John McGraw that a fortune teller predicted that he would help the Giants win the National League championship. Faust was a scruffy, unathletic sort, but he did go on to pitch in the ninth inning of two major-league games in 1911. Soon after, his luck changed when he was diagnosed with early dementia in a mental hospital and died of tuberculosis in 1915 at age 34.

When Dad gasped for air through an oxygen tube, he clung to sports heroes more than ever, rejecting the modern generation of players who faced impossible, unrealistic odds to achieve their dreams. It pained him to hear about the kids who could not afford to be on a little-league team, where all that was needed in his day was a stick and a ball and a good pair of feet to run the bases. Even though he watched television for days on end, he missed the days of the tabletop radios. He felt the media and that thingamajig called the Internet was sucking the life out of players—turning them into false idols they themselves did not even recognize—and he felt sorry for them.

---

[1] Associated Press, January 18, 1935.

[2] Anthony Papalus, "Lil' Rastus Cobb's Good Luck Charm," *Baseball Research Journal 84*, pp. 69–70. SABR Research Journals Archives.

[3] Stuart Miller, *Good Wood, The Story of the Baseball Bat,* ACTA Publications, 2011, p. 170.

He told me many times that he trusted the game of baseball, with its ironclad rules and regulations, representing the remains of what was good and true in an unfair, phony world.

As my father grew more feeble, people connected with his allegiance to baseball, because they, too, missed the simple old-fashioned tradition when people from all walks of life united at the ballpark. During family dinners out, I took notice of the way waiters flocked around him as he talked about the old days of baseball, racing back to the kitchen to field answers to his token riddle, "What are the nine ways a player gets on base?"

Instead of laughing with my father, we laughed at him, sticking wads of wet napkins in our ears. After dinners, we berated him in the car on way home, especially when his stories circled back to his friends at Emerson Field.

Returning to the house, the scenario was always the same. He behaved like a scolded child, deflated, humiliated, and extremely angry. Very quietly, he swallowed up his rage and padded to his bedroom with his head down, falling asleep beside the electric fan from World War II and the hideous purple table. There were times when I heard him cry himself to sleep. We all chalked it up to cocktails and never once asked him why he was so sad.

# Chapter 11

# TED WHO?

As soon as Williams set foot on the Pre-Flight athletic fields, coaches shrugged their shoulders and said, "Oh, so you're the great Ted Williams, huh? OK, mister." And then he was singled out to drill harder and faster and longer in this camp where coaches aimed to do one thing—win the war.

Years later, Ted's good friend Johnny Pesky laughingly said, "Ted took it all."[1]

But there were other reasons why the timing of Pre-Flight training and the atmosphere were such a perfect fit for Ted Williams.

For temperamental cadets like Ted, Pre-Flight was an outlet to unleash the fury that drove them. As long as he did not show disrespect for his new bosses, well . . . Ted could be Ted, and the competitive Pre-Flight spirit fit him like a glove. An entrance test for every man was the torturous sandbag agility drill. With freshly shaven heads, breaking in their new high-tops, yearling cadets strapped one-third of their weight in sandbags to their backs and were pushed to step up and down a ladder at one-second intervals for five minutes

---

[1] Austen Lake, *Boston Evening American,* January 11, 1952, p. 46.

or until they buckled from exhaustion. The time may have sounded brief, but nearly two-thirds of the incoming "Boots" failed to reach the full five minutes, and many collapsed from the strain.

In his first days on base, Ted excelled on the commando course, ultimately gaining his highest marks in military track. Pounds he could barely spare to lose melted off his string-bean frame even though baseball players chowed down on a 5,500-calorie-a-day meal plan at their training table.[2] Ted proved to be a natural leader on the basketball court, too, and officers egged him on to blow his stack within the confines of the boxing ring. The steamier Ted got, the better he performed in his new surroundings.[3]

Falling in with the 25th Battalion, Ted listened to the constant rattle of gunfire at the rifle range, where Marines taught cadets to use bayonets and fire .38 specials and .45 semiautomatic hand guns carried by pilots on missions. With the B-1 Cloudbusters Band playing in the background, he marched double time into classrooms to absorb a hefty load of academics, which he devoured. As Ted made his way to the baseball field each afternoon, he noticed the activity going on at Mangum Hall, where sleeping bags, machetes, packs, and mess gear were doled out for hikes.

Early on, Ted looked forward to being cut lose all alone in the woods with little more than a compass and a canteen. The backwoods military roads and trails surrounding the campus intimidated some of the citified cadets coming from the congested neighborhoods of Chicago and Brooklyn. Even some of the toughest blue-collar cadets who had slaved away in factories and coal mines did not take to the outdoors, but the snakes and the long overnight hikes did

---

[2] "Sandbag test at one-second intervals," F. N. Boney and Gary L. Doster, "A University Goes to War: The Navy at the University of Georgia During World War II," Georgia Historical Quarterly, spring 1993, Volume LXXVI, Number 1, p. 126. *Cloudbuster,* September 19, 1942, p. 2. Proof that Williams was administered sandbag test, with recordings for his health and weight at the beginning of training, Naval Aviation Physical Training records.

[3] Chapel Hill Naval Aviation Physical Training Record Card.

not faze Ted; in fact, his time under the stars in the North Carolina woods would change his life.[4]

He was drawn to the kinetic tension of Hell's Half-Acre. Ted craved the intensity, feeding on the emotional battery that startled boys who were able to grow up slowly in peaceful, stable homes. Ivan Fleser recalled that Pre-Flight instructors aimed to produce fliers who were impervious to fear and doubt. They talked about self-confidence constantly because "if you did not believe in yourself, you would have a difficult time." Though teamwork was stressed, it was an every-man-for-himself attitude aiming toward sheer survival and self-preservation to support the other men. When a reporter for *Esquire* questioned this training philosophy, the commander of a naval base shot back in a resolute tone, "In the air no formation is better than its poorest flyer."

On Pre-Flight sports grounds, friends were turned against friends for the good of the Navy. "One minute you were with your pal in the quadrant. The next you were on the field or in the boxing ring, where your buddy was the enemy. You had to outplay him and out-run him. You had to go full tilt, as fast as you can, as hard as you can, as long as you can," said Ivan, and coaches were merciless to see how much stress the cadets could take.[5]

*Esquire* magazine was one of the first publications to declare that Pre-Flight was not about sports-for-sport's-sake training—it was a sports-for-war's-sake method to "fight any way the enemy asks for it" and to "fight harder, and meaner."[6]

Ted admired the grit of prizefighters and football players, and he looked forward to standing in their shoes.

When Ted was put in a boxing ring with a friend, he was pushed to ignore the bloodshed to "liquidate the foe," and former cadets

---

[4] Chapel Hill station academic and fitness report card on specific sports where Williams excelled, like basketball and survival.

[5] Ivan Fleser interview in Marshall, Michigan, April 25, 2016.

[6] Herb Graffis, "The Sports Scene," *Esquire*, August, 1942, p. 53. Nick Kearns, "They'll Fly for the Navy," *Esquire*, December 1942, p. 252.

would attest that they were practically turned into hamburger meat by guys twice their size when they were left in the ring for five rounds.[7]

Ted quickly realized that football was the most violent sport of all at Pre-Flight, where broken bones, concussions, and dislocations were everyday occurrences. Del Monte Pre-Flight base observed that an ambulance was parked beside each of the four football fields, and 70 years later, one former cadet recalled with absolute clarity that three were often busy rushing cadets off to the hospital.[8]

Little guys who had never played football or any team sport in a uniform were mixed in with cadets who outweighed them by 50 pounds. If players were hurt, or knocked out cold, they were pushed to get back up and work even harder. This strategy came naturally to Ted, who would be sent out on the football field looking clumsy in a helmet and shoulder pads to face opponents who had worn jerseys for the Washington Redskins. Even if Ted's time in Chapel Hill coincided with football season, he was not first-string material for the football squad. Those players could have broken Ted's neck, but that fearless, pile-driving attitude was one of the intangibles recruiters searched for in early interviews, and in most cases officers found men who were willing to take any risk and put their careers on hold for the sake of their country.

Former cadets who were still around to tell me their stories were living proof that this unique culture gave no one any breaks, not even for the greatest baseball stars in the world.

One of the first V-5 naval aviation graduates I interviewed was Frank Selwyn Johnson of Vacaville, California. When I tracked him down he was 90 years old and still rode around town on a Honda 250 motorcycle, "but I stay off the freeways," he said with a laugh. Frank told me that he enlisted in the Navy when he was 17. He wanted to

---

[7] Dale Stafford, *Detroit Free Press*, November 8, 1942, p. 47. Elger August Berkley, July 8, 2005, Veterans History Project Oral History interview.

[8] Conversation with John Sanders, Del Monte Pre-Flight historian, September 6, 2017; Oral History with former Del Monte cadet Edward Deutchman, Del Monte Pre-Flight, May 2, 2011.

fly so badly that he went to a chiropractor who tried to stretch him to meet the V-5's minimum height requirement of 5 feet 4 ½ inches. Being a little guy, Frank vividly remembered being on the football field with professional players for scrimmages, and the baseball players were there, too, getting no breaks. Frank knew full well that he was going to get steamrolled on the field, and he told me that without a doubt, that anticipation of pain and failure was the sensation that changed him.[9]

---

[9] Phone interview with Frank Selwyn Johnson, September 17, 2015. Johnson graduated from St. Mary's Pre-Flight, which also fielded an outstanding baseball team.

# Part III

# THE WORLD'S MOST DIFFICULT TRAINING PROGRAM

# Chapter 12

## THE PRE-FLIGHT SPARK

The mechanics of the V-5 Pre-Flight Navy training formula were engineered by two men and shifted into gear by a third. Under Secretary of the Navy James Forrestal was a high-strung boxer in college who defused his tension with sports. When the war broke out, Forrestal was a 49-year-old man who had maintained the physique of a prizefighter with a hard, wiry frame and a smashed-in nose that never healed after a college match.

One of the highlights of Forrestal's life took place in the boxing ring in 1920. Soon after he was discharged as a young Navy flier, Forrestal took on world champion boxer Gene Tunney at a recreational match at the Yale Club.[1] When Tunney looked away, Forrestal clipped him so hard that he snapped off three of Tunney's front teeth at the root. One tooth died and two remained discolored, causing the vain, matinee-idol boxing legend to smile with closed lips in pictures. When that punch was thrown, little did Tunney or Forrestal know they would be at odds 20 years later when the

---

[1] Gene Tunney, "How I Became Naval Air Training Director of Physical Fitness," *Pittsburgh Press*, April 4, 1942, p. 11.

Navy was pressed to find highly effective training methods for aerial combat.

As the war intensified in Europe, Forrestal championed the use of sports to train pilots. It was something he frequently spoke of behind thick wooden doors of armed services meetings and at cocktail parties with officers. One of the men who tuned into this dialogue most intently was Captain Arthur Radford.

Known as "Raddy," he was a stalwart pilot with ruddy cheeks and frosty blue eyes that "could freeze a can of beans," noted one officer who described his stare. Unlike Forrestal, under Raddy's glacial shell there was warmth and compassion, and he was known for this motto: "Don't be discouraged, stick with it."[2]

Six days before Pearl Harbor, Radford was sworn in as the Navy's head of naval aviation training in Washington. He shared Forrestal's concerns that the Navy was sitting back and waiting for the inevitable attack, while it needed to throw everything it had into pilot training.

Radford experienced a meteoric wartime rise to prominence, working from dawn until nightfall, seven days a week, to take aviation training to unimaginable heights. During those months, he claimed that the walk to and from work from his apartment in Washington was his only exercise. Knowing the war required an all-hands-on-deck approach, Radford lobbied to draw women in naval aviation, and by the end of the war, 23,000 WAVES were in the Navy's aeronautical organization.[3]

As the war shifted from the land and sea to the skies, Radford realized that pilots would be flying long-distance bombing missions over water. Swimming was key, and the Navy needed to find a way to train tens of thousands of able-bodied aviators to survive on land and sea.

---

[2] *Lansing State Journal*, May 24, 1953, p. 19.

[3] Malcolm Muir Jr., ed., *The Human Tradition in the WWII Era (No. 8)*, Scholarly Resources Books, 2001, pp. 161–162.

One of the most practical and cost-effective solutions for training could be found in schoolyards, gyms, swimming pools, watering holes, and hiking trails across America.

From a morale perspective, Radford and Forrestal both agreed that competitive sports bred fighters who would not turn away from the enemy or break the ranks of aerial combat. Specifically, Radford felt the use of sports could quicken the eye, as well as improve judgement and reaction time.[4] Games with fast, explosive violence were laboratories to develop strength, bravery, and concentration under pressure.[5]

While the need for courses such as swimming was never more critical than in the dawn of 1942, there was a huge problem: the Navy did not have a plan or a place to integrate a so-called sports-for-war-training program for pilots.

## The V-5 Program

The V-5 Naval Aviation Cadet Program was created in 1935 for civilian and enlisted aviation cadets with college degrees or some undergraduate education. It was among the many V-branded programs to train pilots, and one of the more difficult training paths. To broaden the pool of pilots at the onset of the war, the V-5 repealed its prewar education requirements of two years of college to high school degrees. With the stroke of a pen, this revision to the rules welcomed professional athletes who never thought they'd see the cockpit of a torpedo bomber, let alone fly one.

To expedite training, the V-5 route was compressed to about one year. The first months of training separated the wheat from the chaff and solidified cadets' resolve to earn their wings. To accomplish this task, Radford wanted the "cream of the crop coaching talent" to run his schools at four regional bases.[6]

---

[4] Admiral Hamilton Oral History Transcript, Annapolis: U.S. Navy Institute, 1983, p. 50.

[5] Tentative Hamilton Syllabus, December 1942.

[6] *Esquire*, December, 1, 1942, p. 250.

Before he could recruit his fliers, Radford had to start from scratch, launching a search for a uniquely qualified individual to design the most difficult physical training program in the world.

Radford didn't have to look far for the perfect man to create the athletic training component for ground training schools, ultimately nicknamed "The Annapolis of the Air." Lieutenant Commander Tom Hamilton was one of Annapolis's most storied athletes and coaches. In 1935, he inspired Milton Bradley Inc. to lend his name to a football board game, *Tom Hamilton's Pigskin*, the same year a real estate game called *Monopoly* flew off the shelves.

Hamilton seemed born for the role, but there was one big problem. He did not want the job—he wanted to fight the enemy. At age 36, Hamilton was one of the sharpest pilots in the Navy. At Anacostia Station, he was ferrying some of the newest aircraft in the skies. Instead of staying put at home, and out of harm's way, he wanted to make carrier landings.

The two officers had flown together many times. It was days after Pearl Harbor, in the cockpit of a Navy plane, that Radford put the hard press on Hamilton to take the job.

Again, Hamilton pushed back on his boss for another week, trying to think of ways that he could do what came most naturally to him—fight. When Radford argued that the aviation training program would collapse without him, Hamilton realized that he did not have a choice. That week, he transferred to the Division of Aviation, rolling up his sleeves to design a brand-new experimental training program from scratch.

The creation of the athletic training program of the Pre-Flight Schools was one of the biggest jobs in the Navy. Tom knew he could not write the plan alone, so he turned to one of the smartest people he knew for help: his older brother, Howard.

# Chapter 13

# TOM HAMILTON, THE FIGHTING AMERICAN

*"To start to describe this man it is not exaggeration to say that he is the epitome of a fighting American with a will to win temperament ingrained by competitive athletics."*
                    —*Robert E. Hooey,* Esquire *magazine, April 1943*

In a childhood scrapbook, Tom Hamilton is dressed in a dark wool football jersey, with a black eye and a scratch zigzagging down his cheek. He was the youngest of five sons, born one day after a white Christmas in 1905, in Hoopeston, Illinois. His father, John Hamilton, was a statesman and one of the first presidents of a small-town bank to take the helm of the American Bankers Association. Though Tom's mother, Mary, was stern and strong-minded, she dressed him up like a doll in dresses with ruffled collars, and family members remembered him with long blond ringlets, perched on her lap on the family's large wraparound porch.[1]

When Tom was in grammar school, his family moved to Columbus, Ohio. When he was a teen, students returning to Columbus

---

[1] Betty Busey interview, June 19, 2017.

from the Great War remembered him wearing that familiar football jersey in a vacant lot beside the house, near the gateway to Ohio State University, where he practiced dropkicks for hours, punting the football over sagging telephone wires strung over the lot.

Though the Hamiltons were wealthy, owning a ranch where they ran cattle in Texas, the family presented an anodyne air of understatement. John and Mary instilled those humble values in all of their boys, who were solid students and exceptional athletes.[2] In high school, Tom's talents lured him to boarding school at Doane Academy, which was associated with Denison University. Following prep school, Tom did not attend Ohio State University like his older brothers, heading instead to the U.S. Naval Academy.

At the Academy, Tom was elected "honorary" permanent class president all four years—quite a feat considering the class had 574 graduates.[3] He swept up every major athletic award on campus, from the Thompson Trophy Cup to the Navy Athletic Association Sword for ability and leadership. Lettering in *nine* varsity sports, it was football where Hamilton truly shined.[4] In 1926, Tom's performance helped the Academy capture the national championship in a game the *New York Times* would call football's "most spectacular pageant."[5]

The post-Thanksgiving Army-Navy game was played at Soldier Field, Chicago's magnificent marble stadium modeled after the Parthenon. Named in honor of the nation's veterans, Soldier Field was the largest stadium in the world with seating for 100,000 spectators. Before that game, a weather reporter poetically described the field as it rose "like a mantle in white" after a series of storms blanketed the city in several feet of snow.

---

[2] *Esquire*, 1942, p. 114.

[3] Hamilton Oral History, U.S. Naval Institute, p. 7. According to *The Lucky Bag* yearbook and other USNA publications, Hamilton was not officially elected class president; it appears to be an honorary position.

[4] Hamilton Oral History, U.S. Naval Institute, p. 4.

[5] Allison Danzig, *New York Times*, November 26, 1936, p. L. 41.

Midway between two world wars, the 1926 match between West Point and Annapolis was an event the entire nation looked forward to all year. World War I was still fresh in the minds of the service academies, and American football fans hungered for heroes. The Army-Navy game was branded by sportswriters as the "Game of the Century." Throughout the fall, newspapers and radio carried stories nonstop, keeping crazed fans posted about the game, which drove an unprecedented 600,000 ticket requests.

It was a game where people from all walks of life pulled together, from local mobsters to the mayor, who hired hundreds of laborers to shovel snow off of the stadium benches. Nearly 1,500 policemen were brought in to direct traffic that day as 18,000 cars parked scattershot on snowbanks and sidewalks along Chicago's Southside. Taxi cabs would make 20,000 trips to the park, where 110,000 fans poured into the stadium.[6]

The game kicked off on a gloriously frozen fall day with the sun cracking through coal-dust smoke and low-lying clouds. Fans were double-layered in scarves and heavy coats to protect them from the bone-blistering wind pushing in from Lake Michigan; ears and noses went numb and teeth chattered as men and women nipped at flasks of whiskey. The excitement of the game spilled outside the stadium with thousands of fans standing on rooftops, water towers, and nearby bridges; and on that frozen afternoon, if they could not see the field, everyone heard Tom Hamilton make college football history.[7]

Late in the game, Army, led by "Light Horse" Harry Wilson and Chris Cagle, maintained a 21–14 lead before Navy mounted a final drive. Alan Shapley scored on a reverse with less than a minute remaining, and Hamilton dropkicked the extra point to tie the

---

[6] Ray Schmidt, "The Greatest Army-Navy," LA84 Foundation, College Football Historical Society newsletter, February 2004, pp. 9–13.

[7] Tip Top 25.com Rating Website Champions of 1926 Army-Navy football game (James Vautravers).

game.[8] To this day, fans and sports historians say it was the greatest game ever played between the academies, but in Tom Hamilton's eyes, a tie or second place was never good enough, and he would inspire one of sport's most quotable lines years later, saying, "A tie is like kissing your sister."[9]

Before Tom won national acclaim, one of the most vaunted men of football had been watching him for quite some time. Twenty years earlier, Walter Herbert "Eckie" Eckersall was an All-American college quarterback at the University of Chicago under Coach Alonzo Stagg. The future Hall of Famer stood only 5-foot-6 and weighed about 145 pounds—and for a moment in his youth, he, too, was a national hero. With speed and finesse, and an unquenchable desire to score, it was not unusual for Eckersall to score all of the points in a game. Under Stagg's guidance, Eckie became a pioneer in the forward pass, hurling the ball 75 yards in one of his first games.[10] He was so fearless and indestructible that President Theodore Roosevelt decided to make football safer after he watched Eckersall getting crushed on the field by players twice his size, then rolling right back up on his feet, without a complaint.

After Eckersall retired in 1906, he became a sports scribe for the *Chicago Tribune*. When he saw Tom Hamilton play, he spotted a leader destined to change the world, and he wrote just that in one of his columns. After Hamilton's performance at the Army-Navy game, Eckersall penned this prophetic passage in his column: "I do not know how far off another war might be . . . but should it come to pass that we must fight again for our rights, I nominate Tom Hamilton, whatever his status may be in the Navy when war darkens the scene, to hold an important post. He will be sure to pull through

---

[8] Ted Patterson, *Football in Baltimore: History and Memorabilia from Colts to Ravens*, Johns Hopkins University Press, 2013, p. 31.

[9] Quote inspired by the 1946 Army-Navy game, when Navy Coach Hamilton unsuccessfully elected to go for a touchdown instead of a game-tying field goal with the Middies trailing by three points late in the contest.

[10] *Corsicana Daily Sun*, April 6, 1951, p. 10.

when the blue chips are piled highly."[11] At age 46, Eckersall died unexpectedly from pneumonia and hard living. Sixteen years after Eckie made his prophetic statement about Hamilton, his vision came true.[12]

There were others who recognized Hamilton's rare leadership abilities when he took the helm at Pre-Flight.

Arch Ward, the "Arch De Triomphe" of sports promoters who hatched the idea for the Golden Gloves and first major-league All-Star Game, made an audacious claim that the V-5's success or failure to train pilots would determine the outcome of the war.[13] Ward cut his teeth as Knute Rockne's PR man at Notre Dame before he became the highest paid sports promoter in America. Ward knew a "dream team" when he saw coaches like Bear Bryant, Jim Crowley, and Bernie Bierman signing up to train the V-5's pilots, and he put his money on Hamilton.[14]

## The Hamilton Brothers—An Impossible Deadline

When I met Betty Hamilton Busey at her home in Virginia, we sat at the kitchen table, where she shared memories from the war. Like her father, Betty is articulate and athletic with a gracious sense of humor. During an afternoon thunderstorm, the grounds of her property blurred outside a bank of windows as we looked through the Navy scrapbook. Instantly, faces and images from the base came back to her, and she proceeded to describe how the war entered their household.

Betty was in the second grade when she watched her father, Howard, who was Tom Hamilton's older brother, take one of the most important telephone calls of his life. At the time, her family lived in a rambling three-story Craftsman house near Indianola

---

[11] William Sullivan, *Daily Tar Heel*, May 28, 1942, p. 2.

[12] *Bremen* (Indiana) *Enquirer*, March 27, 1930.

[13] Arch Ward, *Chicago Tribune*, March 29, 1942.

[14] Gerry Fraley, *Dallas Morning News* report carried in *News-Press Fort Myers*, May 10, 1995, p. 4C.

Avenue in Columbus, Ohio. She was the only child in the room, and she remembered the stricken look on his face, and the way he said, "Yes, yes, yes . . ." over and over into the receiver. Her father knew the country was going to go to war, but as an educator he was taken a bit back by the scale of the job he was asked to carry out.

Betty described her father as a kind man with a sparkle in his eye. Like her uncle Tom, he was one of those guys who had *it*, meaning the ingredients of smarts, sportsmanship, athletic ability, and charisma that could light up a room, be it a train station or a hotel lobby.

In 1941, Howard Hamilton was an attorney and a popular Ohio State University political science professor, holding the most senior position at the College of Arts and Sciences. Betty and her twin sister Barbara were the youngest of four children, including an older brother, Dick, and a teenage sister, Ardis.

Columbus was a place of safety and security, with good schools and a strong church. The Hamiltons were surrounded by earnest people with Midwestern values who respected her family and especially her father. Simply put, the Hamiltons were givers, not takers, who willingly served the community and sacrificed for their country.

On the day of the fateful telephone call, bodies were being fished out of Pearl Harbor, President Franklin Roosevelt had declared war, and Betty's uncle had been tasked to manage one of the most difficult jobs in the Navy. She remembered another wave of shock on her father's face when he heard the impossible deadline to deliver the plan for the so-called Pre-Flight schools in a matter of weeks.[15]

As a leader of one of the nation's largest state universities, her father oversaw huge endeavors, managing attendance of the Buckeyes' home games with up to 60,000 fans. Though Betty and her siblings did not realize it at the time, their father had some highly specialized skills that would come in handy during the war. Professor Hamilton was not an enlisted man. He was an attorney. When that call came in from his brother, America faced a severe pilot

---

[15] Draft plan delivered in December 1941.

shortage, and Betty's father knew how to ramp up classroom training to prep the largest assembly line of pilots ever imagined in the Navy.

Betty's father also knew how to craft academic syllabi. Courses such as nomenclature, physics, and naval aircraft recognition were fundamentals to pilots. In a war fought over oceans, survival training was also key, along with psychological preparation and methods for relaxation to aid stranded pilots and POWs.

The Hamiltons were and still are formal, direct people, so the conversation between Howard and Tom was brief. When Betty's father hung up the telephone, there was little discussion about what was going to happen next. Her father planned to take an immediate leave of absence and enlist in the service, where he would help his brother write one of the most ambitious training plans ever envisioned by the military.

With four children to support and a good job at the university, Betty's father did not want to leave Columbus. Soon after that call, her father said goodbye and headed to Washington, D.C., where the brothers worked around the clock at Tom's two-story brick home located at 1940 South Lynn Street in Arlington, Virginia. Most of the work was hammered out on notepaper on the kitchen table. Page by page, they polished up the syllabus, switching off outlines like a jigsaw puzzle to make sure all of the pieces fit into place.[16] Howard made a quick trip back home to Ohio, where Betty saw him typing up academic portions of the plan at his large office desk with her siblings by his side and her mother bringing him lunch.

To Betty, that is what war looked like, and her father's sense of service stayed with her for the rest of her life.

Tom Hamilton was intent on condensing the program into four campuses to build on solidarity and reduce operation costs. He felt that more than four campuses would "scatter the shot" too wide to attract the highest-grade instructor personnel, which was a huge challenge. The schools would be nicknamed the Annapolis of the

---

[16] Sheet from Howard Hamilton's personal papers, with outline on notebook paper outlining staff, salary, structure for training.

Air, and they would function as powerful athletic plants, training an assembly line of 2,500 cadets in roughly 12 weeks.[17]

The brothers identified four fundamental purposes for training: basic physical conditioning and strength training; knowledge of naval lore; knowledge of military drill and seamanship; and elementary training in communication and other specialties.[18]

Howard also planned to enlist an Ohio State psychologist to create a naval recognition course to help pilots and sailors distinguish between enemy and friendly aircraft and warships in a split second. When Pearl Harbor was bombed, the Navy used the British "WEFT" system, recognizing not the entire body of a plane, but parts of planes' "wing, engine, fuselage, and tail," or slang for "wrong every f___ing time."

For years, Dr. Samuel Renshaw worked in a fourth-floor laboratory on campus to unlock the memory banks of human beings. He believed that people only used about 20 percent of their recall potential for their mind and senses (smell, taste, touch, hearing, and vision). He had pioneered programs with remarkable results for speed reading and was intrigued by the way young men could identify the year and make of automobiles from any angle. He used this theory to develop an experimental method using a slide projector to flash images of aircraft and warships on a screen in a fraction of a second, and Hamilton knew his methods had the potential to give the Allies a huge advantage over the enemy.[19]

To teach the fundamentals of sports and coach varsity teams, the Hamiltons called for an 83-man coaching cadre on each campus,

---

[17] Pre-Flight syllabus, p. 2.

[18] Hamilton's syllabus outline, December 1941, p. 8.

[19] David G. Wittels, "You're Not as Smart as You Could Be," *Saturday Evening Post,* April 17, 1948; Nick Joyce, "Spotting the Enemy," American Psychological Association *Monitor on Psychology,* March 2010, Volume 41, Number 3, p. 24; William Holloway's unpublished manuscript dedicated to and honoring the life of Jim Ashford in Pre-Flight's 64th battalion, pp. 43–44.

with ranks ranging from lieutenant commanders to ensigns for assistant coaches.[20]

In a 20-page directive, they outlined daily activities from 5:30 a.m. to taps at 21:00, with ten minutes of chapel with a fighting parson and one 30-minute break to digest their lunch. There was also a year-round schedule for seasonal intramural and varsity sports with Pre-Flight teams organized in track, football, wrestling, swimming, soccer, basketball, and baseball.

Hamilton's practical techniques for conditioning included a lot of elbow grease with wood chopping, ditch digging, and roadwork. Communal farming with gardens supplied schools with fresh vegetables, which were canned during the winter, and trainees even shot their own turkeys for Thanksgiving. Cadets would clear land for new athletic fields, dig drainage systems, and build rifle ranges. They would use hammers and saws to build their own training equipment, logging timber for obstacle courses, assembling wooden sleds for weight training, and soldering together scrap metal for aerowheels.[21]

Athletics were viewed as laboratories to develop speed, courage, and concentration under pressure. Fouls would not be called on sports fields, and rules would be altered to promote physical aggression. Cadets would be trained to think offensively to break down years of playing by the rules.[22] Depending on the season, two to two-and-a-half hours a day would be allocated to varsity, intramural team, and voluntary sports to develop qualities desired in pilots.

Boxing and rough-and-tumble versions of wrestling and jujitsu or hand-to-hand combat would develop skills for attack and self-defense. Drills in football, basketball, and military track would

---

[20] Donald Rominger, *Journal of Sports History*, Vol. 12, No. 3 (Winter 1985), p. 256, specified number of coaches at 83.

[21] Mary Lane Baker, UNC Thesis, 1976. Also, *The State* magazine, February 27, 1943, Volume X, Number 39, p. 1; Thanksgiving turkey reference from "Naval Flying Cadets Will Work Victory Garden on 35-Acre-Plot," *Athens Banner Herald*, June 11, 1943, p. 1.

[22] James H. Decker, "They Have to be Tough to Win," *Athletic Journal* 23, January 1943.

enhance quick acting; coordination of mind, eye, and body; and agility. Military sports would consist of obstacle climbing, grenade throwing, broad jumping, vaulting, and tumbling. Confidence in the water was a game-changer in the war. Pilots needed to be able to stay afloat for many hours, and they learned to swim blindfolded to simulate darkness should they crash down at night in the middle of the Pacific. They also needed to learn relaxation skills in the water and acquire life-saving skills.[23] To escape sinking airplanes, burning oil, and machine gun bullets, they needed to be able to submerge at least 70 feet underwater—a skill that might have saved hundreds of lives in Pearl Harbor.[24]

Rain or shine, sleet or snow, there would be 21-mile hikes each week and a 40-mile hike to wrap up the program before graduation. And despite blisters, bruises, frostbite, heatstroke, or snakebites, there were no bells to ring or excuses for quitters.

Military arts drills included radio, seamanship, gunnery, recognition, and parachute training. Lectures included mathematics, aerology, and navigation, with instruction in first aid and chemical warfare. With an alarming number of pilots drowning and starving to death in jungles, survival training was another important component to training that had to be mastered.

## A Blood-and-Thunder Speech

Exasperated by lost time and bureaucratic red tape, Arthur Radford rubber-stamped the Pre-Flight plan, giving Hamilton carte blanche to go out and find his coaches.

The mother lode of coaching talent was pouring into Detroit at the end of December for a joint conference with the National Collegiate Athletic Association and the American Association of Football Coaches with a who's who of physical education. That week, news of the cancellation of the Indianapolis 500 automobile race hit close to

---

[23] Hamilton's syllabus outline, December 1941, p. 8; "Pre-Flight Cadets Learn to Swim in War Conditions," *Athens Banner-Herald*, July 4, 1943, p. 1.

[24] Dale Stafford, *Detroit Free Press*, November 8, 1942, p. 47

home, jolting Detroit carmakers with the elimination of another American sporting tradition. Horse racing, tennis, and professional golf were all in a jumble, and the war threatened to throw a wrench into the college football schedule. Rose Bowl organizers were also riled up by the decision to move the game away from Pasadena, California, to Duke University, far removed from the Pacific Coast, where there was talk of another Japanese attack.[25]

In peacetime years, many big-time football coaches skipped the conference to head to the Sugar Bowl in New Orleans. Pearl Harbor changed everything, and reporters were surprised by the important names on the hotel register. That year, more than 1,500 coaches and athletics advocates gathered at the meeting held at the Hotel Book-Cadillac, known as the Fifth Avenue of the West.

Instead of staying up late at night carousing and drawing formations on the marble floors and walls of the hotel, football coaches interacted with members of the Army and the Navy who were integrated into the conference. At the onset of war, Americans played football and baseball better than any other country in the world. Conference leadership knew that sports was the key to military preparedness, and they came to town to figure out a way to do it.

Peacetime living had done America no favors. Samuel Crocker, associate director of a joint Army and Navy committee on recreation, put it more bluntly when he declared that "athletics must end 20 years of slack living."[26] That year, H. O. "Fritz" Crisler, Michigan's athletic director, who was president of the AAFC, suggested that compulsory, across-the-board sports training might be an answer to combat training. He was seconded by Hamilton's good friend Matty Bell, who was stepping in to become the new president of the association.[27]

---

[25] Kenneth Joel Zogry, *The University's Living Room: A History of the Carolina Inn*, University of North Carolina Press, 1999, p. 49; Rose Bowl relocation also mentioned in news clippings about the Detroit conference.

[26] *St. Louis Star and Times*, December 30, 1941, p. 6.

[27] Associated Press, Detroit, December 31, 1941.

Without official authorization from the Department of the Navy, and no staff, Tom Hamilton pulled out his bullhorn to begin recruiting for a training academy that existed in his imagination. Coaches sat on the edge of their chairs, rattling the chandeliers with applause and whistles when Hamilton described how football was going to train the newest generation of pilots.

"Our pilots . . . come from a soft, luxurious, loose-thinking, lazy, peacetime life in our homes and schools," stated Hamilton in a recent memo to Radford. Hamilton believed that America's enemies were stronger, tougher, better physically trained, and indoctrinated from childhood to fight and die for their country.[28]

In his view, the goal of the Pre-Flight program was to "give the Navy the best pilot possible . . . to put learning in his head, muscles on his bones, steel in his soul, and fire in his heart."[29] With an instant pipeline of coaches in Detroit, his proposed schools aimed to train 30,000 pilots a year—many more times the number of aviators who flew Zeppelins and wobbly canoes with wings at the height of World War I.

After his ten-minute speech concluded, there was no need for Hamilton to circulate around cocktail tables to recruit instructors. Three hundred coaches signed up on the spot, including a spry football coach from Vanderbilt, who was the first to charge up to the podium.[30]

In the New Year of 1942, Hamilton announced official plans to install the "most intensive, rigorous and comprehensive program of physical and mental training that the world has ever seen." At the end of his plea he wrote, "Time is short."

---

[28] Lieutenant Commander Thomas Hamilton to Captain Radford, "History of the U.S. Navy Pre-Flight School Chapel Hill," n.d., North Carolina file, U.S. Department of the Navy, Navy Historical Center, Naval Archives, Washington, D.C.

[29] *News and Observer,* "Naval Pre-Flight School," May 18, 1952, No. 4147, University of North Carolina.

[30] Admiral Hamilton Oral History Transcript, Annapolis: U.S. Navy Institute, 1983, pp. 51–52.

Before the locations for Pre-Flight induction schools were designated, hundreds of applications poured into Hamilton's office. The Navy's switchboard lit up like a Christmas tree, overwhelming the new athletics chief and a secretary working out of a temporary office. Anxious to get these schools up and running, a young firebrand, who would one day become one of the great football legends, boarded a one-way train to Washington from Nashville, Tennessee.

## A Bear in the Basement

Come January, a stubborn 29-year-old Southerner who earned a nickname when he agreed to wrestle a bear in a carnival showed up at the temporary athletics office. Long before Bear Bryant donned his famous houndstooth hat as the University of Alabama's head coach, he was a line coach at Vanderbilt who jumped at the opportunity to do his part for Uncle Sam.

William Paul Bryant was the 11th of 12 children, and he grew into a man who was loved, feared, worshipped, and despised. His father was a dirt farmer, and Bryant grew up in a creek town so small that locals called it "Moro Bottom." When the war broke out, Bryant was too old to fly fighters, so he looked for other opportunities where he could make the greatest difference. In Detroit, Bear was in the room with a league of men whose destinies were changed by one speech. When he heard Hamilton's blood-and-thunder rally for his proposed schools, he decided that he would be amongst the first to get the Pre-Flight training stations up and running.

Bryant booked a train to Washington and was waiting for Hamilton by the time he returned from Detroit. Standing in his office, Bryant told him, "I heard your talk, and I'm ready to go to war." Hamilton assured the young coach that his name would be amongst the first to be considered. Hamilton explained that he was merely the "messenger" and did not make the hiring decisions, so he shooed Bryant back to Tennessee. That week, Admiral Radford officially put Hamilton in charge of the Pre-Flight schools and the physical training section. Days later, Bryant showed back up again at Anacostia station with his blue eyes blazing. He said, "I haven't heard from you!

I have left home; I'm not going back. I can't go back now; I've told all my friends that I have gone off to war." Realizing that Bryant was now jobless—and homeless—Hamilton alerted his wife, Emmie, that they had a new houseguest. For the next three weeks, the up-and-coming coach dined at Hamilton's table and slept in his house. As one of the very first Pre-Flight employees, Bryant answered the phones and worked as a civilian until his paperwork was processed as a full-time employee of the U.S. Navy. [31] As Hamilton visited potential Pre-Flight bases around the country, Emmie took classes with Navy wives in cryptanalysis to learn the rudiments of code and cipher. [32]

---

[31] Admiral Hamilton Oral History Transcript, Annapolis: U.S. Navy Institute, 1983, pp. 51–52.

[32] Emmie Hamilton, *Second Fiddle to a Pigskin*, family scrapbook, published February 1984, p. 80.

# Chapter 14

## WINNING THE ONE BIG GAME

Bear Bryant's fingertips touched some of the 25,000 applications received for 2,500 jobs. So much mail poured into Hamilton's small Navy office that it had to be moved to a large garage space.[1]

College coaches were priority hires, and they would be tasked with customizing their respective sports to enhance the skills of pilots.[2]

Gym tumbling adjusted students' equilibrium, getting them comfortable with upside-down flipping, vaulting, and G-force; soccer was important for dexterity, conditioning, and foot control for rudder bars. Boxing promoted speed, reflexes, and the ability to use fists in attack and defense. Rough-and-tumble wrestling and hand-to-hand combat fostered courage and prepared pilots for knife-in-the-teeth fighting; military track enhanced endurance with commando courses designed for combat conditions. Baseball and basketball developed hand-eye maneuvering ability, quickening thought and action. Football, which Hamilton made analogous to "war itself," progressed with two weeks' instruction from fundamen-

---

[1] Hamilton Oral History, U.S. Naval Institute, p. 52.

[2] Hamilton Oral History, U.S. Naval Institute, pp. 51–52.

tal drills to full-scale padded scrimmages. Squadron competition was part of the program, producing six regulation games each week.[3]

Swimming and water polo would prevent Navy fliers from drowning under difficult and hazardous conditions; cadets learned to abandon ship fully clothed, and if they got dumped overboard in the lake or the ocean, they needed to have the skills and the stamina to swim a mile back home.

## The "Man Grab"

The Naval Academy was the go-to source for civilian alumni who possessed the old Navy spirit and highly specialized skills to run these schools. Much of the recruiting was done by word of mouth, and civilian alums, no longer connected to the Navy, were selected. Naval Academy graduates were tracked down in alumni directories and the Academy's *Lucky Bag* yearbook. Every single one of the old friends Hamilton reached out to was anxious to serve, and he was able to recruit old teammates like Frank Wickhorst, former captain and All-American tackle, who played in the great 1926 Army-Navy game.[4]

Many of the Academy's alumni, long retired from sea duty, were quietly working for insurance companies, teaching at universities, practicing law, and poring through the books at banks from Main Street to Wall Street. Future V-5 officers were architects, engineers, physicians, and managers of factories churning out coal, iron, steel, and fuel for the war. They were psychologists, history professors, and physicists with PhDs who taught Theory of Flight to pilots.

---

[3] United States Navy Bureau of Aeronautics, The Aviation Sports Program in the U.S. Navy Pre-Flight Training Schools (Washington: Navy Department, 1944), pp. 3–6; T. Hamilton, "Football in the Navy," in *The Official NCAA 1942 Football Guide*, p. 21.

[4] Hamilton Oral History, U.S. Naval Institute, p. 5.

## The 100

It did not take long for Hamilton to sign his first 100 recruits, and then the Bureau of Navigation cut him off.[5]

Among the 100 was my grandfather, James P. Raugh Sr., who was in his late 30s when he was finally accepted into the reserves after two tries. My grandfather was a corporate warrior who rode a commuter train to the office and enjoyed two-martini lunches. But he was a true patriot at heart. He was the first to enlist after Pearl Harbor, and he took a huge pay cut for a coveted job at Hamilton's school.

The only memory I have of my grandfather is riding in the back of his black Thunderbird, with shiny red interior, when I was about six years old. He was a formal, handsome man of few words who wore fedoras and pin-striped suits. He fancied dark-blue neckties, and there was always a cigarette dangling over an ashtray. My grandfather died at a veterans' hospital of bone cancer in his mid-70s. For reasons I came to understand many years later, he rarely visited us and left behind a small leather case with only a few heirlooms. Inside the box was a France Libre medal, a gold World War II Freedom from Fear and Want medal, and his Naval Academy studs, which defined his legacy.

My grandmother, Eleanor Felty Raugh, was known as Dolly. Truth be told, she is remembered as the one who wore the pants in the family.

She had dark auburn hair that she pinned back into a bun. In the Navy scrapbook, she was impeccably turned out in pictures: pressed linen dresses, pearls, painted nails, and spectator pumps in the depths of the war. Though she was a rather reserved woman, I yearned to know her, and I always wondered why she so rarely visited my family before her death in 1986.

Both grandparents grew up in Altoona, Pennsylvania, a railroad town set high in the blue-gray Allegheny Mountains of Blair County. His father ran a men's clothing store; her father was a high-toned confectioner nicknamed the "Candy Man." In high school, a coach encouraged my grandfather to apply to Annapolis, while my grandmother went on to study piano at Goucher College. He graduated

---

[5] Hamilton Oral History, U.S. Naval Institute, p. 60.

from the Naval Academy in 1926, transferring his friendships and skills from the Navy to a career in the iron and steel industry. They lived a comfortable, quiet-moneyed lifestyle in Rosemont, Pennsylvania. When Pearl Harbor was bombed, their destiny changed.

President Roosevelt's call for war was a dream come true for my grandfather, filling the void of brotherhood that some men never realize they miss. Dusty uniforms from Annapolis were pulled from sea trunks, and patent-leather marching shoes were polished. Former midshipmen struggled to fasten brass-plated buttons, sucking in their stomachs as they looked at a shell of their former fighting selves in the mirror. They may have been henpecked at home and struggling to pay the mortgage. They may have nipped at the brandy to ease their nerves, but that fighting boy was still somewhere deep inside them, just padded and wrinkled and bored stiff by the peacetime years. From the minute men like my grandfather heard about Hamilton's schools, they went on crash diets and started doing push-ups before going to sleep at night. Evening cocktails were shelved for special occasions, and cigarettes were stubbed out to serve a glorious cause far greater than themselves.[6]

By January, Hamilton's class register for prospective athletics instructors read like a royal-blue book of intercollegiate, amateur, and professional sports. In February 1942, a Blue Ribbon advisory council convened at Annapolis to officially recruit base personnel from candidates Hamilton presented. The council included athletic luminaries such as Bernie Bierman, University of Minnesota football coach; Major John L. Griffith, commissioner of the Western Conference and secretary of the NCAA; William Bingham, athletic director of Harvard; and a host of educators from Auburn, Ohio State, Penn State, and Princeton.[7]

---

[6] Stories passed down from Raugh family history.

[7] Navy Department Press Release, April 19, 1942, Physical Fitness Correspondence, Records Group 24, Command file, BuAero Folder. Also, William H. Sullivan Jr., "The Naval Aviation Physical Training Program," *The Journal of Health and Physical Education*, January 1943, Volume 14, No. 1. p. 3.

In March, the Naval Academy hosted the first of four indoctrination courses to familiarize officer candidates with knowledge of naval lore and tradition. Bierman, a Marine major, was the head instructor. For consideration, candidates had to pass a physical fitness test. If these men were going to set the example for cadets, Hamilton insisted that they take the punishment they dished out.[8] Hundreds of provisionary officers lined up in shorts and T-shirts to put their bodies to the test. Since the candidates were approaching middle age, there was plenty of vomiting and passing out, and a few candidates suffered from heat stroke as they vied to earn spots as coaches and instructors. Over the next few months, 200 trainees arrived in shifts, as the Bureau of Personnel fielded a truckload of applications from coast to coast.

As jobs were filled, complaints added up. Some authorities believed that too many assistant coaches were being hired, and that instead of teaching one sport, instructors should teach ten. In one memo, it was suggested that the marching bands should be cut to reduce costs. But Hamilton and other officers were quick to defend the morale-building aspects of their schools. They knew that competition and music were the lifeblood of Pre-Flight, and they dug their heels in to keep the old Navy spirit alive.[9]

## Right-Stuff Recruiters

With Bryant back in Washington thumbing through applications, the Hamilton brothers set out on a tour with officers to select four regional Pre-Flight bases. Recruiting also swung into high gear to find cadets with the right stuff to take the controls of bombers.

Fourteen Naval Aviation Cadet Selection Boards were set up in key cities, including Chicago, Philadelphia, Atlanta, New York, Boston, Dallas, St. Louis, Washington, D.C., New Orleans, and Kansas City. To find pilot material, Hamilton and Radford devised national recruiting teams led by charismatic athletic coaches and officers like

---

[8] *Daily Tar Heel*, January 14, 1943, p. 3.
[9] Memo, n.d., from BUPERS. Believed to be January 15, 1942.

Lieutenant (j.g.) John Glenn, who hit every pocket in the country, from corn belt towns to the south side of Boston. The campaign slogan, "Fly with the FINEST . . . FITTEST . . . FIGHTINGEST . . . THE NAVY," was run in magazines and papers across the country, with an attached "Wings of Gold" application for the Navy's recruiting office in White Plains, New York. Colorful V-5 posters were plastered on post office walls and in recruiting stations, high schools, and colleges. The most enticing recruiting tool, however, was the fleet of legendary college football coaches who barnstormed recruiting offices, declaring, "Men of Action Pick the Navy." Some of the most persuasive recruiters were Hamilton's good friends, such as Bernie Bierman; Bud Wilkinson, future coach at Oklahoma; and George Sauer, who would coach at Kansas, Navy, and Baylor.[10]

The fighter pilot dream was appealing to a generation that romanticized Pan Am Clippers and the once-in-a-lifetime opportunity to fly. But in an unethical war, where the enemy did not hesitate to kill, and kill in the worst way possible, recruiters had to make sure they found candidates with the right stuff. Even some of the most athletic and brightest candidates did not make it to the next round. When an *Esquire* reporter shadowed Lieutenant John Glenn and two other recruiters, a boy marched into the room and stated that he was first in his class out of 455. Before he was rejected, Glenn's counterpart said in a solemn tone, "Son, you *slay* me."[11]

The V-5 offered a $27,000 education for a full year's training. This gold-standard investment included War Training School, three months of Pre-Flight ground school, and primary training at air bases at such stations as Los Alamitos, California, then to intermediate training at Pensacola, Florida, and Corpus Christi, Texas, where pilots mastered hands-on navigation, radio, gunnery, and instrument training. If they passed intermediate, cadets went to advanced training at the Jacksonville and Miami, Florida, air stations. V-5 sought men between the ages of 18 and 26, from 5 feet 4 inches to 6

---

[10] Hamilton Oral History, U.S. Naval Institute, 1984, p. 61.

[11] Nick Kearns, *Esquire*, December 1942, p. 76.

feet 3 inches tall, and between 124 to 200 pounds of lean, mean muscle mass. Cadets were examined by medical staff, described as "sourpusses and grippers," who examined them for perfect vision, good feet, and the ability to hear a whisper at 15 feet. Cadets had to possess 18 healthy teeth with at least two molars and four front teeth opposite one another in upper and lower jaws.[12]

Candidates were asked to bring birth certificates, high school transcripts, and letters of recommendation. Before candidates were even considered, recruiters looked them in the eye and up and down for certain intangible qualities.[13]

## Dear Diary

There was a specific quality that recruiters could sense like bloodhounds: Navy recruiters sought team players willing to risk their lives for their country. They wanted average All-American boys with manners who could become officers. Recruiters rejected the quarterbacks and big men on campus if they sensed they would break formation to save their hide. One candidate applying for a job in the V-5 waited five hours for his interview, entrusting his diary with his humbling experience: "Finally, I wormed my way into the office and got to chat with a fellow who had a carload of gold stripes on his sleeve. He acted sort of funny, like he'd never heard of me before. I guess he doesn't read the sports pages. Another queer thing about this fellow is that he doesn't seem to be listening when I told him my football team won nine out of ten games last fall. This officer was more interested in what other activities I could touch—in fact, he wanted to know a lot of things that didn't seem very important to me. Well, Diary, as I left the office, I began to get the idea that the

---

[12] "The World Behind the Headlines," July 13, 1942, U.S. Pre-Flight School Scrapbook, 1942.

[13] Wesley Phillips Newton and Robert R. Rea, *Wings of Gold: An Account of Naval Aviation Training in World War II, The Correspondence of Aviation Cadet/ Ensign Robert R. Rea*, University of Alabama Press, 1987, p. 50. Also, Hamilton Oral History, p. 58.

Navy is mighty particular who they pledge and initiate. The more I think about it, the more I want to get in."[14]

The V-5 welcomed the sawed-off little guys who could take violent hits and get back up for the fight. They were the guys who were willing to do the little things, too, like make their bed and shine their boots. Just because a guy's face was on the cover of *Baseball Magazine* didn't mean he could swim ten feet or toss a 200-pound caber.

In fact, fame and fortune did not really matter at all when one's life was on the line.

---

[14] "Diary, I'm Doing Graduate Work in the Navy," by Lieutenant (j.g.) DeWitt A. Portal, USNR. Portal was a boxing coach at San Jose State from 1934 to 1953 and also served as an assistant football coach.

# PART IV

# THE RIGHT STUFF

# Chapter 15

# THE RIGHT-STUFF CULTURE

*"You did not go through 13 weeks in the Pre-Flight School without remembering it for the rest of your life," said Dupree Smith, Class of 1944. "They took boys in and made men out of them."*[1]

Ted Williams quickly realized that he was not the best athlete on the field at Pre-Flight. Pccrs included the fastest, toughest, most daring men on land and sea, and they were making extra contributions to the war effort. Swimmer Peter Fick, who broke Johnny Weissmuller's world record in the 100-meter freestyle, served as a coach, missing two Olympics to teach Pre-Flighters how to swim and survive crash landings. Ensign Cornelius Warmerdam, the "Flying Dutchman," held the world pole-vaulting record as the first man to clear 15 feet. World wrestling belt champion Don George not only led hand-to-hand combat classes, he taught females on the base and the munitions plant the art of self-defense. "Willie the Wedge" Turnesa,

---

[1] *Carolina Alumni Review,* "The War Years," September/October 1995, p. 72.

former U.S. amateur golfing champion, trained on base, too, giving golfing lessons before he went to gunnery school in Florida.[2]

With Bear Bryant and Jim Crowley of Michigan State and Fordham coaching on the sidelines, former football players from the New York Giants, Green Bay Packers, Philadelphia Eagles, Brooklyn Dodgers, and Chicago Bears came through indoctrination training. Frank McGuire, a UNC basketball coaching legend whose team won the 1957 NCAA title, was an athletic trainer along with John Wooden, UCLA's future "Wizard of Westwood," and Tippy Dye, a former football and basketball star at Ohio State, who drilled cadets on the hardwoods at Woollen Gym. Future Cleveland Browns quarterback Otto Graham made news when he was named All-American as a cadet at Chapel Hill.[3]

There were Carolina athletes with a story, too, such as Ensign Basil Sherrill, a Golden Gloves champion from Gastonia, who became the youngest commissioned officer in the state of North Carolina.[4]

## That First Week at Pre-Flight

When the Cloudbusters played that May 11 game that ended in a rainout, Ted was in the dugout, dressed in military khakis. That day, he approached Dusty Cooke, like Williams a former American Association batting champion. When Ted walked over to shake his hand,

---

[2] *San Bernardino Sun*, December 5, 1942, p. 7.

[3] *Daily Tar Heel*, January 14, 1943, p. 3; and Seth Davis, *Wooden: A Coach's Life*, Times Books, 2014, pp. 75–77. (Wooden shipped into Pre-Flight April 22, 1943, then he was deployed to the Iowa base, where he was a boxing instructor because the Navy thought it was too hot to play basketball in the University of Iowa's Field House. Students like Ed Orme explained that even then, Wooden, who was a high school English teacher and coach in the South Bend school system, was quite the motivator, who possessed the "ability to get on you when you needed it" and the disposition to have a lot of fun with his trainees.)

[4] University of North Carolina Pre-Flight Photography Archives pictured with Kidd Brewer and March 25, 2017, *The News & Observer* obituary of Basil Lamar Sherrill.

it took Dusty a minute to realize that he was looking at Ted Williams in the flesh.

In their first full week at Pre-Flight, Ted remained on the sidelines as the Cloudbusters won twice, including a 4–1 victory over the NC State Red Terrors. Ivan Fleser got a chance to pitch at that May 12 game. That day his arm held up as he put on a "beautiful airtight hurling duel" against the Red Terrors' pitcher, who gave up three runs in the first inning.[5]

After easy wins on the ballfield, training got bloody and blistered for the new players. None of the Nine had killed a man before they shipped into Pre-Flight, and they learned how to do it from Don George, a barrel of a man who had won several world-champion wrestling belts.

Ted and the newbies observed finger grips to gouge out a man's eyes in hand-to-hand combat. When coaches picked up cadets and flipped them to the ground like suitcases, the potential for injuries, including more than a few broken ribs, became clear. In front of reporters, George routinely announced in a very calm voice, "All right gentlemen, now squeeze your opponent's neck until he's blue in the face."[6] Trainees learned how to strangle the enemy with a piano wire and crush a man's windpipe—it was weird, and violent, and unlike anything Ted had ever experienced, and he absolutely loved it!

---

[5] *Asheville Citizen-Times*, May 13, 1943, p. 12.

[6] *St. Cloud Times*, August 27, 1942, p. 10.

# Chapter 16

## CALDWELL HALL—THE THEORY OF FLIGHT

Having proven himself in the classroom at Amherst, Ted studied very hard with a hunger to master courses that captured his imagination. In his morning classes, he leaned forward from a wooden desk chair at Caldwell Hall, watching an instructor draw vectors and equations on a chalkboard. Classes were hands-on, and instructors passed round model airplanes to explain how objects move through space and all of the forces that impact flight.

Years later, those ground training courses—navigation, physics, aerology, and Theory of Flight—would ultimately shape his understanding of hitting.[1]

The theories first clicked at Amherst, where Professor Harold Irving "Doc" Ewen taught him about wind velocity and took him to a lab to explain why a ball curved. Ewen was a die-hard Red Sox fan

---

[1] The Theory of Flight classes at Pre-Flight outlined and pictured in scrapbooks (St. Mary's yearbook) connect the academics of Pre-Flight to the Science of Hitting. Factors such as speed, velocity, circular rotations, lift, and drag were examined—terms later used by Ted with ease to explain why a ball curved. Classes were held in Caldwell Hall and Manning Hall, where radio code was taught.

who had just graduated from Amherst in 1942. He taught celestial navigation and explained why a bat of certain density would drive a ball farther than one of lighter density. Though Ted was just a high school graduate, he was full of questions, and their minds met when it came to the science of hitting. Ewen explained why a medium-weight bat swung fast would drive a ball farther than a heavier bat with a slower swing, and he explained why a ball curved. When Ted arrived in Chapel Hill, he credited his roommate with helping him master the laws of aerodynamics.[2] Later in his career, sportswriters such as Ed Linn marveled at Ted's MIT-caliber mind and his ability to carry on with ease for 15 minutes to explain how aviation formulas like Bernoulli's method impact how a bat hits a ball, factoring in air, velocity, and weight.[3]

According to Johnny Pesky, as soon as Ted stepped out on the ballfield he checked the direction in which the flag was flying. He routinely reminded Johnny, "If a little bit of wind affects a 100,000-pound aircraft, what do you think it does to a baseball?" With Bernoulli's formula in the back of his mind, Ted adjusted his swing to heat and wind conditions like a weather vane, knowing that more home-run records were broken on blazing hot days.[4]

According to *The Physics of Aviation* textbook, pilots studied Bernoulli's law of the dynamics of fluid motion and Newton's laws of the dynamics of rigid bodies in explaining sustentation and flight.[5]

---

[2] Herb "Huck" Finnegan's series in the *Boston Sunday Advertiser* and *Boston American* and Navy records on classes. In Finnegan's story, he references a Chapel Hill roommate named "Lou Finger," which does not track with University housing records, but it is possible that Lou could have moved in later with Ted.

[3] Ted's interpretations (easily explained to players) were recorded by Ed Linn, *Hitter: The Life and Turmoils of Ted Williams*, p. 184

[4] Ibid., pp. 193–194. Note, Richard Lee, "How Much Effect Does Temperature have on Home Runs?" diamondkinetics.com, March 10, 2016.

[5] *The Physics of Aviation*, 1942 edition, "Aerodynamics for Naval Aviators," H. H. Hurt, University of Southern California, NAVAIR, January 1965, pp. 15–16.

At Pre-Flight, psychologists and psychiatrists indoctrinated war-time thinking, and naval instructors taught techniques to instill hate for the enemy, which came quite easily to Ted. In case he was taken prisoner, he also learned rules for talking and relaxation methods to withstand isolation and torture.[6]

Every night, he fell into the bed exhausted, often with a book in his hand. After all of the studying and the back-breaking drills, there was the chore of double-duty baseball, and a whole lot of it.[7]

On Sunday May 15, the Cloudbusters loaded up on the bus to face both teams in Norfolk. On Saturday, Johnny Sain struck out 12 Naval Training Station Bluejackets, including Don Padgett, a North Carolina boy who had played five seasons for the Cardinals up to that point. From the grandstands it looked like old times, when the Cloudbusters reunited with old friends like Phil "Scooter" Rizzuto and Dom DiMaggio. But it was Norfolk's right-hander Tom Earley, Sain's Boston Braves teammate, who stole the headlines, keeping the 'Busters at bay to win, 3–0.[8]

On Sunday, May 16, the Cloudbusters' luck changed when they faced Naval Air Station's Airmen, besting them, 3–2. Finally, the Navy Fliers got in sync and even Ted got a little more excited about playing in his first game the following weekend.

## One-Year Success Record

On May 23, the Chapel Hill base celebrated its one-year anniversary with a thousand guests at the football stadium.

Hundreds of cadets had since received their wings, and they were headed off to battle as Navy ensigns or second lieutenants. No longer an experiment, the Pre-Flight sports training experiment was producing real results.

---

[6] Syllabus clearly outlines 19 points, including sections 14 and 15 on psychological/psychological training.

[7] Author's father's memories of players being exhausted, drilling and studying until the lights were turned out.

[8] *The Daily Press*, May 16, 1943, p. 17.

In its first year, the V-5's Naval Aviation Cadet Training bases organized 600 football games. They held 4,419 track meets, 9,139 boxing matches, 3,276 swimming meets, 2,828 gymnastic meets, 2,000 basketball games, and 875 soccer matches for a total of 25,000 cadets.[9] Under Coach Jim Crowley, Chapel Hill's football squad made the best showing in the first year, winning eight varsity games, tying one game against Georgia Pre-Flight, and losing two games to Fordham and Boston College.

By the time of the anniversary, baseball was generating the biggest buzz at Carolina.[10]

Following the celebration, the Cloudbusters suited up for a four o'clock game against Camp Butner's 311th Infantry. After sitting on the bench for almost three weeks, Ted was cleared to play part of that game. With the stands packed, he hit a home run to right field his first time at bat. In three games against Butner squads that weekend, the 'Busters scored 40 runs with 37 hits, while allowing just one run and 13 hits.[11]

---

[9] William H. Sullivan Jr., "The Naval Aviation Training Program," *Journal of Health, Physical Education and Recreation* (January, 1943), Volume 14, Number 1, pp. 6–7.

[10] *Raleigh News & Observer,* May 23, 1943, p. 10.

[11] *The Cloudbuster,* May 29, 1943, p. 3.

# Chapter 17

# THE FATHERS OF SURVIVAL TRAINING

Early in the war, the Navy discovered that 75 percent of their pilots who were shot down actually survived the impact of the crash, but many died by the time reconnaissance found them. Pilots perished from the elements or lack of food and water. In many cases, if they did find food it was poisonous. And if they did not die of thirst, pilots drank contaminated water, another fatal, avoidable error. The Navy also determined that Annapolis cadets, and many pilots born to well-traveled families, didn't know how to survive in the wild. To find officers who could train pilots, Hamilton set out to find the most capable survivalists in the world, looking for a few men who could think like mountains, and outsmart a jungle.[1]

The talent pool came from all around the United States—there were burly mountain men, Eagle Scouts, and military officers with experience in survival training. In early 1942, the Navy selected 200 recruits, who were parachuted into four terrains of the Earth,

---

[1] Mike Carlton, *Philadelphia Inquirer*, December 2, 1973, p. 11D, and reference from Kepler's personal speech titled, "Survival," from daughter's files, p. 1.

including the jungle, the desert, the Antarctic, and the Everglades. Two weeks later, they were picked up, and their survival and fitness scores were compared.

One of the top-three candidates was a big game guide from Central Pennsylvania who learned about survival from country folks and Civil War veterans.

The Kepler children were amongst the first descendants of the Pre-Flighters I would meet, once again spending hours at a kitchen table reviewing pictures, letters, and unusual souvenirs from their father's years in the Navy. Like their father, Don, they were modest, soulful people who downplayed his legacy, focusing instead on the family's Sigma Alpha Epsilon fraternity at Penn State, where his sons carried on the membership. But the letters from Gerald Ford, Bear Bryant, and major-league players like Ted Williams put Kepler in a very different category. The family's collection of rare red bearskins and souvenirs signed by some of America's most famous outdoorsmen and fishermen were clues to their father's unique appeal.[2]

Donald Kepler grew up in Pine Grove Mills, Pennsylvania, a mountain village with pine tree groves, abandoned iron furnaces, and lumber mills a few miles east of Penn State. With Tussey Mountain, the Susquehanna River, and miles of underground caverns at his back door, Kepler was raised in a natural incubator for survival training. The Keplers were honest, hardworking farmers. Don's father was a leader in the community who received personal letters from Franklin Roosevelt at the local post office where the Keplers collected their mail at PO Box 1. Like the settlers who came before them, the Keplers built things to last, evidenced by the massive, 200-year-old family barn that stands on their land in the cradle of Happy Valley today. When I journeyed to Pine Grove Mills, I walked the grounds of the old Kepler homestead, where their father taught survival techniques to the armed forces and the first Peace Corps class (including its first troop of females) in his own backyard. The locals were extremely friendly, and they insisted on *showing* me his

---

[2] Interview with Kepler's children, June 17, 2017.

story. Pat Daugherty owns and managed The Tavern, a colonial-style eatery and dine-in museum at State College where Don Kepler dined almost every day of his retirement. The Tavern is a cozy place with burnished brass lamps that cast a warm light on fireplaces and wooden floors. Near the front door is the Keplers' wood-paneled booth, enshrined with framed clippings of the Yanklands war bond game, displaying images of Don with his arm slung around old friends like Babe Ruth. The framed pictures and news clippings have been darkened by chimney smoke over the years. With each generation, fewer kids and visitors recognize the local bear hunter standing beside his friend Jerry Ford. The owner of The Tavern not only knew Don like a member of the family, he has preserved his special legacy just a few miles down the road, behind the pine curtain, where survival training was born.

That afternoon, I jumped in the passenger seat of Pat's all-terrain vehicle—something I would normally never do, but I did it that day for Donald Kepler. Years earlier, Pat had bought the old Kepler place, and he drove me up into the hills to the ravines and the abandoned cabins from the 1800s, where old-timers inspired the Navy's techniques for survival.

As we powered up muddy trails toward the crest of the mountain, cutting through spiderweb veils, I learned that Don started hunting and fishing at age five, near the farm where turkeys and deer were easy prey. During Depression winters, he hunted foxes and wildcats for bounty. He would later become famous for shooting a turkey, deer, and bear every year, earning what locals still call the "triple crown."

Growing up, Don learned survival skills from the Civil War veterans; and, though it was not widely known, their methods, learned from the Indians, were integrated into V-5 training for pilots. As automobiles and refrigeration lured people indoors in the 1920s, Kepler hiked up the mountain with the first men of survival— old-timers who attended Gettysburg reunions. When they took those hikes up Tussey Mountain, with herbs and Indian arrowheads in their pockets, some of Don's friends may have walked with a cane.

They may have been hard of hearing, but their intelligence was vital to pilots in a far-off war. It was the simple farm folks and veterans who showed Don how to find a tiny, extra-strong bone in the ankle of a deer to use as a toothpick or a weapon or a fishhook that could snare a salmon in any hard-running river. They taught him how to find water in grapevines and the angle at which the vines needed to be cut to release a drink. They showed him how to make animal traps and fishing lures out of vines and thorns and hair; how to build shelters elevated from insects and the Nittany mountain lions that roamed Happy Valley.[3]

Veterans not only taught Don to determine the difference between safe and poisonous berries, he learned about natural remedies that spawned a homeopathic business that lasted a lifetime. When an arthritic woman was going to lose her job because she could not move her fingers to dispense change at a store, Don soothed her joints with bear oil. Another elderly neighbor used his "Old-Timer's First Aid Kit" remedy to stand up and walk without using a cane, and cures like these made their way to the Navy.

Don's son Rob explained that when the head survival job was narrowed down to three men, his father was selected because he always carried nail clippers in his pocket. "He had the neat and organized comportment of an officer," he told me, but I knew that was just a small part of the story. The caliber of men he worked with was extraordinary—and that trio of survival instructors in Chapel Hill changed the world.

Don's assistants were identical twin brothers, handpicked by Tom Hamilton, who'd read about their travels to the other side of the world in *National Geographic* magazine. But what really got Hamilton's attention was the twins' reputation for being indestructible and utterly fearless.

John and Frank Craighead, nicknamed the "Brothers Wild," grew up in the wooded suburb of Chevy Chase, Maryland, spending most

---

[3] Interview with Pat Daugherty, The Tavern restaurant owner, and tour of Kepler property, June 18, 2017.

of their time in forests and on the banks of the Potomac River. Their father, Frank Sr., was a forest entomologist at the U.S. Department of Agriculture. Their mother, Carolyn, was a biology technician and a naturalist before the avocation was vogue. Blessed with film-star good looks, the mirror-image brothers had sandy-blond hair and light-blue eyes. The boys were experts with slingshots, and they became Eagle Scouts, developing perfect physiques from years of climbing trees and wrestling. According to family members, they moved as one and referred to themselves as "I" instead of "we." As teenagers, the boys developed an obsession with birds that shaped them into the world's most skilled survivalists. The Craigheads used clothesline and hand-me-down metal spurs from a telephone lineman to shinny up trees, where they studied nests of sparrow hawks, prairie falcons, and great-horned owls. More than a few times the boys were dive-bombed by protective mother birds that sliced open their hands with talons. They spent summers at the family's farm at Craighead Station near Carlisle, Pennsylvania, where they were swept into river currents and toppled from tree limbs, breaking too many bones to count.

By age 15, the Craigheads mastered the ancient sport of kings, when only four American men were engaged in falconry.[4] By 1934, the brothers' wanderlust and fascination with the wild landed them their first paid assignment for *National Geographic*, where they were sent on a mission to photograph the secret lives of falcons and hawks.

After high school graduation, Frank and John headed west in a battered 1928 Chevrolet with heavy folding cameras and a courageous band of friends. Financed by Gilbert Grosvenor and his National Geographic Society, they drove their journey toward Wyoming almost entirely on pitted and crumbling dirt roads. The twins took along their pet hawk, Comet, who dug her claws into the backseat, bouncing along for the ride. That summer, the boys did not call home once, and they slept outdoors, listening to the midnight howl of wolves. In more ways than they could imagine, that pilgrimage to

---

[4] Tom Benjey, *Glorious Times, Adventures of the Craighead Naturalists*, The University of Montana Press, 2016, p. 3.

the Tetons was a glimpse into the brothers' future as they waded through rivers they would one day protect, observing the North American grizzly bears they would help save from extinction.

Their article recounting the trip, "Adventures with Birds of Prey," appeared in *National Geographic* in July 1937, followed by a book on falconry read by people around the world. At Pennsylvania State University, the brothers both lettered as 128-pound varsity wrestlers. When they were enrolled in graduate school, their falconry research got the attention of an Indian prince, who was the son of a maharajah. The prince visited the brothers in Chevy Chase, staying in their family's modest shake-sided bungalow at 5301 41st Street NW. Months later, they boarded steamships and a series of trains and wagons to his palace in Bhavnagar, India, near the Arabian Sea. On another continent, 15,000 miles away from home, the brothers rode elephants and hunted alongside cheetahs in the desert, learning the cruelest lessons of nature from the scorching terrain. On the nine-month journey, they sampled the tropics and scaled the highest mountains in Europe. One of the by-products of this amazing journey was the draft of an academic survival guide being written by the Craigheads when the Japanese bombed Pearl Harbor.[5]

While Hamilton was impressed by the twins' ability to navigate any terrain in world, what he admired most was the way the brothers laughed off the dangers of injuries. When an unnerved spectator called an ambulance while watching the brothers rappel down a cliff, Frank said, "To heck with them. If we fall, a broom is what they need, not an ambulance."[6]

## The Northern Star

According to Kepler's only daughter, Victoria, there were many summer evenings where she and her four brothers lay on the grass at

---

[5] Tom Benjey, *Glorious Times*, 98–100.

[6] Ibid., pp. 112–113. (Original source, the Craigheads' notes that were added as Addendum to Frank and John Craighead, *Hawks in the Hand: Adventures in Photography and Falconry*, Lyons and Buford, 1997, pp. 297–352).

their Pennsylvania farm, looking up at the sky. On those starry nights, the Keplers listened to their father's stories about their ancestor Johannes Kepler, the German mathematician and astronomer who studied the constellations. Their father would spend hours pointing out features of the Big and Little Dippers, Orion the Hunter, and other celestial bodies that had guided men since the beginning of time. One of the sayings they heard most was "Remember, you are never lost. If you have a compass or can see the North Star, you can always find your way home."[7]

Kepler carried the ancient wisdom of the constellations into the Navy. Nearly every day for four years, Kepler took the cadets on long hikes, covering at least 15,000 miles of trails during his years in North Carolina. His trainees were a common sight, marching in formation through Carrboro, where they cut off into the woods for hikes with the ubiquitous pack of dogs that roamed around the base.[8] During the war, stray dogs invaded Chapel Hill, where they were captured in the periphery of Navy photographs—living at fraternity houses, lounging on the sidelines of ball games and running in formation with cadets, who often tripped on them. By spring, there were so many strays that a *State* magazine writer joked that Chapel Hill without dogs was like a circus without elephants.[9]

With the dogs in tow, instructors aimed to expose cadets to danger and discomfort to grow their confidence. In the words of the Craighead twins, "courage is to a large extent self-confidence which is the product of training, accomplishments, testing and acting. Crossing bogs, swimming rapids, scaling high walls, and cliffs, hiking through strange country to an unknown destination, feeling one's way through the inky blackness of the dark woods, and

---

[7] Interview with Victoria Kepler in 2016, and original copy of her father's stump speech delivered to survival training students, Kepler family records.

[8] U.S. Navy Pre-Flight School hiking map and images of cadets in Carrboro.

[9] *State* magazine, Spring 1942.

encountering poisonous snakes and plants, when once experienced, furnish the individual with confidence."[10]

It was this journey into the unknown, forging for food and water, and camping under the North Star that inspired some of the most talented baseball players of all time to reach within themselves and find the confidence to win the war.

---

[10] PEM 39, *The Michigan Alumnus,* University of Michigan, November 7, 1942, pp. 96–97.

# Part V

# GRAHAM'S FIELD OF DREAMS

# Chapter 18

## WHEN THE NAVY MARCHED
## INTO CHAPEL HILL

*"Men marched where boys had strolled before."*
—1943 Yackety Yack yearbook

Chapel Hill's destiny as a flight school was sealed by the little brother of "Moonlight" Graham—a former Marine and president of the University who possessed the self-discipline and the quiet self-confidence that recruiters sought in V-5 cadets. In high school, Frank Porter Graham played football and wrestled, but it was baseball that he loved, and he carried a baseball in his pocket every single day, never going anywhere without it.[1]

Frank called Archibald his "baseball brother," and he was Frank's idol. A head taller, and much faster on his feet, Archibald played college baseball at the University of North Carolina, later using his earnings from professional baseball to pay his way through medical school. In 1905, Archibald played one inning for the New York Giants, winners of

---

[1] John Ehle, *Dr. Frank: Life With Frank Porter Graham*, Franklin Street Books, 1994, p. 3.

the National League pennant and the World Series. Decades later, his story inspired the character of "Moonlight" Graham, in W. P. Kinsella's novel *Shoeless Joe*, which took on a new life as the movie *Field of Dreams*.

But it was Frank, the smaller, less athletic little brother, who truly changed the world.

Dr. Frank Porter Graham was a rat terrier of a man, weighing 125 pounds, standing 5-foot-5 in platform wingtips. Frank had deep-set, rather sad-looking eyes and a receding hairline that made him appear older. He was known to buy his suits at the boy's department of a store on Fayetteville Street in Raleigh, but height never bothered him for a second.[2] When he became president of the University of North Carolina in 1930, Dr. Graham was revered as an intellectual and moral giant of towering brilliance, and some would say his mind was like a glimpse into heaven.

It was a leap of faith, and Frank's eye toward the possibilities of the future, that would secure the university's impactful role during those difficult war years.

Dr. Graham's crusade to convert the campus into a wartime training facility began 18 months before Hamilton's plan was written. This campaign was built on more than a decade of tireless work to position the university as one of the finest institutions of higher learning in the nation. Graham gave his heart and soul to the university, rallying people and gathering resources during the depths of the Great Depression, when North Carolina struggled as one of the poorest, least-educated, and most-starved states in the union. In the leanest years, he worked miracles, earning the nickname of the "New Deal Man of the South." He put unskilled unemployed workers to work through the federal government's Public Works Administration, which allowed men to feed their families as they built miles of rock walls and walkways around campus. Millions of PWA dollars were secured to construct 13 new buildings, including Woollen Gymnasium, three new dormitories, and a significant addition to the Carolina Inn.[3] He also championed for human rights in the legislature, working to keep children out of factories. He fought to enforce legal limits on workday

---

[2] Ibid., p. 23.

[3] Kenneth Joel Zogry, *The University's Living Room*, pp. 41–43.

hours and fair pay amongst factory workers, lobbying for civil rights for African Americans.

In the spirit of "If you want peace, prepare for war," Graham warmed up phone lines with his dear friends Franklin and Eleanor Roosevelt and lobbied Washington to secure his much-improved university as a Pre-Flight training machine. His vision was backed by a battering ram of university trustees, North Carolina politicians, newspapermen, and academics, as well as athletic coaches and philanthropists who saw promise in their world-class university.

The triumvirate credited for pioneering the Pre-Flight campaign included *Raleigh News & Observer* newspaper Publisher Josephus Daniels, a lion of a man who served as ambassador to Mexico. Daniels also served as Secretary of the Navy under Woodrow Wilson during World War I, supposedly inspiring the term "cup of Joe" for strong black coffee that took the place of alcohol on Navy ships.[4] He was joined by university Comptroller William "Billy" Donald Carmichael Jr., a former Army Air Corps private and basketball player at the university, who made a pile of money on Wall Street and Madison Avenue.[5] As officials toured potential bases, Daniels and Carmichael canvassed Washington to lobby the Navy with incentives to sweeten the offering. As Chapel Hill's tour neared, the arm-twisting intensified to outmaneuver other major universities rumored as prospects for the Pre-Flight campus, including the University of Notre Dame, Ohio State University, Purdue University, Michigan State University, and other Michigan colleges.[6]

---

[4] *Cup of Joe* has been a term tossed about since 1914, when Daniels supposedly banned alcohol (lore).

[5] Biographical sketch on NCpedia, https://www.ncpedia.org/biography /carmichael-william.

[6] University of Notre Dame mentioned *The Chicago Tribune*, February 3, 1942; Michigan State and Ohio State, *The Lansing Journal*, February 2, 1942; Purdue University and other unnamed Michigan universities, *The Indianapolis Star*, February 1, 1942. University correspondence, where a few officials loosely mention "keen competition from one or two Eastern universities" in papers, but no specific dates or documents identify specific universities.

In May of 1940, Graham shot off an irresistible telegram to Secretary of the Navy Frank Knox, offering wholesale use of the university's facilities to the U.S. government for defense preparedness. Graham fought to utilize every square inch of campus space for classrooms, athletics, social gatherings, housing, and dining. He drafted detailed training proposals, with enticing graphics and pictures, to recruit young males as young as 16 with tip-top physical and academic training.

Though he was prone to illness, Graham had the constitution of a major-league baseball player. When classes resumed in September of 1940, he mandated physical education training for all male students. He reinstituted the World War I Naval Reserve Officer Training Corps and the ROTC, while members of the faculty continued to join the National Guard. Graham personally organized a sprawling volunteer training corps, spearheading a new department for military science and tactics. In the marbled foyer of the campus's main library named for his dear friend Professor Louis Round Wilson, he created a Civilian War Information Center with diagrammed maps of the Axis's movement. There were current news clippings to help students understand the escalation of the war, along with stacks of recruiting brochures to help students choose the best path for service.

## The Village of Chapel Hill

It was in 1793 when a small farming village inherited its name from a little wooden chapel standing on the site of the Carolina Inn. Almost 150 years later, the town of Chapel Hill was one of the best-run municipalities in the state, with roughly 3,000 residents. The secluded little "Hill" had a progressive and well-run town government with a mayor, a city manager, and an active board of aldermen. The tax rate was low and the town had excellent schools, with fire and police protection and well-functioning utilities providing water, lights, and telephone service. There was a freight depot down the road from the university in Carrboro to ship in supplies for a military base. Durham had a passenger station, along with bus service from all directions, and the campus was in proximity to Washington, D.C., and the Naval Academy.

In addition to mild year-round weather, other than rare snowstorms and short heat waves, the campus offered one of the largest dining halls in the nation, equipped to seat 900 guests in one sitting for meals. Before the fitness goals of the Pre-Flight school were outlined, Graham promoted full use of Woollen Gymnasium, a brand-new, state-of-the art facility featuring varnished basketball courts, adjoining weight rooms, and a seating capacity for thousands of spectators. Kenan Field House, a beautiful Spanish Colonial stadium with seating for more than 20,000, was just 15 years old, and nearby Fetzer Field offered a newly paved track, winding around fields for soccer and lacrosse. The university offered courts for handball and tennis and the use of Bowman Gray natatorium, one of the only Olympic-sized swimming pools in the nation. Emerson Field, with its baseball diamond and moon-tower lighting, functioned as a gathering spot for America's pastime and other spectator sports.

Dorm space with modern plumbing and central heat was in move-in condition. In 1923, the university built a massive U-shaped Quonset hut out of tin for dances and indoor sports that could house hundreds of cadets.

The university owned several thousand acres of forests surrounding campus, including a 1,000-acre farm and botanical preserve with a menagerie of wildlife, flora, and vegetation. Long before Pearl Harbor, Graham requested government funds to expand the landing strip at the airport with a new hangar and buildings for training within walking distance from campus. In the spring of 1941, an armada of steel-tread tractors ripped tree stumps out of the ground like turnips to grade the blood-red land for an airport larger than LaGuardia Field in New York.[7] With three runways, and plenty of

---

[7] *Carolina Alumni Review*, Midsummer 1941, July, "Defense, Alumni—and the University," pp. 289 and 308. Paul Komisaruk, *Daily Tar Heel*, March 9, 1941, p. 8. Note about 3,000-resident population, *Carolina Alumni Review*, *"The War Years,"* September/October 1995, p. 70.

spare acreage for development, by the spring of 1942, it appeared that bombers, interceptors, fighters, and reconnaissance planes might soon accompany the little yellow Piper Cubs buzzing over Chapel Hill.[8]

With Bear Bryant back in Washington, Hamilton and a team of naval officers set out on a national tour to select four Pre-Flight school bases. They looked for ready-made facilities that could be up and running in a matter of weeks without new construction for classrooms, housing, or athletic fields. Nearly 80 institutions applied for the distinction of being one of four schools, with the University of North Carolina on the short list for the Southern or the East Coast campus slot.

Personal correspondence flew between university leadership and Hamilton. William D. Carmichael wrote persuasive letters and memos with the cinematic flair he used as a Madison Avenue advertising executive. Shortly after a meeting with Hamilton, he drafted an enthusiastic memo saying, "You are a great guy! And that goes doubled in no-trumps for the rest of your crew. Dr. Graham, Dr. Cornwall and I certainly enjoyed seeing you, Captain Radford, Captain Thompson, Lieutenant Commander Noren, Pete Cawthon, and your other ship-mates. But now we want that East Coast Induction Center more than ever before."

On April 15, the first Pre-Flight school was selected at the University of Iowa, followed by St. Mary's College on June 12. Carmichael went on to say, "It seems to us that in announcing the selection of Georgia as the Southern Center, at exactly the moment that the committee from the Navy Department was here interviewing us and inventorying the facilities of our institution, the 'higher-ups' must have intended all along to consider us for the East Coast Center.

"In brief, we want to help you fellows win the war; and we believe that we've got what you need." A postscript at the end touched on lingering sentiments from the Civil War: "Don't worry about our

[8] Ernie Frankel, *Daily Tar Heel*, "The Finest College Airport in the Nation," May 10, 1942, p. 16.

Southern blood's building over being considered an East Coast State. NC was one of the original 13 East Coast States. Besides after recent trend of events, we wish that Sherman had done a thorough job instead of mere MARCHING THROUGH a certain state to our south."[9]

## A Student's Remembrance

Ernest Frankel grew up in Charlotte, North Carolina, and made a name for himself in Hollywood, writing and producing scripts for the *Perry Mason* television series. When I spoke with him, the 92-year-old former Marine colonel explained that he always dreamed of attending Carolina after he visited Boys State in Chapel Hill. Growing up, money was tight. After he won a state debate contest and receiving full scholarships to Wake Forest and Clemson, an uncle helped him to pay his way through the University of North Carolina in the days of the Pre-Flight school.[10]

When Pearl Harbor was bombed, Ernie, as he was called, was watching a matinee starring Hedy Lamarr at the Carolina Theater on Franklin Street. That night, Ernie and Sylvan Meyer, his best friend for life who would one day run the *Miami Herald*, borrowed an old car from a fraternity brother and drove overnight to Washington to cover the story. Sylvan was managing editor of the *Daily Tar Heel*, and Ernie was a reporter. Seventy-five years later, Ernie recalled the city's empty streets on that cold, dreary morning on the Capitol grounds, as millions of Americans huddled by tabletop radios to hear President Roosevelt's famous words to the nation. Sylvan had only one press pass to the House Chamber, so Ernie stayed behind, shivering in the car, listening to a crackling radio as members of Congress gathered on the Capitol steps in overcoats, preparing to enter the chamber. Knowing that he was within steps of one of the most historic speeches ever made on American soil, Ernie took a chance, and the car door closed behind him. Within minutes, he was

---

[9] Memo to Hamilton from William D. Carmichael, February 1942.

[10] Ernest Frankel interview, August 4, 2017.

able to inch into the building with a representative from Ohio and find a spot on the balcony with a perfect view of the president.[11]

After that six-and-a-half-minute speech to a nation holding their breath during Roosevelt's declaration of war, the sergeant-at-arms soon found himself alone in a deserted chamber with a few teenage boys serving as pages. Pointing at the two gangly teenagers across the chamber, he shouted, "Well the deed is done . . . you'll be fighting when you are 21." Ernie knew his future had changed, too, and could see the somber mood of the nation in the way the legislators walked down Constitution Avenue in silence, with their heads down—America was going to war.

The next day, Ernie had a hand in authoring front-page editorials in the *Daily Tar Heel*. One of the boldest pieces was headlined "It's here—Let's face it," where students were urged to forget country-club life and the shallow pseudo-sophisticated attitude of unconcern. It was time to stop wasting the state's money and to start training.[12] Christmas came and went, and students returned to school weeks later with a different attitude. *What would become of them? What would become of their school?* Boys who did not enlist after Pearl Harbor wondered, *When will I be drafted?*

In the New Year of 1942, Carolina's undergraduate enrollment peaked with nearly 3,000 students yet to be impacted by the draft.[13] Ernie was a regular at President Graham's house, and he was there on the afternoon of January 31 when Mrs. Roosevelt clomped down the stairs from the upstairs guestroom to greet students before she spoke at a postwar planning conference that night at Memorial Hall. Ernie brought along Louise Lazarus, an exceptionally bright girl from Henderson whom he would marry a few years later. He and Louise remembered the First Lady as extremely warm and unassuming, and they were struck by her height. They had no idea that Mrs. Roosevelt's tour of the campus on the cold and windy afternoon was

---

[11] Ibid.

[12] *Daily Tar Heel*, December 9, 1941, pp. 1–4.

[13] *Daily Tar Heel*, January 22, 1942, p. 1.

inspired by something much bigger than her speech about students' future in the war.[14]

Graham and the powers of the university knew that it was their last chance to showcase the campus as a war-training center. Dressed in a heavy black frock coat and a slouch hat tipped on the side of her head, Mrs. Roosevelt lumbered through campus in the wind, swinging a bowling bag purse. In photographs, the First Lady dwarfed Graham and 79-year-old Josephus Daniels, in his dapper bowtie and three-piece tweed suit. Hugh Morton captured the First Lady's reassuring, crooked smile as she ambled past the baseball field and facilities where university officials aimed to train the next generation of Navy pilots. Her secretary, Malvina Thompson, trailed the group as they dined with students in the campus cafeteria, eating off plastic plates heaping with vegetables and drinking coffee. African American waiters in white uniforms and hats smiled as they served Mrs. Roosevelt, who shared Graham's passion for civil rights.

After Mrs. Roosevelt returned to Washington, the triumvirate—Graham, Carmichael, and Josephus Daniels—lobbied tirelessly for the school. Slowly, mixed news reports trickled out.

On February 3, the *Daily Tar Heel* headlined unofficial news that 1,800 cadets were about to be barracked on campus. Thinking the Pre-Flight school was a shoo-in, campus editors predicted the end of lazy days in loose sweaters and scuffed-up saddle oxfords when the quickened pace of marching feet landed on campus.[15]

One week later, reports about the status of the base were not encouraging. On February 9, Daniels received a sterile memo from the White House saying: "unfortunately when I checked in regard to your telegram of February 7, I found that the Navy had selected Atlanta as southern school; Iowa for the Middle West; and the matter had gotten so far I could not very well change it. F.D.R."[16]

---

[14] Ernest Frankel interview, August 4, 2017.

[15] *Daily Tar Heel*, February 3, 1942, p. 1.

[16] White House correspondence, Franklin Delano Roosevelt, Feb. 9, 1942.

After years of preparation, an exhaustive two-month survey, and a seemingly perfect visit by the First Lady, many feared that the university had been passed over.

Those pivotal months after Pearl Harbor were amongst the strangest in the history of the university, and the "anything could happen" scenario weighed heavily on the shoulders of the campus and the entire town. Students wondered if they would ever graduate, and small business owners feared that they'd shutter for good with shrinking enrollment. The Red Scare invaded campus, and the *Daily Tar Heel* reported sightings of J. Edgar Hoover's G-men at the South Building, digging up records on students.[17] Though the university was located in the center of the state, Dean Francis Bradshaw, chairman of the university's faculty on defense, warned Rotary members that the university could be bombed, with its proximity to Fort Bragg. The timing of that comment could not have been worse, and some feared that it might deter the Navy from selecting their university as a Pre-Flight base.[18]

## The Navy Marches into Chapel Hill, 1942

On the afternoon of February 27, 1942, news arrived by telegram that naval officials formally selected the University of North Carolina at Chapel Hill as the Eastern Seaboard campus, the crown jewel of the Pre-Flight program. Upon hearing the news, Comptroller Carmichael telegraphed Commander Kessing in Washington with this dispatch: "The Navy and Carolina Forever! Come on down. We are raring to go." By 12:30 p.m., the AP and UP wires poured out the news to people across the state who had lost hope for the Navy base that the final Pre-Flight school was Chapel Hill-bound.

From the very beginning, operations within the confines of Hell's Half-Acre were top secret even to campus employees. For the next few weeks, faculty, residents, and students looked for signs that a flight school was actually coming to Chapel Hill. In early March, an

---

[17] *Daily Tar Heel*, January 21, 1942, p. 2.

[18] *Daily Tar Heel*, January 17, 1942, p. 1.

atmosphere of expected excitement prevailed over campus when rumors were confirmed that the small school would commandeer a building or two from the university.

A pair of supply officers arrived on March 24, remaining inconspicuous as they set up a makeshift office on the first floor of Swain Hall. Swain was a white elephant of a building used as a dining hall and office space, and it is the site where the Pre-Flight legacy began. Lieutenant Commander Benjamin H. Micou, USNA, and Ensign Edward E. Mack, USNR, barely unpacked their bags when they arrived on campus, planning to head to Charleston two days later to order supplies. After checking out the building, they stayed just long enough to hire a young inexperienced brunette, Virginia Harrison, as the first de facto commandant of the base.[19]

In his early 20s, Mack had the long legs and square shoulders of a swimmer from his years at the University of Michigan. Mack was working in Chicago before he took a job in the Supply Corps to get the Chapel Hill base up and running. Like Mack, 45-year-old Micou was a former basketball player at Cornell who worked in the transport service during the Great War. When the second war broke out, Micou was an insurance executive in Birmingham, Michigan, with a summer home at Whip 'O 'Will Lodge on the Au Sable River. In a matter of months, he left his wife and children and his comfortable lifestyle behind to open the Chapel Hill base, with no defined date of his return. In his first interview with the campus paper, Micou was tight-lipped about the new base, assuring students that supplies would roll in soon. The school was already a covert work in progress; plasterers and painters hauled ladders in and out of dorms, plumbers renovated bathrooms, and CBS was hired to oversee the installation of loud speakers and an amplification system within the confines of the base.[20]

---

[19] *The Cloudbuster*, September 19, 1942, p. 1. *Daily Tar Heel*, February 28, 1942, p. 1.

[20] *Daily Tar Heel*, March 26, 1942, and *Chapel Hill Weekly*, November 13, 1942, p. 1.

Fresh out of secretarial school, and all of age 23, a bewildered Miss Virginia Harrison was left alone in the temporary office at Swain that smelled of waxed floors and typewriter ribbons. Her official title was Pre-Flight stenographer, and for several days she sat at her desk beside an empty in-box, chewing on her pencil and listening to the *tick-tock* of a wall clock as a cast of uniformed strangers arrived.

With little instruction, Harrison was not exactly sure why she was hired, and for whom she would work.[21] But she soon found herself amongst dozens of female employees nicknamed "lovelies," regardless of their looks, age, or knack for fashion. One-third of the Pre-Flight personnel would include women, and many lived on the third floor of Alexander Hall. Secretaries like Harrison and dozens of WAVES and WACS would take shorthand, beat on typewriters, order supplies, and manage the payroll. Women would operate telephone switchboards that never stopped ringing; they operated mimeograph machines, worked in the medical and dental stations, and crafted some of the most sensitive memos written during the war.[22]

One of Virginia's bosses, Lieutenant Commander John Packard "Packy" Graff, reported for duty from Annapolis while Mack and Micou were in Charleston. At age 46, Graff was a tall, handsome man with a commanding presence and a brisk walk. Raised in Greenville, Pennsylvania, a whistle-stop on the Bessemer Railroad, he graduated from the Naval Academy with the class of 1920.[23] Recruited from Standard Oil, he was an example of a Naval Academy graduate lured to the Pre-Flight School from the private sector.

Like all of the command staff who excelled at one or more sports, including a host of All-Americans and men decorated with Olympic medals, Graff earned laurels as a rower. With height,

---

[21] *Cloudbuster,* September 19, 1942, Vol. 1, p. 1.

[22] *Cloudbuster,* July 27, 1945, p. 1, reported around 30 WAVES.

[23] Though he graduated in June 1919, he was associated with Class of 1920 due to World War I. *Daily Tar Heel,* April 11, 1944, p. 1.

broad shoulders, and long legs, he pulled the number three oar on varsity crew at Annapolis, which won the 1919 intercollegiate title.

After graduation, Packy served on several battleships and cruisers, where he met Oliver Owen "Scrappy" Kessing, a 1914 Academy graduate and career naval officer who scouted sites for potential Pre-Flight bases and assumed command of the Chapel Hill station in the middle of April.

## Launching the Pre-Flight Ship

Kessing was a warhorse with 30 years of service including 22 years of at-sea duty in every sea in the world when he shipped into Chapel Hill. He'd earned medals in the Mexican, China, and Haitian campaigns, as well as the First World War, and like his peers, he was a former athlete. Commander Kessing earned his nickname in the boxing ring, where the lean, 5-foot-10 fighter scrapped through many a fight at the Academy. He was up at 5 a.m., never to bed until 10 p.m., never taking a rest. A roving reporter observed that Scrappy was tough, precise, strict, and demanding—he wore his hat high at an angle like an officer, but he had a twinkle in his eye that won the admiration of the entire base.[24]

When Kessing arrived to inspect the assembly of the station, he was followed by a dozen officers fresh out of indoctrination training at Quonset Point Naval Air Station in Rhode Island. A medical officer and pharmacist's mate were the first to set up shop on campus, along with a lone dentist, with no equipment. Before the *Chapel Hill Weekly* announced the official opening of the Pre-Flight base, the war was rolling into Chapel Hill by the ton.

Convoys of trucks with canvas-covered beds stamped with the U.S. Navy logo came roaring into town. Nosy neighbors and students marveled at the band of men who barely exchanged a glance. A real military base rose like a fortress in the middle of the sleepy Southern

---

[24] William H. Sullivan Jr., "The Naval Aviation Physical Training Program," *The Journal of Health and Physical Education*, January 1943, Volume 14, No. 1, p. 56.

campus with officers stripped to the waist, working side-by-side with laborers from dawn until midnight, unloading desks and chairs and cases of guns.

Farmers on the outskirts of town covered their ears, staring in disbelief at the firestorm of airplanes approaching from all directions with men and supplies.

New employees seemed to come out of thin air, transforming Swain Hall, Alexander Hall, and surrounding dorms into an operation resembling a battleship deck. There was so much to be done in so little time. Until housing was assigned, officers slept in the field house that resembled a Red Cross bunker. Men worked through the night with flashlights to write the regulations to run the base; there were plans for fire drills, air raids, and blackout drills. They drafted charts for regiments, synchronizing schedules to make the base tick like a giant watch 24 hours a day.[25]

Preparing for a major remodel, more carpenters, electricians, and painters appeared with buckets of white paint. Hundreds of mattresses were lined up on the grass along with towers of pillows and towels stamped with the U.S. Navy insignia. There were truckloads of clothing and uniforms, and giant containers filled with thousands of pencils and books. Locals were particularly puzzled by the massive amount of sporting equipment that rolled off trucks. There were wrestling mats, boxing gloves, baseball bats, rubber boats, trampolines, and cargo nets. Balls of all shapes and sizes were unloaded by the thousands along with uniforms and footwear and protective gear for every sport imaginable.

The military brought new sounds to campus, too. The Navy grounds were wired with a public-address system that would chirp day and night for the next four years. Instead of the high-pitched whirl of pea-shooter Cubs, locals began to hear the deep rumble of transport engines from miles away. Windowpanes rattled. With screen doors slamming behind them, kids scattered into yards under

---

[25] Camp Davis vs. Pre-Flight football program, October 16, 1943, p. 17.

Ted Williams, right, communicates with Johnny Pesky during Naval aviation commissions training with 29 other U.S. Navy V-5 enlistees, at Amherst College in December 1942. This training photo inspired 1959 Fleer trading card of Williams. *AP Photo.*

Johnny Pesky, Joe Coleman, Johnny Sain, and Buddy Gremp on tarmac at Turners Falls Airport. *Courtesy of Pesky Family.*

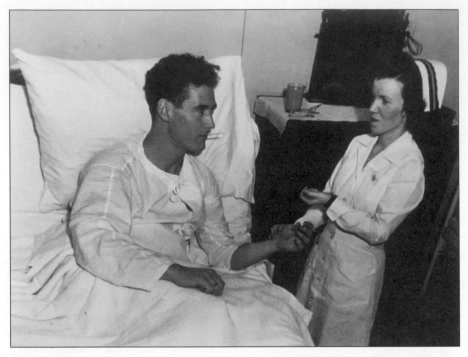

Ted Williams in recovery at Chelsea Naval hospital following hernia surgery before he shipped into Chapel Hill. *National Archives.*

Now naval aviation cadets, a group of former baseball players join a naval officer at Boston's Fenway Park on April 27, 1943, to watch the Red Sox play the New York Yankees. From left are Johnny Pesky, Red Sox; Lt. Cmdr. E. S. Brewer; Buddy Gremp, Braves; Joe Coleman, Athletics; and standing, Ted Williams, Red Sox; and Johnny Sain, Braves. *AP Photo.*

Cadets stepping off train in Durham to begin 90 days of Pre-Flight training in Chapel Hill.

Ted was picked up at Durham station by Lieutenant Donald Kepler (left), his baseball coach and survival school instructor. The two bonded instantly over fishing and hunting and became friends for life.

Three cadets and an unidentified baseball player in their newly assigned quarters. Star players were split up to enforce studying and rest.

Instrument training in Commander Hamilton's retired aircraft without wings parked at Alexander tarmac.

Naval recognition in the classroom.

Cadets hit the ground running with daily conditioning. Here they are running down South Road with the Morehead-Patterson bell tower in background.

Cadets made aerowheels to develop equilibrium and balance for pilots.

Pre-Flight loggers built commando courses, furniture, and other supplies for the base.

Cadets cleared land at current site near Finley Golf Course and installed drains under campus grounds.

Tossing the caber for strength.

World wrestling champion Don George teaching hand-to-hand combat skills.

World heavyweight champion boxer Lieutenant Jack Dempsey casually holds pistol as he visits with cadets. He said, "Get tough, boys, and keep fightin'. The best defense is a great offense, slug it out from the first bell, and never give up. . . Soon you'll be flying the Navy's fast planes and pouring hot lead into our enemies. Keep fightin' boys, and give 'em the works."

Pre-Flight football fields were stationed with four ambulances, and one always seemed to be in use.

Ted Williams (54) on the football field.

An unconventional training drill, diving headfirst into the base fighter-pilot style.

Johnny Sain (far left) watches Ted Williams and Johnny Pesky square off at boxing practice.

Boxing instruction from Lt. (j.g.) A. B. Wolff.

Cadets swimming and climbing cargo nets.

Kidd Brewer with a film director at Kenan Stadium.

Brewer and the Movietone press crew, 1943.

Celebrity visits included "Call for Philip Morris" Johnny Roventini, who sat in dugout at Pre-Flight baseball games.

Buddy Hassett, Johnny Sain, a press agent, Jimmy Raugh, Don Kepler, Ted Williams, and Johnny Pesky before photo shoot at Emerson Field.

Author's father, Jimmy Raugh, in the dugout with Johnny Roventini, Coach Kepler, and Naval officers.

Iconic photo shoot of Ted Williams and Johnny Pesky giving batting lessons to Jimmy Raugh.

Kids collect around Cloudbuster cadets Williams and Pesky on the Chapel Hill Pre-Flight base for this *In The Service* publicity image. *Courtesy National Baseball Hall of Fame.*

Buddy Gremp, Joe Coleman, Johnny Pesky, Ted Williams, and Johnny Sain in Cloudbusters dugout.

Packed stands at Emerson Field in 1943.

Pesky and Williams meet with Dom DiMaggio when the Cloudbusters played Norfolk.

Hillcrest Field in Burlington, North Carolina. *Courtesy of Don Bolden.*

Ted Williams and Babe Ruth in the locker room at Fenway Park for July 12, 1943, benefit game. *Transcendental Graphics/ Getty Images Sport Classic collection/Getty Images*

The Babe took a turn at bat July 28, 1943, in Yankee Stadium, when he managed the Yanklands, a team composed of New York Yankees and Cleveland Indians. Here he fouls off a pitch as his team lost to the Cloudbusters in a Red Cross benefit, 11–5. *AP Photo.*

Teenage Craighead twins, John and Frank, as *National Geographic* writers and falconers. *Courtesy of Craighead Family.*

Lieutenant Kepler and the Craighead twins examine survival school map for hike where cadets were advised on protocol in case they stumbled upon an illegal whiskey still.

Cadets cooling their feet after a hike.

Surviving player Ivan Fleser, born in 1919, who pitched for 1943 Cloudbusters squad. *Courtesy of Fleser Family Collection*

John Glenn (right) with future Rear Admiral Jerry Holland at the Pre-Flight station at the University of Iowa. *Courtesy of Jerry Holland.*

In this 1952 *LIFE* magazine photo, Ted Williams is at a farewell dinner in Boston before leaving to join the Marines that season. According to Chapel Hill Pre-Flight roommate Don Pletts's daughter, her father is leaning on chin to Ted's right. *Leonard McCombe/The LIFE Images Collection/ Getty Images.*

Don Kepler with his fellow Pre-Flight
Coach Bear Bryant in houndstooth at
Penn State, decades after Pre-Flight.
*Courtesy of Pennsylvania State University
Photographic Collections.*

Johnny Pesky, Buddy Gremp, Joe
Coleman, and Johnny Sain on
graduation day

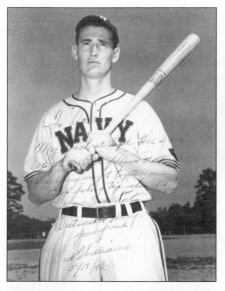

While researching this book, the author
discovered this photo of future U.S.
president Gerald Ford (bottom right) with
Battalion officers.

"To Don, my coach at Chapel Hill
and one of the greatest guys I ever
met. Hoping we get together on a
hunting and fishing trip when this
mess is over. Best Wishes Always,
Your Friend Ted Williams 5/17/43."
*Courtesy of Kepler Family.*

Base artist Gene Aiello, who painted the symbolic cadet painting for Pre-Flight, died in a training accident in Florida three months after he left Chapel Hill. His cadet painting is believed to be a self-portrait.

Rear Admiral Tom Hamilton, 1927 Annapolis graduate who organized and led the Navy V-5 Pre-Flight Naval Aviation Training program. *Courtesy of National Archives-St. Louis.*

The gatekeepers to World War II military baseball, Dr. Bobby Brown (middle), 91, and Eddie Robinson (right), 95, sit beside each other before the Yankees' annual Old Timers' Day game in June 2016 in New York. Also pictured is Don Larsen, the only pitcher to throw a perfect game in the World Series, which he did in 1956. Robinson is the oldest-living former Yankees player. *AP Photo/Kathy Willens*

the shadows of C-47 transporters dropping over the treetops like battleships into Horace Williams Field.

On April 16, 1942, Secretary of the Navy Frank Knox swore in the first V-5 cadet over national radio. David Fairfax Oyster, age 18 of Chevy Chase, Maryland, took the oath in the boardroom of the Bureau of Aeronautics in Washington, D.C., at 11 a.m. Oyster had just graduated from Wilson High School and was a freshman at George Washington University when he became the first and youngest enlistee of the untried cadet training program. The Iowa base was commissioned the day before, St. Mary's was scheduled to open June 11, and Georgia set for June 18.[26]

On May 23, 1942, 5,000 people gathered for the commissioning of the Chapel Hill base at 17:00 nautical time and 5:00 landlubber time, as four motored Flying Fortresses circled over the stadium. Flags of all allied nations fluttered in the breeze, and Old Glory was draped over the podium, where more than 100 radio stations broadcast the ceremony nationwide. It was a beautiful day at Kenan Stadium with dogwoods in full bloom and the smell of fresh cut grass wafting through the air. As the ceremony got underway, the sun rose high above the bell tower as members of the ROTC marched out on the field in dress whites, spelling the word that would define the school's destiny . . . NAVY.

Captain Arthur Radford was there to witness the inauguration of the sports training experiment that he and Forrestal imagined, along with Commander Kessing. Other dignitaries included Captain O. B. Hardison, who entered the university at age 14 and also graduated from the U.S. Naval Academy before he served as an aide to Assistant Secretary of the Navy for Air Artemus L. Gates. Captain Leland Lovette, the Navy's public relations officer who commanded a unit of destroyers at Pearl Harbor, was on the dais, as well as Commander Tom Hamilton and his brother, Lieutenant Commander Howard Hamilton.

---

[26] Camp Davis vs. North Carolina 1942 Pre-Flight Naval Aviation program, p. 11.

The ceremony was one of the biggest who's who wartime gatherings in the state of North Carolina. Governor J. M. Broughton gave the Old North State welcome, tipping his hat to Frank Porter Graham and his powerful troop of leaders who lured the Navy to Chapel Hill. There were beauty queens, and tobacco brokers, and Boy Scouts in the grandstands that day, along with professors and shopkeepers and hundreds of men and women who would run the base.

As former Secretary of the Navy during the Great War, Josephus Daniels had an especially sentimental connection with the base. Daniels was a descendant of the islander who snapped the picture of the Wright Brothers' first flight over the dunes at Kitty Hawk, North Carolina. Almost 40 years later, he delivered the opening remarks at the commissioning to welcome the most advanced pilot training school in the world, just 250 miles due west of the Outer Banks where North Carolina's history as the First in Flight state was born.

"No nation can hope to win in modern warfare unless it controls the air," Daniels said, "The flying Navy is our first line of defense . . . air power dominates the world."[27]

On May 28, the first battalion shipped into Alexander Field with 242 cadets. Dressed in their best suits, boys tumbled out of buses, looking a bit awkward before they registered and took their bags to Manley Dorm.

As Virginia Harrison welcomed the new officers and secretaries, they got little time to rest. The old, easygoing Hey! How are you? was replaced by a quick salute and an Aye, aye sir. The "ladies in blue" at the post office were quickly consumed with one of the busiest jobs on base. Each week, several tons of mail circulated in and out of campus. Cadets received up to three letters a day, often smudged in lipstick, reeking of perfume. Parcels were stuffed with everything from birthday cake to fried chicken, and cadets like Ivan Fleser shipped packages of rationed sugar back home.

---

[27] *Asheville Citizen-Times*, May 24, 1942. Description of planes flying overhead, *Alumni Review* magazine, May 1942, p. 235.

From day one, the publicity office overwhelmed the letter drop with press releases and images of cadets with time-stamped captions for newspaper editors around the world. Some of the most artistic images were inspired at Emerson Field, where an unusual narrative about military baseball was born.[28]

## Betty Hamilton—An Officer's Daughter

In June 1942, after school recessed for summer, Howard Hamilton packed up a few pieces of furniture into the Chevrolet and drove his family to Chapel Hill from Columbus, Ohio. According to his daughter Betty, the family left a large house on Indianola Street, taking along Grandmother North, for the move to Chapel Hill, their home for the next four years. The Hamiltons were assigned to a two-story shingled colonial-style home on a corner lot at 215 West University Drive, just blocks from the Navy headquarters. Built in 1938, the three-bedroom, wood-shingle house became a popular site for entertainment. Every cadet from Ohio was invited for Sunday dinner at least once. Other guests included Bear Bryant, Senator Hiram Bingham, and baseball luminaries such as Ted Williams, who waltzed through the door with Betty's father as a surprise guest at one of the regular gatherings.

Betty recalled that the family had a saying at dinner during rationing, "FHB-NMFIK," translated as "Family hold back, no more food in kitchen." When a neighbor's daughters left for college, they gave Betty and her twin sister, Barbara, a pair of blue Schwinn bicycles, including a bike that Barbara still owned 75 years later. Betty remembered that everyone rode their bikes around base, including her father, who pedaled over to headquarters in his uniform. To this day, she can recall running her hands along the boxwoods on street corners as she biked to the pool.

Betty's mother was an equestrian who never learned to ride a bike. She walked everywhere on campus and drove to Durham for

---

[28] *Cloudbuster*, September 19, 1942, p. 1. Interview with Ivan Fleser, April 11, 2016, regarding sugar that cadets sent home.

shoes and clothes, which were not readily available. There was another stand-alone memory that stood out in her mind of cadets in white uniforms, singing during church service, a breathtaking sight for a little girl during the war.

## Eleanor Roosevelt, Hidden Figure of Pre-Flight

As I explored the development of the Pre-Flight program, it was clear that Hamilton's job was not always smooth sailing, and there were moments when Pre-Flight's sporting competitions were threatened. A debate had smoldered since the launch of the V-5 experiment when Lieutenant Gene Tunney, director of physical education at BUPERS and former heavyweight boxing champion, openly criticized the Navy for diverting men from training and sending them out on the road for needless baseball and football games he considered athletic "boondoggling." When Tunney criticized the "fat, foul-mouthed, and drunken" football coaches selected to train pilots for combat, he went too far.[29]

Tom Hamilton was not aware of the extent of the First Lady's relationship with Dr. Graham when Radford sent him to the White House to visit with Harry Hopkins, President Roosevelt's top aide and decision-maker with the Lend-Lease negotiations. That morning Hamilton checked into the East Wing as a favor to discuss options for Hopkins's son, who was thinking about joining the service. Battling stomach cancer, Hopkins practically lived at the White House for three years, where the Roosevelts treated him like a member of the First Family. For several hours, Hamilton was left alone in the hall while Hopkins was tied up in a meeting. Cool and patient, Hamilton remained in a chair. When the First Lady's staff took notice of the officer with his hat cradled in his lap, they asked Hamilton if he would like to have lunch with Mrs. Roosevelt in the second-floor dining room. His reply was, "I think that would be very fine."

---

[29] *New York Times*, August 20, 1942; Catholic Men's Luncheon Club of Birmingham, Alabama, February 17, 1942, Physical Fitness Correspondence, Tunney File, N. A.

Raw-boned and 5-foot-11, Eleanor Roosevelt was a decent marks-man who bonded with the best sportsmen.

Watching polio rob her husband of his ability to walk, she didn't take for granted the gift of fitness. In her national radio chats, she championed the importance of physical education in schools, stand-ing behind the president's charge to mobilize fitness nationwide.

Bringing along a female newspaper columnist, Mrs. Roosevelt inquired about the Pre-Flight schools, and she was immediately fas-cinated by Hamilton's approach to aviation training. As the lunch concluded, she asked if he was having any problems he couldn't solve. Knowing that Tunney was gunning to cancel the Pre-Flight football schedules, Hamilton paused and said, "Yes, as a matter of fact, there is."

A week later, FDR signed an executive order lifting restrictions that banned V-5 cadets from travel to compete against other teams.

"It was a very notable thing to have that lovely lady go to bat for us," said Hamilton in an interview some 40 years later. Very few peo-ple know that Eleanor Roosevelt was a force behind the continuation of the competition that allowed teams like the Cloudbuster baseball team to leave base for those games.[30]

---

[30] Oral History interview, Tom Hamilton, U.S. Naval Institute, 1983. Also, President Roosevelt's Executive Order 8989 Establishing the Office of Defense Transportation was amended in August 1942 to accommodate this type of travel.

# Part VI

# PLAYING BASEBALL MILITARY STYLE

# Chapter 19

## WALKING BILLBOARDS FOR BASEBALL
## AND THAT AIN'T ALL

Ivan Fleser recollected that Pre-Flight was the most difficult phase of his aviation training because the pressure was always on: "Everything had to be done their way. You always had to be ready to go emotionally and physically." Yet he looked forward to getting up every morning because he never knew what to expect, even on the baseball field.

He described how the baseball team trained for battle, recalling that there was surprisingly little coaching for technique. He also recalled that there were photographers milling around the base but it was not evident that they may have been looking for angles to show how differently the players trained.

"There was no traditional practice sliding into the bases at Pre-Flight. No coaching for skills. They geared us up for speed, reflexes, and power, and quick and *accurate* decisions. We were building muscle mass for combat," he said. Sure enough, when I examined the Pre-Flight photographs, the varsity baseball players were pictured diving headfirst into bases—kicking up a storm of dust. The swan dive was a recipe for bruises and gravel in the palms, but rest assured, it was a good way to practice an emergency dive out of a flaming plane.

"Pesky, who looked more like a football player than a shortstop, could run those bases like a missile," said 92-year-old Bruce Martindale, a Chapel Hill native who worked as an equipment manager for the Cloudbusters baseball team. Martindale described himself as a skinny teenage boy when he managed bats, balls, and other equipment at Woollen Gym: "I barely weighed 90 pounds and the players laughed at me, saying the bags were bigger than I was." Bruce saw players hurling baseballs like grenades, but it was the inclusive spirit that grabbed him. He came to know all of the players by name, and they knew his, too. The cadets carried themselves like officers, and he watched them come in and out of the locker room every day, beaten up and soaked in sweat but smiling. "They were always friendly, very respectful to everyone who worked on base, even the scrawny kid handing out equipment from cages," he said with a chuckle.

Bruce attended all of the home baseball games at Emerson Field and saw Ted knock out "many a window at Lenoir Hall." There were unconventional sports at Pre-Flight, too, like the caber toss, a sport of Scottish lumberjacks; rugby; and pushball, which was played in Great Britain. Bruce blew up the giant rubber pushball and carried it on a pickup truck to Fetzer Field. He told me he'd never seen anything like it when all 22 players went at the ball to push it over the goal line.[1]

## The PR Machine

There were many who left fingerprints on the Pre-Flight publicity campaign. One of those people was William D. Carmichael, who'd made a pile of money on Wall Street and had raised millions for the university through the state legislature, gaining support from the captains of state industry, foundations, and influential families.[2]

---

[1] Phone interviews with Bruce Martindale, November 20, 2015, and May 28, 2017.

[2] Notes about William Carmichael Jr., Howard E. Covington, and Marion A. Ellis, *The North Carolina Century, Tar Heels Who Made a Difference, 1900–2000*, University of North Carolina Press, 2002, p. 214.

One of his disciples was Kidd Brewer, an officer who was too old to become a fighter pilot, so he requested a desk job in a North Carolina spot where the "fighting was the thickest."[3]

Long before Kidd ended up in the psychiatric ward and the state penitentiary for bid-rigging, he was the Pied Piper of the Navy press office. With the help of his editors, Leonard Eiserer and Orville Campbell, Kidd built a crack team of photographers and artists who churned out cartoons, branding Pre-Flight cadets as the Supermen of the war. He was also a charming entertainer who held court with the most influential journalists of his era, and he viciously protected the privacy of star cadets like Ted Williams.

In an official Navy portrait, Lieutenant Kidd Brewer stands on the bleachers of Kenan Stadium with his hands on his hips. He is directing a cameraman aiming a motion picture newsreel camera at the football field like a machine gun. Kidd went about his job as the Pre-Flight publicist just like he played football at Duke, having fun and taking in every single play.

In her mid-80s, Kidd's daughter, Betty Brewer Pettersen, was described by her cousin, Benjamin Kidd Brewer, as spirited, and prone to strong-minded opinions. When I met Betty at a Mexican restaurant with fluorescent murals near her home in Louisburg, North Carolina, she was soft-spoken with a quiet, demure laugh. Like most of the offspring of the Pre-Flight luminaries, she was mystified by her father's stealthy history at the Pre-Flight school. During the war, Betty lived with her mother in Florida during the winter, spending summers on the Navy base, where her father bought her a little brown pony named Tony. She was about ten years old when her father and stepmother moved to 10 Oakwood Drive in 1942, two miles south of campus near the future site of Finley Golf Course. Neighbors included a host of athletes, including Ray Stoviak, an outfielder for the Philadelphia Phillies; and Lieutenant Alexander McLeigh, a hand-to-hand combat instructor, who lived down the road.

---

[3] Kidd Brewer personal papers, written request in application for Navy Reserves, 1942.

Before I met Betty, she offered to give me a box of old letters written by her father when he was stationed in the Pacific and pictures from his years in the Navy that no one wanted. She had considered throwing them away after a recent move but felt the timing of my call was providential.

In person, Betty bore a strong resemblance to her father; she was fair-skinned with sloping blue eyes, and a gentle, warm smile. Though she never said a word about her own athletic pursuits, Betty ranked among the nation's fastest race walkers in her 50s, carrying on her father's genetics. Betty said her father was a wonderful man who made a few enemies after dustups with politicians, but he was "nice to everybody." At least he tried to be.

"My father was good to me. He embarrassed the life out of me, always landing in the newspaper for doing something crazy," she said with a quiet laugh. "Once he drove from Raleigh to Winston-Salem in a Santa Claus costume, waving at people on the road," she said, explaining that he intended to shower people with attention "to lift their spirits."

As we became acquainted, I sifted through the materials in the box, which proved to be a goldmine of information, hinting toward her father's never-give-up Pre-Flight attitude. As a toddler, Kidd was pictured in a ragged gown, barefooted and tow-headed, between two calves on the dairy farm in Cloverdale, North Carolina. There were long emotional letters written to her grandparents from the South Pacific, where Kidd thanks them for teaching him to "hang on like a bulldog to a man's pants" and to learn from the rough rides that follow.[4]

Rare images showed Kidd at the height of his athleticism, testing his strength against a player lassoed with a rope on the Duke University football field. Hundreds of news clippings shed light on Brewer's famous eccentricities: the mansion on Kidd's Hill overlooking a Raleigh shopping mall where his influence-peddling for urban

---

[4] Letter from Lieutenant Kidd Brewer to his parents, April 19, 1945, some content removed.

sprawl began, the garage stocked with yellow Jaguars and electric-red Cadillac Eldorado convertibles, the trapeze hanging from his living-room ceiling, and the *Look* magazine spreads featuring Kidd's adjoining indoor-outdoor swimming pool where he hosted 1920s-theme bathing parties with politicians and Hollywood stars. There were stories about Kidd's campaign against the judge who put him in jail, and his adventures driving around the state seeking votes on a bright-yellow road paver with whitewall tires. Though many of Kidd's publicity stunts were outrageous, they tracked perfectly with the campaigns he led to call attention to the Pre-Flight story.[5]

In mid-March of 1943, the Public Information Office and the *Cloudbuster* newspaper moved to a new building known as Navy Hall. The office resembled a country club with cypress-paneled walls, fireplaces, and gaming tables. The Navy invited bow-tied reporters from the trolley-and-telegram news era to relax in the swanky club chairs and soft leather couches like gentlemen. These historic gatherings merited stories of their own, where sportswriter Grantland Rice was photographed on the couch with reporters, wearing two-toned oxford loafers and a suit before they set out on a behind-the-scenes tour of the base in 1942.

These masters of the Golden Age of Sports, who penned such phrases as "It's not that you won or lost—but how you played the Game," nailed the essence of the Pre-Flight culture. With their clever wordsmithing and gentlemanly vision, the story about this rare training culture was told in newsprint, film, and radio from Tobacco Road to the Pacific.

In an age of concentration camps, burned-out cities, and POW confinement, the Navy's press office pounded the media with uplifting pitches to divert attention from the horrors of war. Kidd's clubby gatherings in the Navy Hall parlor and his truckloads of press kits

---

[5] Kidd ran the office with shoestring staff; he had one ensign, one yeoman, and no secretary, so he hired his sister for approximately $120 a month, working from 8:30 to 4:30, and a half day on Saturday.

paid off handsomely when Ted Williams's lean image caught readers' eyes in unexpected places like boxing rings and football fields. Johnny Pesky, who could not swim, grabbed the media's attention when he paddled like a dog to keep his head above water in the pool.

Pesky, who had gotten his start on a team in nearby Rocky Mount, North Carolina, was trailed by a publicist who captured a typical day in the life of a cadet. With his moonbeam smile, Johnny was pictured happily making his bed, whistling while he combed his hair, and looking a little more serious when he crammed for exams. Like half of the cadets, the rookie shortstop who grew up on the Pacific Coast sunk to the bottom of the pool when he shipped into Chapel Hill. Six weeks into training, Johnny was tumbling off a 35-foot diving platform in full gear cradling a rifle, and doing a cannonball into pools lit with gasoline fires.[6]

Through it all, cadets were playing some grand extra-inning baseball, inspiring UP to write the dream headline: "Johnny Pesky Still Playing Ball, But B'lieve Me, Mister, That Ain't All." In the feature, Johnny gave fans an unvarnished view of his new life, noting that being able to field a baseball had not granted him any privileges—it was up at dawn, train all day, hit the road to trim the Durham Bulls, back on base at 11:30 that night. The next morning, he was up again with the roosters at 5:30, took an exam in class at 7:10, dug ditches in labor battalion from 9:30 until 11:30, went to class and swam until 5:30, studying that night for an exam the next day, after finishing up the day with a 14-mile hike.[7]

Piece of cake, right?

To capture the base's spirit on canvas, the publicity office invited one of New York's most celebrated artists to Chapel Hill. Long

---

[6] Johnny was pictured learning to swim, but according to Veterans History Project Oral History interviews (i.e., Elger August Berkley, July 8, 2005), cadets commonly jumped into pools lit with fire, and they all jumped from platforms in full khaki gear, with rifles. An image from the University of Georgia Navy Pre-Flight archives shows burning gasoline in swimming pools.

[7] United Press story, "Johnny Pesky Still Playing Ball, But B'lieve Me, Mister, That Ain't All" in *Akron Beacon Journal*, June 27, 1943, p. 29.

before Don Freeman charmed millions of readers with his classic children's book about Corduroy the bear, he was a *New York Times* illustrator, earning high praises for his portraits capturing the human story from the subways of New York City to the heights of theaters on Broadway. He sketched the faces of apple sellers, beggars, showgirls, and drunkards down on their luck, shifting to pilot trainees and coaches who defined an American Gothic image of wartime sports.

That summer, Freeman spent a week on campus, camping out under an umbrella with an easel to capture what people were calling a "training miracle" for national magazines. Though he had documented some of the most graphic scenes of humanity, Freeman was astounded by Pre-Flight training. "The public has no idea of the work involved in training Navy fliers," he told a military reporter. "My reasons for coming is to tell the world in pictures what cadets go through," he said. "If I am able to catch their spirit in my artwork, I'll do just that."

When Freeman headed back to New York, he left behind charcoal sketches of boxing matches and colorful paintings of cadets dangling from ropes like acrobats and leaving base on buses. With a touch of artistry, a new breed of superhero came to life on paper and canvas.[8]

## Star Treatment

My father believed in superheroes—at least he wanted to.

In his view, superheroes came in the form of baseball players. Unlike millions of other kids who worshipped professional athletes, he did not just see his idols' faces on trading cards or from a distance in the stands, he saw them up close and personal, and the Navy was there to capture it with a camera.

In one of the most recognizable portraits of Ted with kids during the war, Williams played catch with my father and showed him how to grip a bat. Johnny Pesky taught him how to stand at the plate, and they shared their fears about their return to baseball after the war.

---

[8] Don Freeman official website, https://donfreeman.info.

As tough as he was, Ted confided that he wanted to see the end of the war. Like everyone else, he was sick and tired of the training grind, and he missed a good old-fashioned home-cooked meal. But most of all, he really hated riding in the humming belly of the bus, and he could not wait to get the heck out of "Chapel Hole."[9]

As an only child seeking approval, my father viewed Ted and Johnny like protective big brothers. It is likely that they saw something he needed, too. The Red Sox duo came to his house on Vance Street, where Ted ambled around the den, practicing his swing, throwing left-handed jabs he was perfecting in the Pre-Flight boxing ring. They would have noticed the spit-shine military order, the strict parents, the henpecked commander, and they may have sensed that my father was a bit of a menace.

My father described Pesky as a feisty, fidgety guy with a nervous laugh who walked fast. His best friend Williams was cooler, contained, and extremely kind. The two Red Sox players took my dad to the Scuttlebutt snack bar after practice for lemon custard ice cream, "Ted's favorite," he always claimed. When they took him to the movies on Franklin Street, Ted called him not by his name, but as a "little son of a bitch." At the movies, they would sit my father in the front row with a bottle of Coke and popcorn while they went to the back of the theater with their dates. In Dad's words, Ted said, very sternly, pointing his finger at his face, "Don't you dare come back here—don't even think about looking back, you little son of a bitch . . . not even if you have to go to the bathroom . . . you stay put."[10]

Sportswriters would credit Williams for his ability to make people feel special. Pesky said of his teammate that it was "like there was a star on top of his head, pulling everyone toward him like a beacon and letting everyone around him know that he was different, and

---

[9] According to family lore, Ted called Chapel Hill "Chapel Hole."

[10] College Baseball Hall of Fame interview with Jim Raugh, Texas Tech University, Southwest Collection General Oral Histories by Dr. Jorge Iber, May 14, 2013.

that he was special in some marvelous way, and that we were that much more special because we had played with him."[11]

Williams certainly made my father feel like a star, and he was known to tell rookies, "If you want to see the greatest hitter in the world, just look in the mirror."[12] Ted encouraged kids to visualize success just as he did as a boy, when there was no one there to guide him. He told my dad to block out the distractions and ignore the people who criticized his abilities. He told him to show up early, and be the last to leave the field. He told him to watch the pitcher and to study his swing in batting practice, and my father saw Ted's formula for perfection unfold with his own two eyes when the Splendid Splinter rocketed the ball over campus rooftops like a catapult on a carrier.

As I broadened my search from players to others who were in the dugout with the team, I came across another living mascot who had an identical role as my father at the Iowa Pre-Flight base. This man, who grew up to become an admiral, was the protégé of Ted Williams's most famous wingman in Korea.

## Admiral Jerry Holland, the Other BatBoy

The first time I spoke with Rear Admiral Jerry Holland, he confessed that he never told his seven children or his grandchildren stories about his childhood mascot days at the Iowa Pre-Flight base because they'd heard enough of the "old Navy stories." When he was a kid growing up at 325 Melrose Court, down the street from the University of Iowa campus, Jerry's parents were civilians with no connection to the military. In his words, Jerry's father was a pacifist. When the base opened in early 1942, eight-year-old Jerry fell in line with cadets marching down Melrose because "it looked like fun." He was followed by a scraggly stray spaniel named Blackie Black Bottom, who was also adopted as a base mascot.

---

[11] David Halberstam, *The Teammates: A Portrait of a Friendship*, Hyperion, 2003, p. 15.

[12] Ed Linn, *Hitter: The Life and Turmoils of Ted Williams*, p. 195.

One of the cadets marching down the street was a strawberry-blond, freckle-faced Ohioan named John Glenn, who took Jerry under his wing and helped him land the job as batboy and base mascot. Glenn went after the opportunity to fly combat missions as soon as he was eligible, entering the first Pre-Flight class at the Iowa station in May 1942.

After the Navy bought Jerry a cut-down khaki uniform and service-dress blues, it was John Glenn who gave Jerry the nickname that stuck for life, "Admiral." Pictures in Glenn's scrapbook, taken by Jerry's mother, show the two in matching uniforms, standing beside a large boxwood by the side of their house.

For decades, the Iowa City newspaper followed Jerry's career as a hometown success story. He graduated from Annapolis, going on to became an admiral and a submarine commander in the Navy. Jerry also earned a Master's degree from Harvard's John F. Kennedy School of Government and writes on national defense issues with particular emphasis on command and control and communications, nuclear weapons policy, and submarine warfare. As a naval historian and vice president of the Naval Historical Foundation, he edited *The Navy*, a comprehensive chronology of the history of the U.S. Navy.[13]

When I interviewed Holland, he showed little nostalgia for his years as the base mascot, feeling that he had done more significant things in his life.

As we talked, and I asked more questions, Admiral Jerry cautiously opened up. When I asked if the base had a band, he paused, without an answer. Then, the photographic memory went to work, filing through bands he had served with, and he said, "Hmmm . . . yes, they had a band. I see them now . . . I believe there were about 18 to 24 members." Like the Chapel Hill band, the Iowa band only played at football games, not baseball games, and that memory took us back to the University of Iowa in the spring of 1942.

---

[13] Rear Admiral W. J. Holland Jr., *The Navy*, Naval Historical Foundation, 2000.

Early in the war, he explained, the armed services were recruiting everyone they could get their hands on, especially natural athletes and professional sports stars, who were grabbed off by Army Air Corps and Navy aviation branches. Recruiters wanted men who were already in tip-top physical shape. "If you start with a guy in good shape, training does not take as long," he said. Jerry explained that some commands tried to keep the best players on base, sometimes honestly, sometimes nefariously—and commands battled each other on sports fields. As the pilot preparation line backed up with more cadets than the Navy could train, the great athletes and coaches stayed on bases.[14]

Notable coaches on the Iowa campus included Lieutenant Colonel Larry Snyder, Ohio State track coach, who developed the Olympic track and field star Jesse Owens. Snyder oversaw track meets and the grueling 550-yard obstacle course run by every cadet each week with jagged log fences to hurdle, chutes to crawl though, water holes and muddy canyons to cross over hand-over-hand on ropes, 11-foot walls to climb without help, and steep hills to attack at full speed. While the record was set by a national A.A.U. half-mile champion, it was broken several times over by cadets in training, proving that there is always someone in the wings who is faster and stronger.

Other coaches included Ensign Newt Loken of Minnesota, national all-around gymnastics champion, and a dozen or so All-American football players at any given time.[15]

Coached by Lieutenant Commander Bernie Bierman, who was already white-headed by 1942, the Iowa Seahawks football team would go on to be listed by the Associated Press in 2017 as one of the top 100 college football teams of all time. During the war, the stadium was often packed with 16,000 fans for three short seasons as Bierman and Missouri's Don Faurot, who invented the split-T formation, turned the Seahawks, whose moniker derived from a wartime marriage between the Navy and the Hawkeye State, into a national sensation.[16]

---

[14] Admiral Jerry Holland interview, November 21, 2016.

[15] Paul I. Wellman, Combat Without Weapons, June 27, 1942, pp. 1–3C.

[16] John O'Leary, *The University of Iowa Alumni Magazine,* November 2017.

Like my dad, Jerry served as batboy for the Seahawks baseball team, smiling for the camera as he lugged bats in a spiffy team uniform. Jerry rode on the team bus to games, where the Seahawks played local, rather weak "Three-I League" squads in Iowa, Illinois, and Indiana. He had an official job of riding in the back of the bus to supervise the dispensing of bubble gum to baseball players. Jerry felt like the higher-ups did not see it as a legal operation, so they banned "the kid" from traveling on the road with the team.[17]

For several years, with Blackie the mutt in tow, Jerry was a paperboy who delivered the *Spindrift* base newspaper to officers around the station. The paper's name was inspired by the stinging spray that whips across ships at sea.[18] At the *Spindrift* press office, he befriended a talented young illustrator from Indiana by the name of Theodore "Ted" Drake. Jerry remembered Drake as a pleasant, outgoing editor who wrote the "Who's Who in the Crew" blurb and pioneered the "Woo-Hoo in The Crew" column when the female WAVES arrived.

After the war, Drake sprinkled the gritty Pre-Flight fairy dust on his commercial work for Wilson Sporting Goods at its headquarters in Chicago. He drew Wilson's professional athletes who had trained at Pre-Flight, such as Jim Crowley and Otto Graham from Northwestern and, of course, his good friend Ted Williams. Other athletes who posed for his sketches included Arnold Palmer, Jack Nicklaus, Babe Didrikson, and Chicago White Sox second baseman Nellie Fox. Years after Drake left the Pre-Flight campus, that fighting athletic spirit was channeled into other mascots. For $50, Drake designed Notre Dame's bearded Fighting Irish leprechaun in 1964, which was later copyrighted by the university. Possibly drawing on inspiration of Pre-Flight fliers' bullish, never-give-up attitude, he drew the logo for the NBA's Chicago Bulls in 1966.

Another testament to the Pre-Flight spirt is displayed at the media entrance of Notre Dame Stadium, where Jim Crowley is portrayed in Drake's Four Horsemen painting.

---

[17] Interview by phone with Admiral Holland, November 21, 2016.

[18] *Des Moines Register*, October 11, 1942, p. 50.

Though Jerry downplayed his childhood job, and he certainly did not "roll in" the memory, I could not help but wonder how men like astronaut and U.S. Senator John Glenn, who had shaped the world, had influenced him at an early age.

When I examined Glenn's Pre-Flight records, personality traits began to emerge. After passing through Pre-Flight School, he became a recruiter on the three-member flight board to determine if candidates had, in the words of a 1942 reporter, the right "stuff" to become an officer and a pilot. Recruiters looked for four things: education, exemplary coordination, the spirit of leadership, and a familiarity with aviation. When an *Esquire* reporter shadowed an interview, Glenn dug right into athletics, saying, "You know, the first thing they do is throw you a football suit . . . you understand the hazards, right?" Officers listened to cues on how potential fliers treated women. Knowing that the country was fighting a dirty, unethical war, recruiters looked for intangibles like a quiet confidence and courage. Officers had to know that candidates would not hesitate to kill the enemy if given the chance. If candidates did not possess the grit to do their jobs, they were dropped from the list.[19]

Like Glenn, some of the famous Pre-Flight cadets did not earn the highest scores in the classroom. They did, however, possess an unusually high aptitude for perseverance, endurance, and loyalty— traits that make or break a person in the struggles of life. Getting beaten to a pulp did not faze them; many had a sense of humor and were incredibly resilient, learning to bend instead of break when they were put in stressful situations.

More than anything, the dominant characteristic that determined success as a flier, be it a baseball star, an astronaut, or a future president, was the tolerance for failure.

In fact, the expectation of *failure* is what drove them.

---

[19] *Esquire*, December, 1942, p. 76. Note, the reporter used the phrase *the right stuff* in 1942.

# Chapter 20

## THE SEASON CONTINUES

I had a chance to speak with a few Cloudbusters fans—now in their 90s—and most of their stories circled back to Ted.

On Saturday, May 29, Irwin Smallwood sat in the press box on top of Memorial Stadium's grandstand in Greensboro for one of the most anticipated games of the 1943 season. He was a teenager, working about 30 hours a week at the local paper as a copywriter, when he was sent to cover the eight o'clock game between the Cloudbusters and Norfolk Naval Air Station's Airmen.

At age 91, Irwin described the parking lot at Memorial Stadium as packed with so many fans "you couldn't stir them with a stick." People had ridden bikes to the game. Some walked for miles, and they waited in the parking lot for the team bus to pull in, hoping to get autographs from players.

Ted had played at Memorial Stadium back on April 5, 1940, when he blasted a home run over the short right-field wire fence in the second inning of an exhibition game against Cincinnati. The Red Sox lost, 12–10, but locals never forgot that long-range hit as he became the hottest player in spikes.

Earlier that week, Norfolk Naval Training Station participated in one of the most lucrative war bond games ever recorded, raising $2 million when they defeated the Washington Senators, 4–2. With Babe Ruth, Bing Crosby, and Kate Smith performing at Griffith Stadium, this game showed the sway of service-league teams.[1]

Drawing 6,500 fans, Memorial Stadium had not seen such a lively crowd in years. Stadium lights turned the diamond into a blaze of neon green; a light breeze cooled the stands; bronze plaques honoring the dead from World War I shined in the moonlight, making for a beautiful night. That day, the *Saturday Evening Post* debuted its famous cover of "Rosie the Riveter" on newsstands. Rosie was the very kind of girl who changed out of her overalls after her shift at the Fairchild Aircraft plant, putting on lipstick and a dress for the Cloudbusters game.[2]

For weeks, reporters wrote teasers about the contest to build crowds for Ted's first complete game.[3] The Naval Air Station nine had Brooklyn Dodger Pee Wee Reese at shortstop, with his Brooklyn teammate Hugh Casey on the mound, along with Detroit Tigers infielder Moe Franklin and players from the Cincinnati Reds and the Philadelphia A's. Casey had appeared in 50 games as the Dodgers' bullpen ace the previous season, and he had just pitched a no-hitter against the Naval Training Station's Bluejackets. The 'Busters' Johnny Sain had hurled in 40 contests for the Braves, and he was expected to give the Airmen a run for their money.

That night, Airmen pitcher Emil Lochbaum limited the Cloudbusters to five hits, including a two-run homer by Ted in the ninth inning, for a 5–4 Norfolk win in the first game.[4]

It was not the score that people remembered, however.

Like any boy who witnessed that game, Irwin remembers how Ted Williams clipped the ball into "Never-Never Land," for that

[1] Associated Press, May 25, 1943.

[2] Rosie the Riveter debuted on cover of the *Saturday Evening Post* on May 29, 1943.

[3] Associated Press, May 28, 1943.

[4] *The Sporting News*, June 10, 1943, p. 6.

two-run homer toward the end of the game. Other fans described the way the ball sailed like a bomb over the scoreboard, landing in the trees behind right field. They never forgot the sound of that hit, the roar of the crowd, or the look on Williams's face as he circled the bases, waving with his familiar home-run grin.[5] In the words of Philip Hammond, who grew up in Greensboro, "At age 12, I saw Ted Williams play at the stadium . . . even now, I clearly remember him hitting a monstrous home run."[6]

There was something else reporters noticed that got picked up in the headlines. Though the 'Busters lost that night, good-natured reporters wrote about the spirit of players like Williams and Pesky who spent more time in the stands signing autographs than on the field. Unlike in Boston, where reporters knocked one another over to take a jab at Ted, he was a little more relaxed at those games wearing the Navy jersey. His sense of humor returned, and one might venture to say the Southern hospitality made him feel at home.

Irwin told me that he got on his bike around midnight to ride home a few miles across town. As Irwin passed the bus pulling out of the restaurant, Ted stuck his head out the window, and he yelled in that deep booming voice, "Sonny, does your mother know you've been out so late?"[7]

As the team headed back to Chapel Hill, they were followed by the Cloudbusters Band, who traveled in another bus to make a rare appearance at that game. Six months before he passed away, I spoke with 94-year-old Abe Thurman, a piccolo player for the base's all-black B-1 Cloudbusters Band. Abe lived in the port town of Beau-

---

[5] Irwin Smallwood phone interview, June 26, 2017. Smallwood became managing editor of the *Greensboro News & Record*. He was also a golf writer and is a member of the North Carolina Sports Hall of Fame. Smallwood was also a *Daily Tar Heel* reporter, covering Ration-League games during World War II.

[6] *Our State* magazine, June 2014, p. 11. Quote used in letter to editor about Memorial Stadium story by baseball fan Philip C. Hammond Jr. of Charlotte.

[7] Irwin Smallwood phone interview.

fort, North Carolina, where he taught chemistry, physics, biology, and music at East Carteret County High School, also serving as a county commissioner and mayor pro tem.

The Pre-Flight base's first commandant, Commander O. O. Kessing, loved nothing more than to listen to jazz with a good cigar. In early 1942, he set out to build an all-black band to entertain cadets and to boost morale at the station. The band went on to break the color barrier in the modern Navy, becoming the first African Americans to rise above the rank of stewards or messmen, and Abe took me back to the day he was recruited.[8]

In the spring of 1942, he was a teenage student at Greensboro's Agricultural and Mechanical College (now North Carolina A&T State University) when a band director came through campus looking for 45 black musicians to field the Pre-Flight band. Thurman's bandmates did not just play jazz, they were trained by three of the best classical musicians of the 20th century; Bernard Mason, Warner Lawson, and Nathaniel Dett. With other recruits from Dudley High School, the band trained in Norfolk before they shipped into Chapel Hill that summer.

By spring of 1943, the band was an institution in Chapel Hill, where their music served as the campus's soundtrack. Every day, they could be spotted marching up and down Franklin Street, rain or shine, in blue-and-white uniforms to raise the flag at Navy Hall. There were times when locals threw rocks at the band, hitting them so hard that they their faces bled and their instruments were dented. But the band persisted, faithfully playing marches and grinders for cadets switching classes, serenading officers and cadets as they entered the dining hall for meals. In the evening, the Cloudbusters' live music and big-band jazz poured through open windows into the campus, and some of their most majestic performances took place on the Sabbath. Every Sunday morning at ten, the school hosted three religious services for students and cadets from all of the

---

[8] Alex Albright, *The Forgotten First: B-1 and the Integration of the Modern Navy*, R. A. Fountain, 2013, p. 11.

military branches. It was an unforgettable sight when thousands of worshipers marched behind the band from the Pre-Flight zone toward Cameron, where they gathered near the Old Well. Columns of men, accompanied by chaplains and rabbis, peeled off for services: the Jewish faith headed to Graham Memorial, the Catholics marched to Hill Hall, with Protestants heading to Memorial Hall.

Though the band played at war bond rallies, along with football and basketball games, they were not welcome to play at Emerson Field. During that historic May 11 baseball game, they practiced in the Quonset Hut, not even realizing the level of baseball they were missing. But for reasons Abe could not recall, the band was ordered to follow the baseball team on the bus to Greensboro for that game at Memorial Stadium, where they performed behind home plate. He did not recall any other performances at Pre-Flight baseball games, and he certainly did not expect to reunite with the Cloudbusters' most famous players on an island five thousand miles from home.[9]

The next day, the Cloudbusters couldn't wait to face Naval Air Station on their home turf in Chapel Hill. Since the Amherst Five shipped into campus, the revamped 'Busters had scored 61 runs in seven games. Buddy Hassett led the club with 11 hits in 20 trips to the plate for a .550 average, with Ted Williams just behind, batting an even .500.[10]

To capture the reunion amongst big-league stars, the Chapel Hill base had already fired up press releases, getting photographers ready for a photo shoot that came to symbolize the old camaraderie of military baseball.

## From Mills to Military Bases

On Sunday, May 30, the 'Busters came back strong, finally beating Norfolk Naval Air Station, 3–1, scoring three runs in the eighth inning. With 4,000 fans watching, Hugh Casey held off the pilots for seven innings. After Joe Cusick reached first on Eddie Shokes's first

---

[9] Phone interview with Abe Thurman, April 23, 2016.

[10] *Cloudbuster,* May 29, 1943, p. 3.

error in 28 games, Harry Craft bunted him into scoring position, and the 'Busters edged ahead with a single by Pesky, a triple by Hassett, and Williams's single.[11]

With that game, the gritty texture of those service-league games began to appear in photographs—chipped concrete bleachers and a torn up, all-dirt field.

Evidence of friendships also blossomed. Ted was pictured with his arm slung around Coach Don Kepler, described by the press as his "new baseball boss." They were two of a kind, and perhaps the mischievous smile was based on stories they exchanged about Ted's experience in the frozen tundra of Minnesota, hunting wolves, and Coach Don Kepler's unusual trophy collection of wildcats and bears.

That weekend my father suited up for the photo of a lifetime in an extra-small uniform stained with grass and caked with dirt. Johnny and Ted, dressed in plain white T-shirts, taught him to hit. The headline of the feature, which ran in the *Cloudbuster* and other military papers nationwide, was "The Champs Show Jimmie." The caption under the photograph said it all: "From the expression on Jimmie's face, he's determined to hit the pitch out of the park."[12]

That watershed moment marked the highlight of my father's life, when he had that imitable expression of a young ballplayer who sees it all ahead of him. For a few minutes he stood at home plate between two of the best teachers in the business—far removed from the failures and disappointments that come with real life, far removed from the limits of time and age that put an end to childhood dreams.

## From Hosiery Mills to Aircraft Factories

Later that week, the 'Busters entered a new phase of play, squaring off against a mix of industrial league teams to give blue-collar workers a thrill they deserved. When the factory whistles blew at the end of the work day, the 'Busters drew the largest crowd ever to Burlington's Hillcrest Field on June 3, where they faced a hosiery mill team

---

[11] *New York Times*, May 31, 1943, p. 11.

[12] *Cloudbuster*, June 5, 1943, p. 3. Image also ran in *The Sporting News*.

called the Alamance County Cameos. Don Bolden, who was editor and publisher of the Burlington newspaper for 60 years, was a kid when he walked three miles with his father to see the game, promoted a week earlier in the newspaper. People came from all directions to Hillcrest Field, funneling through the maze of textile mills in the center of town. The old wooden grandstand with chicken wire fencing was packed 20-deep with approximately 2,500 fans. People fanned out all around the park, with arms slung over a wooden fence along the foul lines, where skinny barefoot kids draped in overalls sat cross-legged watching every play. A Gibson's Ice Cream truck was parked near the dugout, doling out bars for a few pennies. It was a paradise for a ten-year-old boy like Don, sitting in the stands with his father with the sun on their cheeks.

That day, the Cloudbusters won, 15–3.

Days later, the team squared off against Army and Marine teams, both of which they soundly trumped—17–3 against the Army Finance School in Wake Forest, North Carolina, on June 5 and a 6–0 win over Camp Lejeune's New River Bombers on June 12.

When a game was arranged against Fairchild Aircraft on June 13, a reporter said the match was between the "boys who build the planes and the boys who fly them."

As if on cue, the pilots won that game, 6–3.

After another 10–6 win against the New River Bombers with 2,000 Marines roaring in the stadium at Camp Lejeune on June 20, the Cloudbusters achieved five more victories to close out the month. On June 23, the 'Busters defeated Wake Forest Army Finance, 8–1. They beat the Durham Bulls of the Piedmont League the next day, 11–4. On June 25, they defeated Naval Air Station, 4–2, followed by victories over the Newport News Shipbuilders, 6–3, and 8–2 against Wright's Automatic Tool Company, which manufactured gunfire control equipment in Durham.

## Discovering New Talents beyond Baseball

Initially, Williams loathed the attention from the PR office. He resented being followed around by a skinny, pimple-faced deputy who asked him to smile for pictures in his baggy uniform. Ted wasn't excited about hitting the road to play baseball, either—in fact, he was downright belligerent about it, but his attitude mellowed when he learned new skills and got in the best shape of his life.

By midsummer, Ted and the Nine felt at home in Chapel Hill. If they were not playing baseball during liberty on Wednesday and Sunday afternoons, players blended in with cadets in the Village Theater, watching *Tarzan Triumphs* and *They Got Me Covered* with Bob Hope and Dorothy Lamour.[13] Ted could be spotted on Franklin Street with Pesky and the team, canvassing trinkets at souvenir stores. Cadets kept bicycle rental shops busy, pedaling bicycles to Sparrow Pool with girls riding sidesaddle on the frames. They guzzled milkshakes by the gallon at the Dairy Bar and hung out at Brady's Diner, where northerners got their first taste of grits-and-honey and fried gizzards. Because the ballplayers were so busy with training, they were often oblivious to the celebrities who were also amongst them.

In late June, Doris Duke Cromwell, the richest woman in the world, arrived on campus after a messy separation from her husband.[14] That summer, the tobacco heiress lived in Room 235 at the Carolina Inn, and she was none too pleased that the *Daily Tar Heel* reporters published the telephone extension to her room in a story. Campus reporters described Doris as she slipped through the lobby every morning at 6:45 in sandals with a plait in her hair to report for work for Dr. Harold W. Brown. Familiar with exotic islands like Hawaii, Doris volunteered as a tropical disease researcher at the School of Public Health. Not a girl to sit on the hot concrete bleachers at Emerson Field, Doris surely knew that Ted Williams was on base, but she avoided crowds and cameras. As she burrowed in her room, hiding from the *Daily Tar Heel* photographers, there was no escape from the sound of marching boots and the nonstop sports dominating the campus.[15]

---

[13] *Cloudbuster,* June 26, 1943, p 1.

[14] *Raleigh News & Observer,* July 11, 1943, p. 6. Duke arrived on June 23.

[15] *Daily Tar Heel,* July 1, 1943, p. 2.

That month, baseball players did hard labor, digging drainage ditches with picks and shovels, and they were tasked to build more training equipment for the base. Players were also thrust into half a dozen different sports, where they got kicked around, submerged in water, pinned on a wrestling mat, and knocked out cold. Boxing pavilions were constantly set up in the middle of Emerson Field for Navy smokers and exhibitions.[16] There was not enough time to teach cadets polished fighting techniques, so instructors focused more on drawing out aggression and improving reflexes in three-minute matches with 16-ounce gloves. One day, a boxing coach noticed a tall, whippet-thin cadet who reacted with unusually quick reflexes in a session. At the end of class, the coach, who'd been a professional fighter, lured Ted into the ring and said, "Let's see if you can hit me." The trainee took a few punches with the big gloves and initially missed, but pretty soon he got the hang of the routine, then . . . *pow!* Ted unloaded on the guy with the grace of a Madison Square Garden boxer. When Coach Lieutenant Alfred Wolff approached his student, telling him he could make a quick million bucks after the war, Wolff found out that he was talking to Ted Williams.[17]

When Ted was finally back out on the baseball field full-time, his passion returned for hitting. Don Kepler's children laughed about the "Ted Williams diet" when he skipped meals to take batting practice. During survival lectures to get his trainees through tough times, Kepler often cited an example of why Ted Williams performed so much better than his peers. During training, all of the major-league cadets on the team took one day off a week from practice. Four days a week they would have mess hall after practice, where all of the guys relaxed and ate dinner except Ted.[18]

---

[16] *Cloudbuster*, April 3, 1943, p. 4.

[17] Account by Johnny Pesky, who reported name as Allie Clark; I strongly suspect it was Alfred Wolff, head boxing coach. Leigh Montville, *Ted Williams: A Biography of an American Hero*, p. 109; Captain Clifford Thuot interview with Michael H. Gelfand, March 31, 1994.

[18] Interview with Rob Kepler, August 14, 2017.

Many evenings, as the sun went down, Ted summoned his coach to the field to throw low pitches, where he felt weak. In letters to a friend, Ted complained that he was having an awful time hitting pitchers in the Navy . . . hitting all the balls on the end of the bat and little grounders to first base, but he did not mention that he was working overtime and missing meals to regain his skills.[19] "For hours, Dad threw low inside pitches until his fingers blistered. Without gloves, Ted wrapped his hands in rags and swung the bat until his hands cracked open and bled. Tore his palms to shreds," said Kepler's son Rob, "and he just grit his teeth and kept swinging." Johnny Pesky was never far away and he was often in tow because he had trouble with sharp grounders as shortstop. Getting those line drives from Ted improved his game, too.

Everyone knew that Williams and Pesky were natural athletes, but Kepler always believed that they were *great* because of their work ethic.[20]

Soon, the old calluses returned to protect Ted's hands. Pitch after pitch, night after night, Ted's twisting barber-pole swing came back. He flexed his wrists, and it looked as if sawdust might roll off the bat as he knocked balls over the roof of Lenoir Hall like cannon fire.

Kepler's daughter, Victoria, said that Ted was always a gentleman, even when girls watched him from behind the fences. "He was polite and completely focused on his training," she said, "Always respectful when he was with my dad. He was a natural born officer."

## Moonshiners

One of the highlights of Ted's time in Chapel Hill was survival training, the most intense and unusual course in the school. The course blended academic courses, including Celestial Navigation, Communication and Principles of Flying, Ordinance & Gunnery, and Aircraft Engines, and it was taught throughout the 90-day stay.

---

[19] Letter to June Friest, June 14, 1943.
[20] Interview with Richard Kepler, December 6, 2017.

The intention of this class was to maximize the chance that pilots shot down at sea or over hostile territory could evade capture, live off the land, and eventually make their way to a friendly location to fight again. The final requirement of the course, which followed the classroom periods, involved each cadet undergoing a simulated survival experience as a type of final examination. Taken 20 to 30 miles out into the rough countryside around Chapel Hill, each cadet carried only the material for survival that a pilot would normally have with him. Deposited and instructed to find his way back to Chapel Hill using dead reckoning and survival skills learned during the course, each cadet was on his own.

There was one unusual caveat. In the early to mid-1940s, it was not unheard of to have illegal whiskey stills operating in the woods. A chance encounter by a cadet coming upon such a still could present a real danger. Backwoods moonshiners did not take kindly to interlopers, assuming all such intruders to be federal agents. If cadets were to stumble upon such an operation, they were to remain calm, pick up a branch, stir the cooking fire, and place their branch on it as additional fuel.

Moonshiners were the true masters of the woods. Long before a cadet stumbled on their still, they were alerted to the intruder and watched from the bushes with a loaded shotgun. The sign of the branch made a cadet a willing accessory to the process. Though there is no record of such an encounter having occurred, and no record of a cadet being lost or shot on the survival trek, bootleggers were running all over the Carolinas. In the final analysis, it may have been one big snipe hunt set up by the instructors as a classic joke to play on the young, gullible cadets, but even Ted was part of the ruse and never would have known the difference.[21]

After the long hikes, with 50-pound packs on their backs, when sunburned baseball players fully realized that they were helping

---

[21] William Holloway's unpublished manuscript dedicated to life of his friend Jim Ashford in Pre-Flight's 64th Battalion, pp. 40–57.

people, and especially kids, to get through the hard times, they found a second wind to play another game.

Families were still recovering from the Depression. Fans included farmers struggling to feed their children, factory workers pulling double shifts in sweltering plants, and civic officials looking to the team to boost morale for families and their children who had walked for miles on bare feet to get a glimpse of Ted Williams. If anyone knew that narrative, it was Kidd Brewer, because he lived it.

## Reunion Images

On Saturday, July 3, they faced the Red Springs Flying Robins at Chapel Hill. Though the Flying Robins were considered one of the best semipro teams in the state, the Cloudbusters slayed them, 9–0, for their 13th consecutive victory—just a warm-up for their busiest and most unusual month of play.

Kidd had a vision, and he powered up his PR team to photograph a reunion for the history books. On Wednesday, July 7, Naval Training Station rolled back into town for the biggest home game of the season, and they ended the 'Busters winning streak, 6–2. Before the game, Red Sox players from both teams were reunited, sitting on a wall in their Navy jerseys. Hassett and Rizzuto paired up for a Yankees photo, and 75 years later these images would come to symbolize the camaraderie of service-league ball.

Though players like Ted Williams looked noticeably thinner and exhausted, with scratched-up arms, they were persuaded to put on a smile to show the Pre-Flight spirit to the world. If anyone knew how hard he was training, it was the Pre-Flight press office. Ted ran commando courses with Orville Campbell, a deputy editor of the *Cloudbuster*, who became a lifelong friend. Based on the photos they took together, hamming it up with Johnny before a publicity session, it was obvious that Ted was having a great time, even in front of the camera.

Another posed publicity shot ran in the military section of *The Sporting News*. It featured Williams and Pesky amongst a crowd of boys, including my father, who sat on the ground in a blue Navy cap, looking skyward.

As images circulated from the Norfolk reunion, Chapel Hill's commander Packy Graff was working with Captain H. S. McClure and the Raleigh Jaycees to put the final touches on one of the most memorable games in North Carolina that season.[22] People knew they were going to lose their diamond fliers in a matter of weeks, so the Navy filled up their dance card.

## To Fenway and Back

On July 12, Ted left for his first off-base celebrity appearance at Fenway Park for an All-Star game to raise funds for artificial limbs and glass eyes and to furnish milk and food for undernourished school kids. The All-Star team was managed by Babe Ruth, and with the help of Dom DiMaggio, the team bested the Boston Braves, managed by Casey Stengel, 9–8, as Ted blasted a three-run homer. The media wrangled to capture fresh angles for Ted's homecoming—it was the first time Babe and Ted met in person—and photographs of them holding a bat in the locker room and the field circulated around the world.

Reporters also projected how far "The Kid" could catapult a deadweight balata ball, and Ted delivered, thrilling the crowd with his homer into the bleachers.[23]

Right after the All-Star game, Ted zoomed back to Durham on the train for a July 14 twilight game against Norfolk's Bluejackets. The exhibit to raise funds for the United War effort drew 7,000 fans to Devereaux Meadow in Raleigh, the second-largest crowd for the Bluejackets that season. Space was so tight that the public address announcer, Phil Ellis, came over the intercom asking fans in the grandstand to "sit a little closer" so that "those standing can get a seat. Exhale," he exclaimed to laughter. With heavy rain soaking the field a few days earlier, it was all hands on deck for the city recreation department to ready the park for the game. It was quite a patriotic presentation, with 1,500 Army cadets from NC State marching in

---

[22] *Raleigh News & Observer,* June 27, 1943, p. 9.

[23] Fred Barry, *Daily Boston Globe,* July 12, 1943, p. 6, and July 13, 1943, p. 14.

and out of the park. Jaycees wound through the stands, selling pea-nuts and soda pop that ran out before the five o'clock game began. Josephus Daniels, former secretary of the Navy, roared up the micro-phone as a special guest. After getting pressed by his grandson to keep his remarks short, the man who helped bring the Pre-Flight base to North Carolina settled on two words, "Play ball," and the game began.[24]

Reporters called Ted the "Stringbean Slugger"—a comment they might have withheld had they known that he was skipping meals and drilling nonstop to earn his wings. Though Ted was physically and emotionally drained, he asked for more batting practice as soon as he arrived. That night, Johnny Sain started off with some of his most brilliant pitching for the first seven innings. The game was tied, 2–2, in the eighth inning—Ted did not connect for a decent hit all eve-ning, then Dom DiMaggio connected for a two-run homer in the ninth.

The Cloudbusters were humbled, 4–2, that night, but their hearts were set on a much bigger War Relief game at the end of the month if the Navy allowed them to travel.

One reporter who cracked Ted's inner shell with behind-the-scenes stories was the *Greensboro Record*'s "Sporting Along" columnist, Smith Barrier. After an exhibition game was rained out in Norfolk earlier in the month, Smith recounted an incident where Ted and a buddy were roaming around the main drag and approached a mag-azine stand. Williams bought *Hunting and Fishing*, and beside his out-door bible was a spanking new copy of *Baseball Magazine* with its bright-red banner. Ted's face bannered the cover as Player of the Year when the New York writers selected him in 1942. The owner of the stand glanced over at him, comparing his face to the cover, and said, "Say, you know you look exactly like that guy on the *Baseball* cover." Ted did not crack a smile. He eyeballed the cover with a dead-pan response. "There is a resemblance, isn't there?" he said, before he walked away with his hunting magazine tucked under his arm.

---

[24] *Raleigh News & Observer*, July 15, 1943. p. 9.

Barrier also reported a story about Ted's first day out for baseball at Pre-Flight. He had not touched a ball since the previous September, and Johnny Sain nudged Williams while pointing to the right-field fence. In a dare, he said, "Betcha can't hit three of the first ten pitches over that." Pete Appleton was pitching batting practice that afternoon when Ted eased up to the plate and whispered a few words to Appleton. He said, "I've just made a bet with Sain that I can't hit three of the first ten pitches over right field. Now you know we American Leaguers can't let the National Leaguers get anything over on us. You know where I like 'em, Pete." Of course, Ted won the bet.[25]

When the North Carolina State League shuttered during the war, another unofficial Victory League was assembled to boost morale.[26] On July 17, a game was scheduled against a team based out of Concord, a textile town that fielded some rising major-leaguers. The Victory League had a colorful lineup, with yearlings too young for the service and too athletic to stay home. That summer, Victory League fans filled every seat in the park for most games. Tickets went on sale at drugstores such as McDuffie-Eubanks and Crutchfield's at 40 cents for bleachers, and 60 cents for grandstands. Soldiers could sit in the bleachers for 25 cents. If fans were feeling extravagant, reserved box seats could be secured at Younts-DeBoe clothiers for a dollar.[27]

That night, the flyboys did not disappoint. Ted got three hits and batted in four runs before 4,000 fans, helping win the game for the Cloudbusters, 11–3.

On Saturday, July 18, at 2:30 in the afternoon, former teammates once again reunited at Chapel Hill for the third match against the Bluejackets. Bluejackets pitcher Charlie Wagner, a former Red Sox who played with Pesky back in Rocky Mount, posed for the cameras. Other locals included infielder Crash Davis from Duke, who played for the Philadelphia A's from 1940 to 1942 and was the namesake of

---

[25] Smith Barrier, *Greensboro Record*, July 16, 1943, p. 10.

[26] Chris Holaday, *Baseball in North Carolina's Piedmont*, Acadia, 2003, p. 33.

[27] Advertisement in *Greensboro Daily News*, July 17, 1943, p. 4.

Kevin Costner's character in the movie *Bull Durham*. Eddie Shokes, another ex-Duke player, wore a jersey for the Reds, with Hugh Casey starting on the mound and his fellow Brooklyn Dodger Pee Wee Reese at short. Maybe it was the extra rest—maybe it was the hometown field, maybe it was good luck. Finally, after three attempts, the 'Busters beat Naval Air Station, 8–3, with their sights on New York.

After the victory, a photograph of Coleman, Kepler, Sain, Pesky, and Williams made national sports pages. As far away as the Des Moines cornfields, fans got tipped off about the Yanklands game in the caption under the headline, "Help Beat Norfolk Nine."[28]

When Ted came home, he got a real workover from photographers. Trailed by a publicity escort, Ted had to repeat the poses three times, climbing a "commando-type obstacle . . . crawling under barbed wire." Ed Rumill of the *Christian Science Monitor* made the crack that they put him through a grind, thinking back to the verbal abuse he had dished out at the "lens boys" in his younger unmuzzled days.

There was a great deal of speculation whether the Yanklands benefit game would even take place. In fact, no one knew if Ted Williams or the Cloudbusters could get cleared for the trip, destined to banner sports pages across America. Greensboro baseball reporter Smith Barrier knew that the war bond game would be the homecoming of all homecomings. When he approached Ted for some insider scoop, he shrugged his shoulders and acted like he did not know anything about it. Barrier even called Lieutenant G. E. "Bo" Shepard, the assistant athletic director of the Pre-Flight School, who gave him the silent treatment, saying it was Navy protocol not to discuss Ted's travel off base.

Apparently, Ted's one night in Boston required special permission in the rigid flight program. Early on it looked like he would stay on base while the rest of the team headed to New York. That night, Barrier did extract details about Ted's experience with Babe Ruth in Boston. "I surely did enjoy seeing the Kid up there. I'd never met

---

[28] *Des Moines Tribune*, July 19, 1943, p. 11.

him before, and at 42, he can still hit that ball a long piece," he boomed, either being polite or not realizing that Babe was 48 years old. While Ted credited Babe for being the best left-handed hitter of all time, he zeroed in on Jimmie Foxx instead, saying, "But now you take Foxx . . . Wow, there is a real hitter."[29]

When the Yanklands game was organized, Pre-Flight experienced a sea change in leadership. Commander Tom Hamilton had gone back to sea to serve as executive officer of the USS *Enterprise*, a dream come true. According to the latest *Esquire* Sports Poll, the 1926 Army-Navy game was still ranked as the number one football game its voters ever saw.[30] It could not have been more fitting that his replacement was an old Navy classmate and former captain of that football team, Lieutenant Commander Frank Wickhorst.[31] He would prove to be a fine leader to guide the schools. The handoff was seamless, but it was Hamilton's imagination and love of athletics that planted the seeds for one of the best baseball teams to ever take root in North Carolina.

---

[29] Smith Barrier, *Greensboro Daily Record*, July 19, 1943, p. 8.

[30] *Esquire*, September 1, 1943, p. 78.

[31] Oral History, USNI Hamilton, p. 5.

# Chapter 21

## BABE'S LAST AT-BAT—THE YANKLANDS

By mid-July the 'Busters' season record was strong: 21 victories in 25 starts. The climax of the season was confirmed by the United Press when the Red Cross benefit game was announced for Yankee Stadium. It was set for July 28, 1943, pitting the Cloudbusters against the Yanklands, a one-time-only team of Yankees and Indians players managed by Babe Ruth.

Long before that Yanklands game, Babe had proclaimed that he'd "always wanted to manage a big-league team."[1] That wish made headlines a few months before the stock market crashed in 1929, when Harry Grabiner, secretary of the White Sox, sat Babe down in the Yankees locker room to sign a contract to manage his team the following season. Of course, that job never happened.

In October of 1934, the man who bought Babe from the Red Sox set out to make him the boss of the Brooklyn Dodgers on the condition that Connie Mack didn't beat him to the punch and sign him as manager of the Philadelphia A's. Colonel Tillinghast L'Hommedieu "T. L." Huston, the harbor magnate and former coowner of the

---

[1] *Chicago Tribune,* July 24, 1929, p. 15.

Yankees, made the exclusive announcement to the *Los Angeles Times* before he left for his hunting lodge in Georgia. Once again, no job materialized.[2]

Four years would pass before the Bambino inspired one of his most sensational managerial bids. In June of 1938, Babe was coaxed out of retirement and hired for $15,000 a year as a coach for the Brooklyn Dodgers. Stories pictured him in a Dodgers uniform in the dugout. Sportswriters forecast him as a manager by 1939, but Babe quit by the season's end.

The last managerial rumor appeared in the *New York Times*, when Don Barnes, president of the St. Louis Browns, leaked the news that Babe telephoned, asking for a job to manage the team the following year. Due to poor behavior and bad luck, it was another failed negotiation. The home-run king's dreams as a manager would not jigger the telegraphs until World War II.

The Yanklands game was a job audition for Ruth, who jumped at the chance to manage the team. Some questioned if he would even show up for the game. After his antics at Fenway Park, when Babe declared to the *Boston Globe* that his appearance at the All-Star Game would be his last, *New York Times* sports columnist Frank Graham assured fans that the Yanklands game was still on.

University benefactor Josephus Daniels leaped at the opportunity to use the game as a hook to pitch the stellar success of the V-5. In the *New York Times*, he wrote that the cadets' unstoppable will to win was turning the war.

As headlines seesawed between Williams and Ruth, the team loaded up to play one of the best mill teams in the state in Burlington. On July 24, the Cloudbusters rallied for five runs in the last two innings to beat the stubbornly determined Burlington Mills Weavers, 9–4, before a crowd of 3,000. Buddy Hassett was the star of the game, hitting a triple with the bases loaded in the eighth inning to break a 4–4 tie. Ted Williams collected a single in four at-bats, as Harry Craft and George Moriarty gained notice by slamming home runs.

---

[2] Associated Press, October 31, 1934.

On July 27, UP reported that 22 players from the Yankees and the Indians were chosen by Ruth for the benefit game. The Yankees on the squad included shortstop George "Snuffy" Stirnweiss, one of the most decorated athletes from the University of North Carolina and a close friend of Buddy Hassett; center fielder Roy Weatherly; Bud Metheny, right field; Charley Keller, left field; Nick Etten, first base; Bill Johnson, third base; Oscar Grimes, second base; Ken Sears and Rollie Hemsley, catcher; Tommy Byrne and Marvin Breuer, pitcher. Cleveland's players included Oris Hockett, center field; Russ Peters, shortstop; Hank Edwards, right field; Jeff Heath, left field; Mickey Rocco, first base; Ken Keltner, third base; Ray Mack, second base; Gene Desautels and George Susce, catcher; Ray Poat and Pete Center, pitcher.

Babe's Yanklands had a player with a true-blue North Carolina Tar Heel history. Stirnweiss was the son of a New York City policeman. Built like an anvil, he was a 5-foot-8, 175-pound wonder. Stirnweiss was the first athlete to captain the football and baseball team at UNC, winning the Patterson Medal as the most outstanding senior athlete on campus in 1940. Pre-Flight Coach Jim Crowley had watched Snuffy come up when he coached at Fordham. Crowley recognized his unusual energy, calling him a jackrabbit with the ball. During his senior year in college, Stirnweiss was a second-round draft pick of the NFL's Chicago Cardinals. But Paul Krichell, the Yankees' top scout, was determined to sign him, and on the day of his graduation, the lifelong Yankees fan signed with his hometown team. For the next three years, Stirnweiss played for several minor-league teams, earning the nickname "Snuffy the Bear" after a teammate watched him stuff his mouth with chewing tobacco and light up a cigar, saying, "What, no snuff?" As he broke in with the Newark Bears, Snuffy was one of the league's most aggressive base stealers. At age 23, he received his first call up to the majors, starting at shortstop for the Yankees on opening day.

## Babe's Last At-Bat

The gates opened at 11 a.m. for the doubleheader festivities. There was the Seventh Regiment Band concert at 12:30 to warm up for the 1:30 Indians-Yankees game. Contests were planned to bring fans and officials out on the field. Catchers competed in a throwing accuracy contest, pitching balls into a barrel. There was a 60-yard sprint, a relay race around the bases, and a fungo-hitting contest among the pitchers.[3]

After the band's opening performance, the regular league game started. The Indians defeated the Yankees, 6–2.

The *New York Times* reported, "The Indians rushed over four unearned runs on the Yanks in the first inning through an error by Frankie Crosetti, and that was more than enough. But, to make doubly sure, Lou Boudreau drove a homer with a mate aboard in the fourth. Crosetti hit an inside-the-park homer in the eighth. Spud Chandler was striving for his 13th conquest but went down to defeat before Mel Harder."[4] Winners of individual events won $50 war bonds, as relay winners picked up bonds in $25 denominations. Yankees catcher Bill Dickey did not participate in the catcher's throwing contest, won by the Indians' Gene Desautels with teammate Buddy Rosar coming in second. Roy Weatherly, Spud Chandler, Johnny Lindell, and Tuck Stainback won the relay around the bases race for the Yanks. Tommy Byrne won the fungo-hitting contest with a drive of 365 feet, while Jim Bagby came in second at 358 feet. Charlie Keller beat Yankees teammate Stirnweiss to win the 60-yard sprint.

When the field was cleared for the exhibition, factory workers were leaving shifts, and thousands of fans clicked through turnstiles to see one of the most unusual war bond exhibits of the year.

On a toasty summer afternoon, thousands of fans nestled into the grandstands, decorated with American flags and red, white, and blue bunting. The lords of baseball had hoped for a full house that day, but people were not disappointed, as the game drew one of the

---

[3] Jesse Abrahamson, *New York Herald Tribune*, July 28, 1943, p. 20A.

[4] James P. Dawson, *New York Times*, July 29, 1943, p. 14.

largest midweek crowds of the season. Even though the stadium was only partially filled, the crowd and the press were excited to get a view of the Babe, who had not been at the plate in a year. Game organizers made sure workers from the local defense plants and factories could attend the game and bring the kids. Hot dog and peanut vendors bounced up and down the stairs as peddlers hustled souvenir buttons and pennants commemorating that special game.

Fans brought the roof down with cheers as an older, heftier Bambino trundled onto the field to face the Navy pilots. That day, neither manager Joe McCarthy of the Yankees nor Lou Boudreau of the Indians was on the bench—for this time only, Ruth was the boss of everything, opting for Art Fletcher of the Yankees and Del Baker of the Indians as his coaches.

Babe Ruth was Don Kepler's idol, and though it was not picked up by reporters, the two shared a special history. "When I was a kid I used to lie around on the farm under an apple tree and read *Colliers* magazine," Don reminisced decades later. "Babe Ruth was everything to me . . . a farm kid . . . I never dreamt that one day I'd be in Yankee Stadium managing against him."

He met his idol for the first time in 1930, when he broke in as a minor-leaguer. And Babe called him "kid," just like everybody else. "There was something about him that immediately made you like him . . . he was very warm, especially to kids . . . he could make you feel like you were ten feet tall.

"Before the Yanklands game, the Babe and I had to go out and exchange our lineups with the umpires. We got to home plate, and there must have been 100 photographers that descended upon us. They had Babe and I posing there with our arms around each other for 15 minutes. They kept crowding in, there wasn't any breathing room. And Babe was chewing tobacco and couldn't find a place to spit. Then he spotted one of the photographers who was wearing a pair of white buckskin shoes. Babe gave me a little nudge in the ribs and winked. And of course, by that time he had a mouthful of tobacco juice and let loose on this fellow's shoes. They were all brown—just like that. After they got enough pictures and started to leave I went over to apologize because Babe didn't have any room to spit. The guy said, 'Oh, don't apologize, I'm gonna take these shoes home and put them on a plaque.'"[5]

## Surprise Package

That afternoon, baseball scribes and fans got the surprise of a lifetime. Ted Williams was on the overnight bus ride to New York after all, and the ballpark trembled with applause as he strolled out on the field with a wide grin, waving his Navy-blue hat and wearing a number 39 jersey.[6]

For two and a half hours, the war stopped. Sportswriters, radio announcers, and cabbies listening to the game were overcome by emotion, knowing Babe came home for the special game. When Captain Sutherland's band played "Anchors Aweigh," generations of fans sang together, waving flags and pennants—painting a picture of American baseball at its finest.

Decades later, when the Navy pilots were in the autumn of their lives, all of them highlighted unique memories of the Yanklands in bright lights to biographers. Signature stories abounded. In the clubhouse, Williams asked his hero, Babe Ruth, to sign a ball before the game. It was the only time that Williams ever sought an autograph from another person, and that ball, which was stolen years later, was one of his most prized possessions.[7]

Buddy Hassett was finally back home in New York with Babe Ruth, who coached him in 1938 with the Dodgers. Even then, Ruth's eyesight was failing. He was packing on weight but could still crack balls over the right-field fence. Hassett would call Ruth the best

---

[5] *Sunday Mirror,* September 30, 1973. Also references in Harrington E. Crissey Jr., *Athletes Away: A Selective Look at Professional Baseball Players in the Navy During World War II,* self-published, 1984, pp. 29–30.

[6] Rud Rennie, *New York Herald,* July 29, 1943, p. 20A. Yanklands scorecard with handwritten number lists Ted as number 39.

[7] Ben Bradlee Jr., *The Kid: The Immortal Life of Ted Williams,* Little, Brown and Company, 2013, p. 229; also reported the ball was signed at Yankee Stadium, "To my pal Ted Williams from Babe Ruth."

player he ever saw because he could hit, pitch, and play outfield, and he was thrilled to see him bat one last time at their old park.

Johnny Sain never forgot when Babe Ruth left the coach's box to pinch-hit in the sixth inning. Seeing the game as a sort of audition in front of big-league officials, Sain angled to retire the Bambino, but catcher Al Sabo came out and told him not to throw Ruth any curves and risk embarrassing him.

After the game, Sain said, "Taking away my curveball was like cutting off two of my fingers, but it was Babe Ruth in Yankee Stadium. Then, it became obvious that [Ed Rommel] the home plate umpire wasn't going to call any strikes on him. So, I threw five medium fastballs, almost batting practice pitches. Ruth took one, then hit a long foul ball, and then walked on the last three pitches."

When Babe got to second base, he was huffing and puffing. He was upset with himself for having to call a pinch-runner off the bench, but that was the least of his problems. As he stormed off to the shower before the game ended, Babe wanted to manage a team more than ever, and he would be the last to realize that he'd been used as a pawn to draw in the crowds.

The Yanklands scored four runs during that sixth-inning rally to take a 5–4 lead, but the Cloudbusters responded by sending 11 men to the plate in the seventh inning, scoring seven runs on six hits, including a double by Hassett and a single by Williams.

Newsreels and teletypes pumped out pictures with updates on the Yanklands game, reporting a victory that wrapped itself around the world. Headlines shouted: "The Cloudbuster Nine Handily Defeat Babe Ruth's Yanklands, 11 to 5, raising $35,000 for the American Red Cross." Baseball scribe Charles Segar summed up the victory with this line: "The Cloudbusters, who demonstrated what navy training can do, ran all over the lot."[8]

Other headlines were not so kind: "Babe Ruth Tried His Hand at Managing—Not So Good"; "Babe Ruth; Chipper at Start, Tires Fast

---

[8] "Yanks Bow to Tribe; Ruth Bats in Fund Tilt," Charles Segar, *New York Daily Mirror,* July 29, 1943, p. 30.

in Manager's Role"; "Babe Ruth gets Big 'Headache' as Yanklands Lose to Cloudbusters," and "Ruth Returns in Roly-Poly Pilot Roll."[9]

The game was a Mount Rushmore-sized memory for the batboys, too. Dick Hamilton, one of the teenage assistants Pre-Flighters nick-named "Navy juniors," recalled the visit to New York prior to the game in a family memoir. As an executive officer, his father, Howard Hamilton, made arrangements for him to accompany the team and ride along as the batboy on the trip to New York. While in the city, he went to see the Rockettes at Radio City Music Hall. They headed over to the Yankee Stadium early to watch the first half of the dou-bleheader between the Indians and the Yankees. At the center of his memory was Babe Ruth, sitting cross-legged on a trunk in the locker room before the Yanklands game. Not only was Hamilton able to meet him and talk to him, but Babe was the first player to sign his baseball.[10]

For Ted Williams, that game was a declaration of his maturity, and he was surrounded by men who treated him like the family he never had. In the stands, American League president Will Harridge sat next to Williams's commanding officer, who gave Ted a glowing endorse-ment. He said, "You are going to be surprised by the boy we are going to return back to you when activities are over. He is one of the finest young men we have in our entire school. He is idolized by the men for what he had proven to be . . . I understand he had ideas of his own in baseball. Ted has different ideas on life now, and I am sure his naval training has added greatly to a remarkable personality."[11]

It was a compliment that followed the Splendid Splinter for the rest of his life, affirming friendships that blossomed when he put his career on hold to serve Uncle Sam. Yanklands players also fondly

---

[9] "Tries His Hand At Managing," Chip Royal, Associated Press, July 29, 1943; "Tires Fast," and "Gets a Headache," Associated Press, July 29, 1943; "Roly Poly Pilot," *The Sporting News*, August 5, 1943, p. 2.

[10] Dick Hamilton's family records shared with author, 2017.

[11] Jack Malaney, *Boston Post*, July 31, 1943. Malaney's son had just won his aviation wings and was stationed at an Oklahoma base, inspiring the sports-writer to defend the Navy players. *Berkshire Eagle*, April 29, 1943, p. 16.

remembered that game, especially one player with a special connection to Chapel Hill. After a ten-year major-league career with the Yankees, Browns, and Indians in which he played in three World Series, Snuffy Stirnweiss hung up his cleats to manage in the minor-leagues for two seasons. After the 1955 season, he left baseball to work in the finance industry. Snuffy boarded train number 3314 of the Central Railroad of New Jersey, bound for Manhattan, on the morning of September 15, 1958. For unknown reasons, the train flew off the tracks at the Newark River lift bridge, and Stirnweiss's passenger car landed in the deep dark end of the bay. He was 39 years old, with six young children, when he died.[12] Like Buddy Hassett (who did not receive a major-league pension), Stirnweiss was cut from the Cleveland Indians six weeks before his 10-year pension kicked in, but he never lived to fight for his payment or to advocate for the players who shared his plight.[13]

Babe Ruth hoped that the game would enhance his managerial prospects. On August 5, Chip Royal of the Associated Press wrote an article headlined "Babe's Bench-Eye View as a Manager." Recapping the game, Royal reported, "As he dragged his tired body down the stairs to the locker room, we asked him if he was still interested in being a baseball manager. 'You bet I am,' he answered, 'I have every afternoon open, and I don't know where I would rather be than in a ball park.'"

After the Yanklands game, Babe didn't get one serious call, even after he offered to manage a team for a dollar. When bad news came in envelopes, instead of telephone calls, he put his head down on the kitchen table and cried.[14]

His co-manager Don Kepler did get a nice surprise about four months after the game when he returned to New York on business for the Navy. In the press room, he ran into the reporter wearing the

---

[12] Time Out column, with Joe Marsico and Joe Maurer, *Journal News* (White Plains, New York), September 19, 1958, p. 10.

[13] *Elmira Star-Gazette*, September 21, 1958, p. 42.

[14] Eddie Deezen, "Babe Ruth's Final Years," *Mental Floss*, August 6, 2012.

white bucks at the game and asked, "Hey, aren't you the guy who said he was going to bronze his shoes after they were soaked with Babe Ruth's tobacco? That was pretty funny." Sure enough, the guy pulls out a photograph of the shoes on a mantel bronzed with big wads of Babe's tobacco on the toes.[15]

When the war was over, Babe said he wanted to visit Kepler at his farm in Pine Grove Mills for some "big-time" hunting and fishing, but never made the trip on account of his health. In June of 1944, Ruth was too ill to attend the unique Tri-Cornered Baseball Game at the Polo Grounds involving the Yankees, Giants, and Dodgers that raised an unprecedented $5.5 million in war bonds. Over the next few years, throat cancer and hard living took a toll on his body. When he was still mobile, Babe puttered around on the golf course and hit local bowling alleys until he was too weak to pick up a ball. One of his last sports trophies had nothing to do with baseball. In 1946, he caught a nine-foot sailfish in Acapulco, and his El Mirador Silver Sailfish certificate hangs in the Cooperstown Hall of Fame museum.

For as long as he could walk and talk with a gravelly whisper, Babe continued to make appearances to benefit kids. Like Ted Williams, he never forgot his lonely latchkey days when he roamed the streets of Baltimore and was sent away to the St. Mary's Industrial School for Boys. His nature was such that he could not resist any charity.

On June 13, 1948, Ruth's pin-striped number 3 uniform was retired at a ceremony marking the 25th anniversary of Yankee Stadium, the "House That Ruth Built." He was reduced to a bag of bones, knowing death was imminent. Before 50,000 fans, he found the strength to mince out on the field wearing a baggy raincoat over his jersey, using his long yellow bat as a cane.[16]

The Sultan of Swat died of cancer two months later at age 53.

---

[15] Interview with Richard Kepler, December 6, 2017.

[16] Joe Reichler, Associated Press story in *Burlington Free Press,* June 14, 1948, p. 12.

## End of an Era—The Ultimate Sacrifice

When the bus hauled it back to base to beat the 48-hour deadline, some of the Cloudbusters knew the Yanklands game would be their last appearance in a major-league park.

Harry Craft was approaching his 30th birthday. His joints hurt, and, though he was drop-dead handsome and tough as nails, old Harry was getting a few wrinkles around his eyes. Dusty Cooke and Alex Sabo were others who knew their big-league days were long gone, but the most painful goodbye was reserved for hometown favorite Buddy Hassett. That season, Buddy was almost 32 years old. As he watched the New York skyline disappear behind the bus, he had a good reason to sing the blues, knowing that he had played his last game at his home stadium.

When the Navy fliers left New York, service-league baseball was being scrutinized. Even contests reeling in millions for War Relief were susceptible to cancellations because of gas rationing, public perceptions of cadets goofing off, and personal preferences of command staff who may or may not have been baseball fans. It was not long before the military reluctantly took action about complaints that had come in since the start of the war, reducing game schedules and appearances with celebrity players and even canceling the most harmless scrimmages.

At age 91, Dr. Bobby Brown, a retired cardiologist and an eight-year veteran of the New York Yankees who played in four World Series, walked me up a long stairwell to show me his wall of fame as he reminisced about the way the service picked off the best players. When I spent a half day with him, the "Golden Boy," as he was known, smiled and seemed to look through me when I tried to understand how these men felt about putting their careers on hold during the war.

Bobby opened up the conversation with a story about his experience as a child in Seattle, when he and his father watched Al Ulbrickson coaching the University of Washington's fabled 1936 U.S. Olympic rowing team celebrated in the best-selling book *The Boys in the Boat,* in the estuary that came off Lake Washington. He remembered George

Yeoman Pocock, the designer who built the racing shells, and the stroke, Don Hume. It was a moment that took him back to a place and time that my generation longs to understand, but for Bobby it was just a story that inspired him, when he was about 12 years old.

When Brown was a freshman at Stanford, he played baseball against the St. Mary's Pre-Flight team, the Air Devils, coached by Charlie Gehringer, and he said they were a darn good team. He went on to serve in World War II and again as a doctor in Korea. Early in our conversation, Bobby enlightened me to a profound truth at the center of service-league baseball: "No one said anything about *it*—we just played through *it*—it's just the way it was," he said in a casual tone. Bobby explained that Ration-League ball in Chapel Hill "was great duty for players because they could keep their hand in baseball." To him, that brotherhood among teammates was unforgettable because "everyone wanted to serve," and that sense of service was the glue that bound players together forever. "People lied about physical infirmities to get in uniform— men too old to serve sold war bonds," he said. "There were no strikes or protests, no running off to Canada. It was an all-out effort by the whole country, because we knew if we did not win the war we were done," Bobby said. "Regardless of who they were, players were united by that sense of service, and everyone willingly did their part," he said. "Games could be canceled at the last minute because of a higher-up. It was just the way it was." In his view celebrities were not treated much differently, because everyone had to be on the same team when America went to war.

Deflecting from his own accomplishments, he was quick to say that every kid should watch the movie about his friend Hank Greenberg, "a terrific guy" who was discharged from the Army on December 5, reupping right after Pearl Harbor. "Now that is a hero."

From 1984 to 1994, Bobby served as president of the American League. He and Eddie Robinson returned to Yankee Stadium for Old-Timers' reunions, and they were amongst that rare fraternity of players who knew the Cloudbusters quite well, from their early playing days to the ends of their lives.

Bobby shared the same uniform number as Johnny Pesky, number 6. When he was approached by a man in a business suit after a high school game who asked if he would like to train that summer with the Cincinnati Reds, Bobby found himself on the same field with Harry Craft.

During his first year with the Yankees, Bobby rented Buddy Hassett's house up in the Bronx, above 205th Street, where he took the D train to 161st Street, getting off at Yankee Stadium. He became good friends with his brother, Billy Hassett, whom he remembered as a terrific basketball player at Notre Dame. There was the diathermy whirlpool machine and a new-fangled shocking device used by a trainer to contract muscles for healing. When the trainer tried to get Johnny Sain to use it, he looked at Bobby, who was in medical school, and said, "We have a doctor playing third base for the Yankees, when he gets in I'll do it." There was a story about Pete Jablonowski, who changed his last name to Appleton. The reason why guys like Pete changed their names to begin with an A was because they thought they got paid alphabetically and worried the team might run out of checks.

Bobby told me a story about his friend Jerry Coleman, another Yankee and a Marine pilot who won the Distinguished Flying Cross. Coleman went to visit Ted a few months before he died. When he walked into the intensive care unit in San Diego where Williams was hooked up to all sorts of tubes, Ted did not say, "Hi, how are you?" or "I feel terrible"; instead he bellowed, "That f____ ing hit you got . . ." It was a moment harking back to a game during the last weekend of the 1949 season when Boston held a one-game lead over the Yankees. The bases were loaded in the eighth inning when Coleman's base-loaded double broke open a tight game.[17]

In Bobby's living room, he displays just a few trophies with special meaning. As I listened to his final story about one of the smaller trophies he won on the day Pearl Harbor was bombed, he told me that he broke his ankle that day. He remembered that it rained four Sundays in a row and he kept on playing with a cast on his foot.

---

[17] Interview with Dr. Bobby Brown, January 11, 2016.

That is when I understood the power of baseball, and the old-fashioned work ethic that distinguished players like Ted and Bobby and Hank Greenberg, who were always striving for perfection. I realized how baseball brings people together as a morale booster, dissolving loneliness, quieting pain, offering small unpredictable moments of anticipation that inspire hope.

And in the end, hope is what my father lost.

# PART VII

# GRADUATION

# Chapter 22

## TED'S NEXT STATION

As graduation neared, three out of four cadets washed out of the program. The Amherst Five faced three more weeks of training and a final 40-mile overnight hike alone in the woods before they could move on to the next station.

On Saturday July 31, the cadets' exhaustion showed. After returning from New York, they got nipped, 7–5, by Erwin Auditorium, a cotton mill team out of Durham.

On August 1, the Pre-Flight team faced the Carolina Victory League All-Stars on their home field for the second time. After an embarrassing 11–3 loss to the pilots in mid-July, the All-Stars were gunning to make a comeback, but the Cloudbusters, feeling the sting from their loss a day earlier, dug in their heels.

Even with a few gangly 16-year-old players, the All-Stars held the advantage until the eighth inning, when the 'Busters scored three runs on three hits and two errors. Joe Coleman pitched a complete game for the Cloudbusters, allowing a total of 11 hits. The final score was 7–4, Coleman's ninth victory of the season against two losses. Thirty-three-year-old catcher Alex Sabo grabbed the lime-light, scoring three runs in one of the final games of his career.[1]

As players like Ted and Johnny got excited about graduation, the tides were shifting on rules for military ballplayers. On August 2, Smith Barrier of the *Greensboro Record* reported that the Navy and Pre-Flight universities had revisited the status on travel limits. Football was the focus of the biggest rule set forth by Rear Admiral Randall Jacobs, chief of Naval Personnel, who moved to limit games to assigned NCAA districts. Another ruling was also issued, stating that well-known athletes in the Navy "could not engage in exhibits or games away from their stations except as members of a team representing the activity."

That season the Iowa Seahawks were forced to cancel games against their biggest competitors, including Notre Dame, Illinois, Ohio State, Marquette, and Minnesota. Even Wake Forest's football coach Peahead Walker penciled in just one out-of-state game against the Naval Academy, staying close to home to play against NC State and Duke.

With their major-league veneer, the Cloudbuster Nine had done something special, proving the value of sports as the ultimate morale booster. Because of the overwhelming success of their two exhibitions at Memorial Stadium, the Cloudbusters football team reserved an October 30 date at the stadium to face a major, yet-to-be-named team. Johnny Pesky also received special permission to make an appearance with a Rocky Mount club in a war bond game before he left the station.[2]

One of the Nine's last games was set for August 7, where they were pitted against the Army paratroopers at Camp Mackall in Hoffman, North Carolina, a sandy, tree-lined base that looked more like a golf resort than a military station. The winged soldiers' new baseball field was pristine. One writer compared it to a billiard table "where

---

[1] *Greensboro Record*, August 2, 1943.

[2] Smith Barrier, *Greensboro Daily Record*, August 2, 1943, p. 8. Middle East Cairo edition of *Stars and Stripes*, August 6, 1943, p. 7.

pebbles were picked out by hand" by lads doing time in the guard-house. The paratrooper players had the best of everything: cus-tom-made uniforms, lighting better than that of the bus circuits, and the finest equipment in the land. Still, they were no match for the gritty major-leaguers, even without their best players.[3]

On that picturesque field, the 'Busters tallied three runs in the first inning, two in the second and fourth, and four in the sixth. Sain, pitching his last game for the Cloudbusters, went eight innings, striking out 13, and holding Mackall hitless until the seventh inning. In the final frame, a bored and feisty Pesky made a rare appearance on the mound and "retired the side in order, fanning one."[4]

The final score was 11–1, and the team boarded the bus focusing on one of their last home games against the Durham Bulls two days later. Even with Ted Williams limping on the sidelines with an infected blister on his foot, the Cloudbusters handily defeated Durham at Emerson Field, 10–3, on August 9. Buddy Gremp drove in three runs with a double and two singles, and Pesky had two hits and scored twice.

Immediately after the game, Williams, Pesky, Gremp, and Cole-man left on a ten-day leave. Harry Craft left earlier that week to report to the Del Monte, California, V-5 School, while Johnny Sain left for Glenview Naval Air Station outside of Chicago and George Moriarty packed his bags for his next training station.

Before they left, Kidd Brewer snapped images as they gathered for the last time in their Navy whites for a group shot at the conces-sion stand beside crates of Coca-Cola bottles. Photographers cap-tured Johnny, perched on a rock wall, beaming with a self-satisfied grin. He was pictured one last time with Sain, Gremp, and Coleman as they walked down the steps at Navy Hall as changed men.

Days after the players left Chapel Hill, FOX Movietone film crews descended on campus, recording some of the only existing footage of cadets in training. That week, filmmakers captured 1,600 cadets

---

[3] *Baltimore Sun,* June 6, 1943, p. 31.

[4] *Asheville Citizen-Times,* August 8, 1943, p. 14.

running the six-mile loop around campus like an army of ants. Cadets strapped to aerowheels rolled through the quad, and incoming Boots were initiated on film with the sand pack test, with the commander pounding on a drum.[5]

On August 15, the remaining players faced the Burlington All-Stars on their home turf. Without Ted, attendance was as thin as the season of 1942. That afternoon, old-timers Lieutenant Alex Sabo and Lieutenant Robert "Ace" Williams grabbed headlines in an easy 6–0 victory. Williams, a former Boston Brave, was on the mound and limited the All-Stars to five singles, while Sabo hit two home runs to account for half of the 'Busters' tallies.[6]

The ballfield felt like a furnace when the 'Busters closed out the season on August 21. This time they were rested and prepared and took care of business, swamping the Erwin Auditorium nine, 20–1, gaining revenge for losing to them three weeks earlier. Ensign Ray Stoviak, an outfielder who had played ten games for the Phillies in 1938, collected three singles and a home run, driving in five runs. The real star of the game was a newcomer named Ray Scarborough, a sizzling pitching sensation from Mt. Gilead, North Carolina, who played for the Washington Senators. Ray was one of seven children born to a mail carrier, who also ran a general store and worked in the cotton exchange. His father, a left-handed pitcher who had played semipro ball, built a baseball field for his kids on a patch of land behind the house. Earning a scholarship to Wake Forest University, Scarborough graduated Phi Beta Kappa in 1942, going on to teach biology before he joined the Navy. That day, Scarborough held the Erwin Nine to five hits and struck out a dozen players.

It was the reported 30th victory of the season for the Navy pilots, who lost only six sanctioned games. Including scrimmages, War Bond exhibits, and appearances at All-Star games and other fundraisers, the Cloudbusters played a grand total of 45 games that

---

[5] University of South Carolina, FOX Movietone film archive. Paramount newsreel made films of cadets in July, 1944.

[6] *Greensboro Daily News*, August 16, 1943, p. 8.

season. With Ted's special appearances at games like the All-Star charity gala at Fenway Park, the team helped raise close to a million dollars.[7]

When Pre-Flight training results were quantified in a study, V-5 officers, coaches, and physicians knew their hard work had paid off. In three months, each and every graduate gained sufficient capabilities in ten required sports, and they stood a better chance of surviving the roughest waters and the cruelest places on Earth.

A study from Chapel Hill indicated the average cadet was 22.7 percent more physically fit upon graduation.[8] On average, cadets would grow half an inch in height, gain one and a quarter pounds, lose two and a half inches around the waist, and expand their chests by two inches. Physicians reported better posture and a gain of 16 percent in overall strength for each trainee.[9] In the first year, tests showed that Pre-Flight pilots gained a five-to-one advantage over enemy combat fliers.[10] But most important "was the change in their attitude," according to Lieutenant Commander Harvey Harman, who compiled before-and-after comparisons of the first four battalions. "We see them grow daily in poise, aggressiveness and discipline."[11]

According to Johnny Sain, on the base's Muster Day, where cadets could pick their branch in the service, he chose the Navy because it was the biggest branch. Ted chose arguably the most difficult and selective path—the Marines—where he could fly alone.[12]

---

[7] A 1945 *Daily Tar Heel* story accounted for 45 games—including Ted and Johnny's Fenway appearance, Yanklands, and local games.

[8] William H. Sullivan Jr., "The Naval Aviation Physical Training Program," *The Journal of Health and Physical Education*, January 1943, Volume 14, No. 1, p. 54.

[9] *Cloudbuster*, May 22, 1943, p. 5.

[10] Camp Lejeune versus North Carolina Pre-Flight program, p. 45; *Cloudbuster*, February 23, 1945, p. 3, based on Pacific (CNS) news report.

[11] *Cloudbuster*, October 10, 1942, p. 4.

[12] Bill Nowlin, *Ted Williams: A Tribute*, p. 78.

Ted earned a 3.28 grade point average at Pre-Flight, leaving with a few bruises and scratches but ten pounds thinner, whittling an inch off of his chest and waist.[13] As he advanced through training, Ted stated that he could run like a deer and he was in the best shape of his life.[14]

Many have claimed that Ted's secret to hitting was his better-than-perfect vision. It was said that he could read the writing on a spinning record, but there were other lesser-known tales that gave credence to his extraordinary vision. According to Don Kepler's son Rob, pilots took Ted up in an airplane for a game called "What color is the man's necktie?" High above Horace Williams Airfield, Ted looked down, and he could often identify the color of a man's tie when he stepped out of the hangar.

Ted's ability for recall was certainly heightened by naval recognition methods introduced in Pre-Flight classrooms.

Dr. Samuel Renshaw, the mild-mannered, pipe-smoking professor Howard Hamilton recruited from Ohio State, created recognition methods that enabled pilots to differentiate enemy from friendly planes travelling at 400 miles per hour, with near-perfect accuracy.[15]

Flashing silhouette images of planes and ships on a screen at one-hundredth-of-a-second shutter speeds, Pre-Flight cadets were amongst the first to unlock the power of their minds with this technology. By early 1943, every Navy ship that left port had a recognition expert schooled in the Renshaw method on board.[16]

For his next station, Ted was given a choice between Chicago, a more glamorous city where he felt reporters would be all over him, and Bunker Hill Naval Air Station in Peru, Indiana, a place where

---

[13] Ted Williams Naval Aviation Physical Training report card, weight chart, entered as 185 pounds, left at 176 pounds; chest 38 and one fourth inches, left at 37 inches; abdomen entered at 32 inches, departed at 31 inches.

[14] Ted Williams personal website, noting his shape during military training.

[15] David G. Wittels, "You Are Not As Smart As You Can Be," *Saturday Evening Post*, April 17, 1948.

[16] Ibid.

pilots stood ankle-deep in mud with dust blowing in their eyes. Pesky was cleared to join him. He said, "I didn't give a shit where I went," so he followed Ted to the flat patch of farmland pilots called the USS *Cornfield*.[17]

Raring to fly, Ted shipped into primary flight training on September 11, without his baseball bats, near the end of the season. With the majority of his service-league baseball behind him in Chapel Hill, he halfheartedly played in four games at Bunker Hill to appease his bosses while Johnny eagerly trotted onto the field. A few weeks earlier, Ted's younger brother Danny was discharged from the Army for dishonorable conduct, putting more pressure on him to send money back home to his mother.[18] Fortunately, the matter did not make the papers, but it likely motivated Ted to work even harder, and that is what he did, perfecting his takeoffs and landings on four- and five-thousand-foot airstrips and a wide concrete pad set in the middle of pastures. Initially, he complained about the air being streaked with planes and a tarmac so crowded that it looked like flies on a garbage lid. The plains of Indiana were bitterly cold, with powerful wind shears that jerked around the aircraft. Wearing his green uniform, with authentic flight gear, Ted looked like a real navigator, and he performed beautifully in the air, earning about 100 flight hours, including 60 solo runs.[19]

From the snow-covered pastures of Indiana, Ted headed to the sunny beaches of Pensacola, Florida, in December, earning his wings as a second lieutenant in the U.S. Marine Corps on May 2, 1944. On his transcript, Ted earned his highest marks for cooperation, attitude, moral courage, initiative, and reaction in emergency situations. His academic marks grew higher as he entered more advanced

---

[17] Ben Bradlee Jr., *The Kid: The Immortal Life of Ted Williams*, p. 230; *Cloudbuster*, November 28, 1942, p. 3.

[18] Bill Nowlin, *Ted Williams at War*, pp. 20, 46.

[19] Ted Williams, *My Turn at Bat*, p. 100.

levels of training, and Ted's superiors described him as "excellent officer material."[20]

## Johnny

When I met Johnny Pesky's son, David, and his wife, Alison, in Gloucester, Massachusetts, the interview requests had slowed since his father's passing in 2012. David and Alison had spent several years whittling down an entire house filled with baseball memorabilia to the possessions that meant the most to them. They live in a Cape Cod–style shingled house on a cove with a glassed-in observatory that looks out over sailboats floating beside the docks. In the garage are cars with Johnny's vintage Red Sox license tags promoting the Jimmy Fund, a children's cancer charity.

Like a naval officer, David has meticulously "curated" his family's heirlooms, and he embodies his father's jovial, self-deprecating personality, fondly describing himself as the "chunky kid on the bus" when his father spent years on the road as a coach and a manager. He told me he got hit by a car in Victoria, Texas, around the time my father played for Johnny. "See this scar on my temple," he said, laughing, "I was running after a toy or something in the street and got clipped."[21]

We spent a three-hour session looking over hundreds of images laid out on the dining room table from Johnny's years in the Navy. Some of the first portraits were taken in March of 1942, when Johnny was photographed by a woman named Alice Winters in front of a biplane parked on the runway at Turners Falls. Johnny is wearing heavy winter boots, dungarees, and a sweater, and he appears to be throwing a baseball. Another image captured Johnny Sain, padded in full winter gear and a sheepskin aviator's hat; and there was a portrait of Buddy Gremp, Joe Coleman, Johnny Sain, and Johnny Pesky in street clothes, standing on the tarmac, while Ted may have been in the air.

---

[20] Naval Aviation Cadet Training transcript, May 1944 (author's files). Analysis offered by current Mariner pilot and researcher at NARA. Also, Bill Nowlin, *Ted Williams at War*, p. 47. Notes from General Larry Taylor, December 27, 2004.

[21] Interview with David and Alison Pesky, June 14, 2017.

It occurred to me that a few of the most casual images, with the players cutting up on the tarmac, were warm-ups for some of the most iconic photographs of major-league baseball players during the war.

Poring through tattered scrapbooks, with postcards and pictures crumbling to dust, I asked David what Johnny would want people to know about his time at Pre-Flight. "He'd tell you that it was the best time of his life. Johnny loved the Navy. Always said he was prouder of getting his commission in the Navy than his years with the Red Sox. He was a squared-away military kind of guy. Even if the sheets were not washed that day, he made his bed every morning, and you could bounce a quarter on it. And he washed his socks religiously in the sink as ball players did on the road—it was a symbol that said, 'I care about this.'"[22]

That "I care about this" sentiment was evident in every Pre-Flight cadet.

Though Ted described Johnny in *My Turn at Bat* as a terrible pilot with "stone arms," Pesky was a natural for the military, scoring in the top ten percent of his class on his abilities to work with others and boost morale.[23]

Johnny's road to success in the Navy was bumpy. When he climbed into the cockpit in Indiana, instructors scratched their heads, questioning his previous flight training. Johnny had issues with air speed and altitude control, and he was a menace to pilots on a small airfield. After 10 days of testing at Bunker Hill, Johnny could maneuver loop-the-loops but he barely passed muster, neglecting to engage the rudder and overshooting the runway in seven out of seven landings. In one test, he stalled out three times, leading one exasperated instructor who was pulling for Johnny to write, "Knows what to do but does not know when to do it."[24]

---

[22] Ibid.

[23] Atlanta, April 30, 1945, record rating by Commander Wm. H. White.

[24] Flight grading report, Naval Aviation records, from as noted from September 11, 1943, through late October. L. M. Sapp questioned his previous flight training on September 14, 1943. On October 20, 1943, instructor William D. Barwick noted that Johnny seemed to know what to do but not when to it. On October 29, 1943, the check pilot M. H. Cromer gave Johnny his lowest marks, scratching one test altogether, saying he "crowds small fields."

One of Pesky's most famous flying mishaps occurred toward the end of his training days in Indiana when he ran low on fuel. "I thought I was a hotshot acrobatic flyer—a regular Eddie Rickenbacker," he said with a laugh in an interview at age 88. It was a blustery day when Johnny looked at his watch, realizing he had to get back to the airport, but he could not find it. Looking down on the ground, he saw a farmer putting up a snow fence on a nice long field. Johnny waved at him, circling at about ten feet off the ground before he set the plane down, "making a good landing, too!" From the other side of the field, he taxied toward the farmer. Johnny got out of his plane and pushed up his goggles, and pulled the hand brake up with the engine running. He tucked his parachute under the wheel to keep the plane from running away and walked toward the good-natured farmer, who asked, "What's the matter, Sonny, you lost?"

As if the farmer knew he was speaking to a ballplayer with a healthy appetite for humor, he said, "Son, you are about the fourth boy who stopped by here this week."

Pointing toward a wooded area, the farmer sent Johnny on his way. As soon as he pulled back on the stick and cleared a stand of trees, the airport was on the other side.[25]

It is not known if the farmer knew who he was talking to, but when Johnny got back to base an hour late, his instructor, Bill Barwick, shook his head, grinned, and cracked, "You goddamn ballplayers get every break around here."

When Johnny took on formation flying and navigational work, his instructor told him he was 150 miles off course. His comment was, "Look, I could pass you but suppose you got involved in something. Not only you, but you might take somebody with you." Night flying came next, and in Johnny's words, it was "a bastard." Even with extra help, Johnny was thinking of the safety of that other guy when

---

[25] Johnny Pesky, Oral History interview, National World War II Museum, New Orleans, November 8, 2007.

Captain Roy Callahan, who was a Yankees fan, steered him toward other meaningful work to gain his commission.[26]

On December 4, 1943, Johnny wrote an earnest letter from the heart admitting that he did not have the qualifications to become a Navy pilot, but he wanted to help the Navy in another field where he might be more useful.[27]

That one-paragraph declaration sealed Johnny's destiny as an operation officer, and one of the best athletic instructors in the Navy.

After Bunker Hill, and a pit stop in Bainbridge, Johnny ultimately settled at (NAS) Gordon Field in Atlanta, where he met a little blonde spitfire from Lynn, Massachusetts, who worked as an aviation machinist mate on a service crew of WAVES. Ruth Catherine Hickey, known as "Ruthie," stood 5-foot-2. She had blue eyes, with pert Debbie Reynolds features, and looked adorable in heavy-soled boots riding shotgun on the sideboard of fuel trucks zooming along the tarmac. Johnny said there were thousands of people on the base where he first laid eyes on his Ruthie, whose job was to rev the engines of planes. Ruthie did not know much about baseball when they met, but she liked to fly. Johnny used to take her up in a Cub and scare her to death, cutting the engine in midair, then climbing back up in the nick of time.[28]

Seven months later, on January 10, 1945, he and Ruthie were married in Lynn, Massachusetts, with Red Sox coach Tom Daly as the best man. Three weeks later, he was in Pearl Harbor.[29]

For the rest of his years, Johnny never turned a kid down for an autograph. He would go to spring training with a chaw and fungo bat, leaning on it like a tripod, so he could sign autographs for hours.

---

[26] Bill Nowlin, *Mr. Red Sox: The Johnny Pesky Story*, Rounder Books, 2004, pp. 66–67.

[27] U.S. NAS Bunker Hill, Indiana, memo "Request to be dropped from Flight Training," signed by John M. Paveskovich, AvCad, V-5, USNR, December 4, 1943.

[28] Interview with David and Alison Pesky, June 14, 2017.

[29] Bill Nowlin, *Mr. Red Sox*, p. 71.

In the middle of meals, he'd get up to say hi and talk to fans. The whole celebrity thing rested easy on him because he genuinely liked people. In David's words, his father was "raised in a big family like a basket of puppies," and I am certain he brought that friendly energy to Pre-Flight.[30]

## Secrets of Survival—September 1943

After the baseball players headed to other bases, the publicity office hosted one of its most successful media tours in September when the major media outlets sent reporters to Chapel Hill. The Monogram Club welcomed the Associated Press, United Press International, the *New York Times, TIME* magazine, *Washington Star, Pittsburgh Post-Gazette, Reader's Digest,* and CBS News. Motion picture producers were there, too.

The tour began at the baseball field with a display of wooden boxes containing copperheads and rattlesnakes gathered from nearby woods. Following cadets on foot, reporters plunged into the forest with haversacks to learn the survival secrets of fliers. Jack Sell, from the *Pittsburgh Post-Gazette,* wrote an exclusive on the 27-year-old Craighead twins and their boss, Donald Kepler. Sell's story was picked up around the world. That fall, the Self-Preservation course was being expanded to all four Pre-Flight schools, where most cadets had never struck a tent or lit a campfire before they arrived at their stations. Cadets showed reporters how to make fishing line out of tree bark and shrubs. They demonstrated how to make hooks with bird's claws and thorns, and rabbit traps with woven vines. Reporters learned about the final exam, too, where cadets were taken 30 miles out and dropped in the underbrush without arms or food. For days, cadets were left to fend for themselves as if they were stranded in Burma or the South Pacific. None of the cadets stumbled across an illegal whiskey still, and all of them made it back to base safely.[31]

---

[30] Interview with David and Alison Pesky, June 14, 2017.

[31] *Pittsburgh-Post Gazette,* September 15, 1943, pp. 14–15.

Reporters were intrigued by the manual that Kepler and the Craigheads co-wrote that became the bible of survival for pilots, foot soldiers, and everyday hikers. Like the Keplers' barn, the 300-plus-page guide titled *How to Survive on Land and Sea* was written to last, and their guide is sold online and in bookstores to this day.

The Pre-Flight bases never lost a single cadet to survival training. Many men knew full well that Kepler's survival course saved their lives, and they thanked him. Over the years, letters from airmen who survived plane crashes and made their way home arrived at PO Box 1 in Pine Grove Mills. One of those men was Michigan All-American football player Tom Harmon, whose Kepler-Craighead wrist compass brought him home safely twice, leading him out of the South American jungle and the mountains of China.[32]

Another famous survival story can be traced to the youngest pilot commissioned by the Navy, who shipped into Pre-Flight in the 6th Battalion on August 6, 1942. On a yellowed memo from the Naval Aviation Cadet Selection Board, George Herbert Walker Bush's name is the 15th listed among 21 men registered at 150 Causeway Station in Boston as Seaman Second Class, V-5, U.S. Naval Reserves. Theodore Samuel Williams's name is recorded at the top of the list on this little-seen memo dated June 15, 1942.[33]

Lieutenant George H. W. Bush was 18 years old when he shipped into Hell's Half-Acre, settling into Room 317 of Lewis Dormitory. Though he was the son of a Wall Street scion and a rising U.S. senator, Bush received no perks or free passes at Pre-Flight and grubbed stumps head-to-toe in the mud, training like a pack mule like every other cadet. Bush may have been a shoo-in for the baseball team, had he arrived in the spring. He played varsity soccer instead, earn-

---

[32] A Quest for Survival, *Penn State Magazine*, pp. 41–44.

[33] Naval Aviation Cadet Selection Board memo from the Senior Member, NACSB, The Chief of Naval Personnel. Subject: Enlistment papers. Reference (a) BuNav ltr. Nav 1641 LW., Subject: Recruiting Procedure. Dated June 15, 1942. E. S. Brewer initials. Source: National Archives.

ing praise in the *Cloudbuster* newspaper for his "scoring punch" when the team defeated Duke, 3–0.[34]

Almost a year after he graduated from Pre-Flight school, Bush was shot down during a bombing mission over the volcanic island of Chichi Jima, some 150 miles north of Iwo Jima, when his plane's engine was hit by intense anti-aircraft fire. The date of the attack was September 2, 1944. Bush was then 20 years old and a member of Torpedo Squadron VT-51. His fellow Avenger crewmen, radioman second class John Delaney and Lieutenant Junior Grade William White, perished in the attack. Ditching his Avenger near the aircraft carrier, the USS *San Jacinto*, he managed to swim to a life raft as American warplanes opened fire on Japanese gunboats bound for downed pilots. Bush not only managed to destroy the radio tower on the island and complete his mission, he was the only one of nine airmen who escaped from their planes and evaded capture by the Japanese after being shot down in that bombing raid.[35]

That rescue, captured on granular 8mm film, shows a lanky Lieutenant Bush, soaked and shivering as he climbed aboard the ribbed hull of the USS *Finback* submarine. Bush's head was bleeding after hitting the plane's tail when he bailed out of his cockpit at 3,000 feet. He had been vomiting up gasoline and seawater and his arm burned from the sting of a Portuguese man-of-war, but he was focused on the loss of crew he could not save. In typical Pre-Flight form, Bush passed on the chance to rotate home, hitching military rides back to the *San Jacinto* to put in another eight bombing runs.[36]

The Chapel Hill Pre-Flight cadets tended to move together from station-to-station and carrier-to-carrier as the war progressed,

---

[34] *Cloudbuster*, October 24, 1942, p. 5.

[35] Charles Laurence, *The Telegraph*, February 6, 2017.

[36] Multiple Sources: Walt Harrington, George H. W. Bush, WWII Navy Pilot, www.History.net, originally published in May 2007, issue of *World War II Magazine*; Joe Hyams, *Flight of the Avenger: George Bush at War*, Harcourt, 1991. pp. 108–120. It is believed that Bush may have moved to another station, right before Boren made his miracle landing on the Jacinto, but he certainly would have been aware of his heroics.

deepening friendships that lasted a lifetime. Several Pre-Flight cadets who trained with Bush were on board the *San Jacinto* when he was shot down, including Sixth Battalion platoon leader from Chapel Hill, Lieutenant (j.g.) Howard G. "Buck" Boren Jr., a member of torpedo squadron VT-51.

Boren was a born maverick, getting in trouble at summer camp in Pennsylvania for buzzing right over the camp with an airplane. On the morning of October 24, 1944, Boren won a Navy Cross for overcoming impossible odds to strike and likely sink an enemy destroyer, making it back home to the carrier with a nearly totaled aircraft.

Former Pre-Flight cadets were often invited back to campus to share their experiences with trainees, and Boren returned to Chapel Hill nearly six months later, addressing an auditorium of wide-eyed cadets. Boren flew number nine in his squadron—tailman on the runs. During his speech, he described how his Avenger flew so close to the Japanese battlewagons that the men could have thrown rocks at his plane. That morning, his gas tank was nearly empty, and his flaps did not work. Anti-aircraft fire destroyed his port stabilizer and elevator, riddling the rudder and fin. Oil covered Boren's windshield, and his landing gear was frozen down when he circled back to carry out his mission.

Getting back home to the carrier was equally difficult, and he was waved away twice for coming in too fast, without flaps. Fire engines were readied when Boren's Avenger came in hot for a third and final landing attempt, blowing out a tire as he engaged the tail hook and jerked to a stop. When Boren stepped out of the cockpit without a scratch, he felt like the luckiest guy in the Navy.[37]

One month after Buck's speech in Chapel Hill, he was killed at age 24 during a training exercise at Quonset Point, Rhode Island. Back home in Ohio, his father, who had been a school superintendent, died from a prolonged illness and heartbreak 17 days after he

---

[37] Description of Boren Flying Number 9 Tailman, *Cloudbuster*, February 2, 1945, p. 3.

lost his only child. Buck's mother donated an organ to the YMCA chapel to honor his memory.[38]

Forty-five years after Bush's rescue, he admitted that he had an awakening on the *Finback*. He thought about all of the people he knew from different backgrounds and felt as if his life were spared because he was destined to do something on Earth that his friends like "Buck" and "Del" and "Ted," nicknames for deceased members of his crew, would be denied. George H. W. Bush flew 58 combat missions during the war, earning the Distinguished Flying Cross for his valor.[39]

Because Pre-Flight cadets were a rare breed, a little-known brotherhood lives on quietly through memories of men who made great sacrifices during the war. Decades after the Japanese surrender, when Bush served as president of the United States, he would have an opportunity to thank the children of the officers who toughened him up in the war. When Richard Kepler mentioned his father's name to President Bush during a happenstance meeting in Kennebunkport, Maine, he immediately remembered Don Kepler and smiled when he heard his name. Bush not only invited Richard and his family onto his marina, he credited his father for saving his life, saying with a wink, "The one course I am glad I did not sleep through was your dad's survival lecture because *I needed that*," referring to the day he was shot down over the Pacific. After they looked through some old Navy pictures, Richard was struck by the way Bush recalled specific details about his father's class, as if he were right back in those woods surrounding Chapel Hill.

Over the years, Richard, who was the youngest of five kids, observed that the hugs, tears, and expressions of friendship were exactly the same amongst the Pre-Flight alum, whether they were

---

[38] Camp Fitch website, Legend and Lore, Fitchipedia http://wiki.pygmyisland.net/fitchipedia; also, Boren is pictured with Squadron VT-51 in Flight of the Avenger.

[39] World War II Distinguished Flying Cross database; History.com; Flight of the Avenger, p. 134–135.

down on their luck or the president of the United States. He shared a story about a former cadet hitchhiking through town who knocked on the door at the Keplers' farmhouse looking for his old officer. When Richard answered the door, he could see that the young man was poorly dressed in a ragged T-shirt and probably did not know where his next meal was coming from. But he spent hours with his father in the basement, talking about the old days in Chapel Hill. Over the years, letters and phone calls came from buddies like Gerald Ford, when he was flying in for fundraisers near State College. Bear Bryant asked Kepler to pick him up at the airport when he came to Penn State, and the gestures and conversations were identical.[40]

## Military Baseball Leaves America

By 1944, every ounce of the armed forces' energy was plowed into the war effort. Some of the best service-league baseball teams disbanded as players scattered all over the world.

Dusty Cooke was the Cloudbusters' only marquee player left in Chapel Hill that season. When Kidd Brewer shipped out to the South Pacific to serve as an aide to Rear Admiral Paul Hendren, his publicity machine dulled to a slow burn with less focus on baseball. My father stayed on as a batboy, looking slump-shouldered and bored in photographs where he no longer wore a uniform. That year, the baseball team was not allowed to play in the service tournament due to regulations. Most of the factory teams were eliminated from the schedule, and the majority of Cloudbusters coverage consisted of *Daily Tar Heel* stories.

Over and over, the old-timers I interviewed described how military players and the big stars were pulled off the field and games were cancelled when it was not "politically correct" to horse around playing baseball when other kids were dying.[41]

---

[40] Interview with Richard Kepler, December 6, 2017.

[41] Per interviews, many players knew about cancellation of games, but there was little written in newspapers about this trend.

Ivan Fleser experienced the pullback in baseball from his first-hand experience in Pensacola. "We practiced three times, and on the fourth day Charlie Gehringer walked out on the field and said, 'I have bad news for you. They are not going to allow us to have a team.' There was criticism . . . we [meaning ballplayers] were getting all this attention. Families thought we were getting special treatment, and we were getting special treatment . . . there's no doubt about that. If you have a son that's not getting all these perks it makes a difference in a parent's mind. There's a war out there and there are all these guys playing baseball—the feeling was controversial and justified," he said.

As the year wore on, the pilot shortage lessened, leaving America with a surplus of skilled aviators. When my grandfather James P. Raugh Sr. took command of the base, training was extended from 12 to 25 weeks. A new generation of training machines was introduced to campus, like the famous Dilbert Dunker (featured in the movie *An Officer and a Gentleman*), where cadets were strapped into a sawed-off cockpit of a plane and submerged in water.[42] Courses had a similar flavor, but the physical training and the varsity sports were not as intense as the original program that branded those first battalions.[43]

The soulful sound of the station also faded away when the Cloudbuster musicians were shipped to Hawaii. At the request of Admiral O. O. Kessing, the B-1 Cloudbusters Band shipped out of Chapel Hill on May 14, 1944—a date that 94-year-old Abe Thurman always remembered because it was Mother's Day.[44]

Most of the musicians had barely been out of the state of North Carolina or dipped their feet in the Atlantic Ocean, let alone the Pacific, when they were loaded onto a Dutch cargo vessel, converted to a troop carrier in San Diego, California, and shipped out to Pearl

---

[42] Former cadets I interviewed such as Charles Kahn explained that the Dilbert Dunker became synonymous with the Pre-Flight training experience.

[43] Raugh took command in the fall of 1944.

[44] Alex Albright, *The Forgotten First: B-1 and the Integration of the Modern Navy*, p. 106.

Harbor. Abe claimed that his friends grieved the long-distance assignment to the other side of the world, where they traveled in a ship with sailors and Marines transporting ammunition. Ninety-three-year-old Calvin Morrow, a French horn musician from Greensboro, said the freighter bounced up and down like a rocking chair for an entire week as they headed toward Hawaii. "Fifty or 60 of the men were getting sick in the dining area while the rest were running up to the upper deck," Calvin recalled, with a laugh.[45] When clarinetist William E. Skinner went to see the doctor, "he was sick, too," he said in an interview with Alex Albright, who wrote *The Forgotten First: B-1 and the Integration of the Modern Navy.*

More than anything, band members struggled with an even more severe bout of homesickness as they left the United States and headed to the island where the Japanese attack had begun.

About a week later, 45 exhausted, seasick, and nervous boys from North Carolina wobbled off the ship in white uniforms at Pearl Harbor. Coming from Tobacco Road and small Carolina towns, the musicians were mesmerized by the tropical wonder of the islands with thatched roof huts, wide beaches, and palm trees swaying in a warm breeze.

In Hawaii, the B-1's destiny changed when they were reorganized and renamed the Manana Meteors, living on a base carved out of sugar cane fields outside Pearl City. Band members hopped from island to island, playing for men returning from combat who treated them like "royalty," and they performed on national radio with stars like Kate Smith, who sang *God Bless America.* Toward the end of the war, the B-1 became the largest band in the Pacific, playing for more than 500,000 people in one year, counting Admirals Chester W. Nimitz and Bull Halsey amongst their biggest fans.

Though the Pre-Flight band never got to enjoy the baseball games on their home base in Chapel Hill, the musicians were destined for a grand reunion with some of the biggest stars of the Cloudbuster Nine.

---

[45] Interview with Calvin Morrow, December 5, 2017.

When the calendar flipped to 1945, Americans still felt like they were battling a war without end. The heartache was brutal on the home-front. More than five times as many Navy men had died in action in World War II than all previous wars of the United States combined. As gold stars were sewn onto banners in windows across America, the Pre-Flight Schools offered a silver lining. About 60,000 pilots had funneled through the sports-based ground training program, and seaborne aviators were crushing the enemy. It was reported in February that Japanese aerial combat losses were 20–1 against American pilots in the Pacific.[46]

Though Frank Porter Graham was a man who lived and breathed for the principles of freedom and democracy, he served as the first president of the Oak Ridge Institute of Nuclear Studies, a non-profit association of Southern universities at the atomic weapon plant in Tennessee.[47] Created by the Atomic Energy Commission (AEC), the committee was spearheaded to counsel and assist the Manhattan Project (the production of nuclear weapons), the Army, and the Corps of Engineers with research, education, and develop-ment of programs related to atomic energy. The Chapel Hill naval base had its fair share of PhDs and physicists on staff who were aware of the Manhattan Project's clandestine operations.[48] If the United States did not utilize atomic weapons, leaders feared they would face the worst casualties in the history of battle with the invasion of Japan. All of the training and all of the sacrifices built up to that moment, when a decision had to be made by the new president, Harry Truman, who took office following President Roosevelt's death on April 12.

---

[46] *Cloudbuster,* February 23, 1945, p. 3.

[47] *Daily Tar Heel,* January 14, 1949, p. 1.

[48] Julian M. Pleasants, "A Question of Loyalty: Frank Porter Graham and the Atomic Energy Commission," *The North Carolina Historical Review,* Vol-ume 69, No. 4, October 1992, p. 4141; charter of Incorporation, Oak Ridge Institute of Nuclear Studies, President's Office Records.

## Little Boy and Fat Man

On the morning of August 6, 1945, Iowa's base mascot Jerry Holland was on a Boy Scout retreat when the atomic bomb was dropped on Hiroshima, Japan.

At precisely 8 a.m. Eastern Standard Time, Major Thomas Ferebee, who grew up on a farm near Mocksville, North Carolina, was the lead bombardier on the mission, opening the doors of the *Enola Gay* to release the 9,000-pound bomb nicknamed "Little Boy." With 63 missions under his belt, Ferebee realized the magnitude of his actions and never regretted them.

At least 60,000 people immediately perished. Another 20,000 would die as a result of burns, radiation, and malnutrition. Holland was home with his family three days later when a second plutonium-based bomb was dropped on Nagasaki, leveling the city and killing another 40,000. Days later, Truman announced to the waiting nation that the Japanese had surrendered. UNC student Harold Hansen raced out of a steak dinner at the baseball banquet to capture the reaction to the surrender on Franklin Street. Within an hour of the news, he photographed some of the most moving images ever recorded on the Navy base, running a story with the headline "When Peace Came . . ."[49] On August 15, Emperor Hirohito announced Japan's surrender on national radio at noon to millions of people around the world—the war was coming to an end.

---

[49] *Cloudbuster*, August 24, 1945, p. 3.

# Chapter 23

# A CLOUDBUSTERS REUNION IN HAWAII

After the Japanese officially surrendered, church bells rang out across the country. Car horns blew and fireworks exploded as people spilled out into the streets, filling out town squares. In Chapel Hill, bonfires lit up Franklin Street, where people said the mood was like a national championship times ten. Millions of Americans came together on Victory over Japan Day—black and white, young and old, rich and poor. Barefoot kids without shirts raced down Franklin Street, where cadets threw hats into the air celebrating the victory and uniformed trainees rode bareback through town on horses used for parades. Drugstores served free ice cream across the state, giving away flags inscribed with the immortal words *V-J Day*.

Frank Porter Graham walked out of his house and headed toward Franklin Street to join the masses. While America joined together in celebration, most of the major-league baseball players who trained at Chapel Hill were scattered throughout battle stations around the world. With much of the Allies' air power stationed in the Pacific, some of the best players were on the islands where the war started.

## Hawaii's All-Star Game

It was no coincidence that Williams and Pesky were both stationed in Hawaii in the fall of 1945 when the Navy assembled its baseball firepower on the islands for the so-called "Service World Series." A year earlier, Phil Rizzuto and Dom DiMaggio were flown in from Australia; pitchers Schoolboy Rowe (Phillies) and Virgil Trucks (Tigers) were brought in from Great Lakes Training Station; and Bill Dickey, the catcher for the Yankees, was brought in as the top dog from Memphis, Tennessee, where he was a reservist. Special cargo ships, nicknamed "cattle boats," were converted to carry a continuous stream of players across the Pacific, where they scattered all over Hawaii and Guam.

In September 1945, Pesky was the manager of Honolulu Naval Air Station team. Williams was sent to Honolulu, where the 14th Naval District hosted an all-Navy World Series between American and National League squads on a sandy diamond with packed grandstands at Furlong Field on the island of Oahu. The baseball field was built by Navy Seabees at the civilian housing area on Pearl Harbor Naval Base, where shipyard workers lived in tents and barracks in a sprawling company town.

The *Honolulu Advertiser* wrote that the series would present "more individual stars than even the World Series on the mainland . . . a titanic battle between some of the best-known players of baseball."[1] The entertainment called in to perform at the games was none other than the B-1 Cloudbusters Band.

Admirals Bull Halsey and Scrappy Kessing were at the series, as were ballplayers who never knew the band members' names but had listened to them every day while they trained at Chapel Hill Pre-Flight. With the afternoon sun on their cheeks and the breeze blowing across their faces, band members rose in their uniforms and played for their home team 'Busters and fans.

Though he wasn't a great pilot, Johnny hit his stride as a coach and an athletics officer at Honolulu NAS. Before the series, the

---

[1] Gayle Hawes, *Honolulu Advertiser*, September 25, 1945.

American League shortstop finished in second place in MVP voting in the 14th Naval District League behind Brooklyn Dodger Billy Herman, pilot and second baseman of Alea Barracks and a future Hall of Famer.

Ted played in about 40 games with service teams in 1943, representing the Cloudbusters in the majority of those games. He played only 20 games in 1944 and seven games in 1945. He felt rusty and was unusually quiet during the opening games at Furlong Field. In game three, he managed to hit a home run. Ted missed game five because of a bad cold that left him hoarse. Confined to his quarters, he whispered that he wanted to play in the sixth game.

Ted and Johnny's American League team won three of the seven games. Truth be told, Ted's mind may have been on fishing, as he was looking out at the most beautiful fishing hole in the world. He finished the series with a .272 batting average (3-for-11), while Pesky batted .346 (9-for-26). After the series, Johnny went on to become the business manager of the base's All-Star football team. By December, Ted was on an airplane back home, where he picked back up with his life, refocusing his thoughts on his comeback to baseball.[2]

## Decommissioning of the Pre-Flight School

Like a CEO shutting down a company, my grandfather oversaw the base's closure, as classrooms and dorms were dismantled and converted to peacetime purposes. Admiral Jerry Holland joked that it took about 15 minutes to close down the Iowa City Pre-Flight bases, and such was true for the Pre-Flight base at the University of North Carolina. In three years and four months, 75 battalions of American and French cadets cycled through Chapel Hill Pre-Flight, including at least 23 major-league baseball players and a host of minor-leaguers. More than 1,200 American officers and athletic instructors in nine classes passed through indoctrination training on Hell's Half-Acre, along with 78 French officers who were trained on campus in 1945.

---

[2] Duff Zwald, SABR research of *Honolulu Star Bulletin* and *Honolulu Advertiser* for Bill Nowlin in *Ted Williams at War*, pp. 68–72.

Hundreds of other military officers and enlisted personnel from the Coast Guard, Marines, and other service branches also utilized the campus for special courses, such as photographic interpretation, which was used for military aerial reconnaissance missions.[3]

When fall arrived, the trees shed their leaves, and the military faded into a distant memory. Downtown crowds thinned, war bond posters and articles with names of service members killed in action were scraped off storefront windows. Uniforms disappeared from displays, and the Navy stationery with engraved golden wings was pulled off shelves. The Scuttlebutt commissary, which doled out the famous lemon custard ice cream that Ted lapped up, was restored to a civilian snack shop for students. The *Cloudbuster* newspaper, printed commercially in Durham, published its final issue on October 3, 1945.

The "No Admittance" military barricades were consigned to the woodpile along with barriers and sentry huts as government jeeps and canvas-tarped trucks pulled away from the base. Bunk beds and government-issued furniture were rapidly disassembled and shipped back to Washington and Charleston on trains and flatbed trucks. Navy planes with stars on their wings lifted off the airfield, and they never returned, leaving behind a silent field, bordered by weeds and waist-high grass.

In the final issue of the base newspaper, my grandfather wrote this parting salutation:

TO ALL HANDS:
Our work here has ended—our mission has been fulfilled and the time has come for saying our goodbyes as we decommission the Pre-Flight school and fit ourselves to the new pattern of living which lies before us and a world no longer at war.

---

[3] *Cloudbuster*, October 3, 1945, p. 1. (Reports that 1,220 officers and coaches came through indoctrination training between August 1942 until September 1943.)

On behalf of the Ship's Company I extend congratulations to all the young men who have trained here. Your purposefulness in training has been our inspiration and your valorous record in combat has been our pride. Those of you who are now in training measure up in every respect to your predecessors, and yours will be a vital contribution to the continuing greatness of Naval Aviation. You have chosen a career of usefulness and honor.

I wish to express all hands, Naval and civilian, my appreciation for the fine spirit of cooperation and devotion to duty which has earned high praise for us throughout the Naval Service. It has been a distinct privilege to serve with you and I shall always cherish the pleasure of having been your shipmate.

With Frank Porter Graham's steady lobbying, dorms were renovated, and the university inherited a three-story fireproof naval hospital that was to be used as an infirmary with 105 beds.[4] Other buildings bequeathed by the Navy included O. O. Kessing Pool, an undergraduate admissions building, the Scuttlebutt canteen, and a women's gymnasium. The Navy cleared land used for athletic fields and outdoor basketball courts, and a labor battalion cleared the land that is now Finley Golf Course.[5]

The last of the cadets left campus by October 1, 1945, and the Chapel Hill Pre-Flight School officially closed its doors on October 15. Athletic supplies that had rolled in by the ton were sold to the University of North Carolina or donated to high schools and charities such as Baptist Orphanage in Thomasville, North Carolina.[6] Kids would never realize that they were swinging a bat held by Ted Williams, throwing a baseball that may have been pitched by

---

[4] *The State*, September 29, 1945, p. 18.

[5] *Chapel Hill Weekly*, November 13, 1942, p. 1.

[6] Interview with Ray Jeffries, July 8, 2017, *Chapel Hill Weekly*, November 2, 1945, p. 1. Also, classified memo written October 31, 1945, by James P. Raugh Sr. concerning decommissioning of school.

Johnny Sain, or wearing a glove that may have been used by Buddy Hassett.

Funds from the Cloudbuster Athletic Association were turned over to the Navy Relief Society. Savings from the Welfare and Recreation Department were turned over to the Navy ROTC and the V-12 units on campus.[7]

Just as Ted Williams described in letters to friends, Chapel Hill turned back into a quiet town in the middle of the country. When classes resumed in January 1946, the annoying intercom that chirped with bells and announcements was dismantled, and the sounds of combat boots had disappeared. Military khaki was replaced by colorful sweaters and two-toned bucks. Without military inspections, rooms were messy, with clothes strewn on floors, and racy posters of Hollywood starlets plastered on the walls. Loud music flowed from radios, and easy laughter echoed across courtyards under the giant oaks. Classrooms were once again filled with coeds and regular Joe college students, fraternity and sorority rush selected incoming pledge classes, and students looked forward to their traditional college baseball games in the spring.

The grass slowly grew back on Emerson Field by the start of baseball season, and the concession stand was reopened for ballgames. The Tar Heels had a good season that year, but the old Navy spirit disappeared, and that patriotic feeling from that extraordinary season of 1943 never returned.

In its humble understated manner, the Navy quietly faded away, leaving behind a few modest bronze plaques and framed editorials in the halls of the Navy ROTC building on South Columbia Street, where an armory cannon stands on the lawn. During college, I was oblivious to my family's history with the university and the Navy and cringe when I remember those nights when I climbed on that cannon after court parties following football games.

---

[7] Classified memo written October 31, 1945, by James P. Raugh Sr. concerning decommissioning of school.

A modest granite and tarnished bronze marker rises from the South Quad on the Iowa campus commemorating the legacy of Pre-Flight. Former mascot Jerry Holland recalled that the rejoicing in the school was unparalleled after the surrender. When the war was over, he said, "The Navy did not fool around with bureaucratic bunk . . . they went to work to close up shop and to send people home."

When Jerry returned for the Pre-Flight base's 50th anniversary reunion, there were no "old Navys"—just civilians who had worked on the base. Having been there and watched these people as a kid, Jerry said they did a great job—in fact, he couldn't imagine anyone doing any better, even with old sailors who may not have conformed so nicely to the desires of the Pre-Flight program.

Ted Drake's career as an artist took off when he left the Pre-Flight publicity department. After designing iconic sports mascots and creating the first American children's show, *Kukla, Fran and Ollie*, Ted Drake kept up his Pre-Flight work ethic and painted every day in his studio in Elkhart, Indiana, until he died at age 92 in 2000.

## The Craighead Twins and Don Kepler

I had the opportunity to speak with John Craighead Jr. several months before his father died at age 100. For years, John Jr. lived next door to his parents in a ranch house in Missoula, Montana, near the silver tips of the Tetons. His father was nearly blind and deaf in his final years, but he still managed to get up in the middle of the night to carve a squash for dinner.[8] Little John had saved stacks of World War II letters that had never been published. He was hoping to compile them into a book to round out their years in the Navy when we first spoke. After the Craigheads completed their statewide assignments, they left for more training at American bases in the Marshall Islands and the Philippines toward the end of the war. They were groomed as special agents for the Office of Strategic Services (OSS), the precursor to the CIA, and just before the brothers

---

[8] Conversations with John Craighead Jr. in 2016.

were scheduled to be dropped into territory behind Russian lines, they received news that the war was fortunately coming to an end.[9]

The Craigheads went on to become world-renowned conservationists who co-authored the National Wild and Scenic Rivers Act of 1968, legislation that protects 208 rivers in 40 states. Their pioneering research also helped rescue the North America grizzly bear from extinction. They went on to become fixtures in *National Geographic* circles, and they were both named among America's top scientists of the 20th century by the National Audubon Society. When Dr. John Craighead received the Wildlife Society's Aldo Leopold Memorial Award in 1998, he encouraged people to think like nature and look at the fundamentals. He said, "That philosophy has guided me in my work; I have listened to the voice of the mountain for most of my life." He passed away peacefully in September 2016, one month after his family gathered to celebrate his 100th birthday. His wife, Margaret, died several weeks later.[10]

After the war, Don Kepler returned to the sleepy hollow of Pine Grove Mills, where he began to experiment with waterproof hunting boots to prevent trench foot. When he came home, he pulled a design out of the drawer for a waterproof boot with a built-in steel shank arch and a stub-proof toe cap insulated by thick inner rubber layers for warmth. Kepler designed his boots with trademark red jungle cloth tops, a precursor to the brilliant blaze orange that was introduced to the public in a 1960 article in *Field and Stream*.[11]

In the spring of 1947, the Kepler boot prototype was introduced to the market with his cursive signature written on the heel. He spent a year developing the boot, which resembled a cross between an L. L. Bean gumshoe and a combat boot. Kepler made 500 pairs,

---

[9] Vicki Constantine Croke, *Washington Post*, November 11, 2007.

[10] John Craighead Jr. conversations with author, July–August 2016; Sherry Devlin, *Missoulian*, September 17, 1988 (Leopold quote).

[11] Frank Woolner, "Hunter Orange–Your Shield for Safety," *Field & Stream*, October 1960. Also, Associated Press article in *Altoona Tribune*, July 11, 1947, p. 12.

which received national press coverage in publications such as the *Philadelphia Inquirer, Grit,* and *Outdoorsman* magazine. Kepler also created a fishing boot with the same design and sold them from the basement of the Penn State Hotel. When he went into the boot business, his best friend was George W. Harvey, America's "dean of fly fishing," who was inducted into the Pennsylvania Fly Fishing Hall of Fame. Mr. Harvey took presidents Dwight Eisenhower and Jimmy Carter and other dignitaries fishing on Pennsylvania trout streams, and he would have been the best judge in the world to know what kind of footwear was needed for the river.

One advertisement for Don's red hunting boot read, "the long trail from the pitcher's mound was the longest walk of all." More of a hunter than a businessman, Kepler sold a couple hundred pairs for $12.95 each. Today, the last remaining pairs of his bright red boots with the Kepler signature are in the closets of his children and grandchildren. His boots are remarkably well preserved, looking as new as they did in the 1940s because they were designed to last by one of the greatest survivalists of all time.

To this day, Kepler's children treasure the handwritten letters he received from presidents, and professional athletes like Ted Williams, and the most decorated naval officers in history, who all appreciated their father as a coach and a loyal friend they trusted with their lives. Many of the daughters and nieces of players and baseball coaches carried on the modest Pre-Flight legacy as healers, offering something unseen yet invaluable back to people that continues to thread its way through the generations. Victoria Kepler Didato counsels trauma survivors, while Addie Beth Craft Denton, Harry Craft's niece, volunteered to counsel 9/11 victims. Claudia Williams, a triathlete and author, returned to school to earn a degree in nursing at Duke University, where her father shipped into training at dusk in the spring of 1943. When I had the privilege of speaking with Claudia, she mentioned that she works to advocate for female athletes with strong father figures, and my study of his Pre-Flight training reaffirms that there is no better man for today's youth to study and emulate than Ted Williams.

Claudia Williams considered her father to be the most principled and ethical man she ever knew and a role model for hard work. In jest, she told me that if she had a son, he'd be the best baseball player on the team, he'd make straight A's, he would have a job and work, and "don't even think about getting a car when he turned 16. He would walk or take a bus" like her father, an attitude that molded the character of the World War II generation.

Like many of the cadets and officers profiled in this book, Claudia said that her father had the courage to be bold. He had the ability to recreate greatness—he strived to prove to others that he was better than the competition. His attitude was "You'll be so damn good at it if you dream it, live it, eat it, and own it," and that is exactly what the Pre-Flight cadets took away from those three months in Chapel Hill, where baseball players took on a third job, riding from bases to ballparks in the belly of those uncomfortable tin-can buses to boost morale.

I knew her father would be proud that she had followed his example, championing the Jimmy Fund and caring for patients, just as he did when he visited kids suffering from cancer and other illnesses that strike the most innocent victims. As a nurse, and the daughter of a World War II veteran, Claudia enjoys caring for seniors, "the gems of our country." Her way of giving back is being beside a patient who might be a foul-mouthed grumpy old man, but one she respects because he may in fact be a war hero and she wants to take care of him.

Like her father, and the men who wore the Cloudbusters uniform, Claudia urges today's kids to be independent. She said, "My father knew what he stood for and he carried that spirit into the military as a fighter pilot, standing up for his country."

Though Claudia was born during the Vietnam War, she is the daughter of a World War II veteran. She inherited her father's intuitive inner "compass" that Donald Kepler referred to in his survival speeches, that keeps her grounded, guiding her like the North Star to carry on her father's legacy.[12] After Hall of Famer Jimmie Foxx's

---

[12] Interview with Claudia Williams, November 6, 2017.

daughter read Claudia's book, *Ted Williams, My Father*, she wrote her a letter saying, "You are our voice."[13] Through my writing, I have realized the profound power and truth of this statement, as we need to remember the humble lessons of the Old Leaguer whose pictures line the back walls of Boshamer Baseball Stadium in Chapel Hill.

---

[13] Wright Thompson, "The Greatest Hitter Who Ever Lived On," *ESPN the Magazine*, May 5, 2015.

# Chapter 24

## THE NINE—AFTER THE WAR
## AND THE .5 PERCENT

The 1944 Cloudbusters baseball team won 24 games, lost 12, and tied one, seizing the Ration-League crown. That year, the 'Busters faced more military squads such as Oceana Air Field, Camp Davis, and Cherry Point, dropping civilian competition against most of the factory teams. The 1945 team fell below the .500 mark, racking up 17 wins against 25 losses.

The Pre-Flight schools left behind a legacy as the first sports academies in the United States.[1] In the billion-dollar industry of baseball memorabilia, relics from the Cloudbusters team have been overlooked by collectors because so few people are familiar with the team's name.

But images of the team and their batboys are everywhere—they cover walls of military and sports museums across America, are featured in Major-League Baseball films, and live in the collections of the Hall of Fame memorializing the spirit of World War II baseball.

---

[1] Donald W. Rominger Jr., "The Impact of the United States Government's Sports and Physical Training Policy on Organized Athletics During World War II," PhD dissertation, Oklahoma State University, 1976.

I made several attempts to acquire the Yanklands baseball signed by 31 attendees and players, including Hall of Famers Babe Ruth, Bill Dickey, Ted Williams, and Mickey Mantle (who signed the ball with a ballpoint pen at a later date). According to inspectors, the "Official Reach" ball bearing the notion "*War Relief—July 28, 1943—Yankee Stadium*" shows evidence of use with scattered scuffing and soiling. It last sold in 2016 for $4,600 at an auction house in Pennsylvania. Babe Ruth's gray wool road jersey recently auctioned for more than $4 million, and collectors routinely value baseballs signed by Hall of Famers for tens of thousands of dollars.[2] I own an original red, white, and blue Yanklands scorecard and a barrelful of autographed baseballs representing every player on the team. I acquired a series of original advertisements from Wheaties featuring Cloudbuster players, along with Jack Armstrong Pre-Flight Kits that inspired the next generation of fliers. My scrapbook swells with trading cards and original images of every single famous player who wore the Cloudbuster jersey, along with souvenirs from the other immortals who trained at Pre-Flight, including Bear Bryant, John Glenn, and Jim Crowley. I've acquired original artwork sketched by Ted Drake, and last but not least, I own a copy of the Pre-Flight training syllabus outlined on that kitchen table in Arlington, Virginia, and polished up with handwritten notes in Howard Hamilton's office in Columbus, Ohio.

Though they have never been commercialized or branded as a training guide for civilians or kids, elements of the Pre-Flight Fighter Pilot Training Formula have been passed down through the generations by every officer and cadet who cycled through a Pre-Flight base. After the war, these men assimilated back to civilian life, never realizing how this training experiment built on teamwork and competitive sports would impact millions of people in the future.

James Forrestal and Arthur Radford were credited for their crusades to call in the most talented coaches in the nation to train pilots, and they certainly left fingerprints on the Pre-Flight Training

---

[2] Richard Sandomir, *New York Times,* May 22, 2012, p. B12.

Formula. Howard Hamilton was credited for his academic contributions to the Pre-Flight Schools, but the man who deserves recognition for the success of the program is Tom Hamilton.

In December 1942, Tom Hamilton was voted "Man of the Year" by the National Football Writers Association, which recognized him as the individual who did the most to keep football operating at full tempo when the world went to war. For the rest of his years, he took that spirit to aircraft carriers, military bases, sports fields, campuses, and athletic foundations. In July 1943, Hamilton was the commanding officer of the USS *Enterprise*, an aircraft carrier that took part in the invasion of the Philippines, Palau, Hollandia, Formosa, and Iwo Jima. In 1946, he returned to the Naval Academy to serve as head coach until 1947, where he also served as the Navy's athletic director until 1949. The mystique of the V-5 remained, and that year he helped form the V-5 Association of America to mold young people through competitive athletics.[3]

Hamilton moved to the University of Pittsburgh, where he took on similar roles until 1959. Early in his career as athletic director at Pitt, legislation was introduced to allow television stations to broadcast football games at schools supported by state funds. Long before Jumbotrons and million-dollar halftime commercials dominated primetime, he understood and anticipated the enormous, potentially dangerous power of television on athletic programs. As a man with an appreciation for public relations, Hamilton hoped to protect the good clean integrity of college sports. In a 1951 story printed in the *Pittsburgh Post-Gazette*, Hamilton, who was president of the NCAA television research committee, brushed off legislators' threats, stating, "We certainly don't want to destroy the goose that lays the golden eggs."[4]

Hamilton was chairman of the President's Council on Physical Fitness, served 16 years on the U.S. Olympic Committee, and was

---

[3] V-5 Association Constitution of Bylaws of the V-5 Association of America, Annapolis, Maryland, U.S. Naval Academy. 1947.

[4] *Pittsburgh Post-Gazette*, April 6, 1951, p. 20.

vice president of the National Football Foundation, which named him to the Hall of Fame as a player in 1965 and awarded him its Gold Medal in 1970. He received the Theodore Roosevelt Award from the NCAA and the Amos Alonzo Stagg Award from the National Association of College Directors of Athletics.

Forty years after he helped launch the Pre-Flight schools, Hamilton recorded his life history for a naval historian. Early in the interview, he expressed concern that the athletic programs of yesteryear had deteriorated in the Navy, where service members were frequenting beer joints and massage parlors to boost morale. He yearned to see young people return to the old days of sports, where airmen and sailors had pride in their teams. Going back to the days of the Pacific Fleet, he reminisced about men losing a month's pay to bet on a baseball game. Hamilton certainly did not advocate gambling, but he did appreciate the sense of pride and the wholesome recreation demonstrated by teams like the Cloudbuster Nine.

Hamilton died on April 3, 1994, in Chula Vista, California. He is buried next to Arleigh Burke, former chief of Naval Operations under Presidents Eisenhower and Kennedy, at the U.S. Naval Academy cemetery.

His brother, Howard, returned to Columbus in 1945. For years, he served in the reserves, and his daughter, Betty, remembered how he wore his uniform to meetings every Thursday night. Because of his absence during the war and a lost opportunity to earn his PhD, Howard was passed over for the deanship, but he held a number of influential positions at Ohio State. After a long career with the university, Howard was recruited by the national Presbyterian Church to start the department of Ministerial Pastoral Relations. After giving a speech for the church in Alaska, he had a stroke. As a lifelong runner and a handball player, Howard was in excellent shape, but he died a year later at age 65.[5]

---

[5] Interview with daughter Betty Hamilton Busey, July 2017. Ancestry.com and State of Ohio death records, December 8, 1968.

Bear Bryant transferred from Chapel Hill to Georgia Pre-Flight before he shipped out to the Pacific. At the height of his career, he was regarded as the number one coach in the game. Sportswriters believed that the secret to his success was his ability to inspire athletes, drawing out the potential of scrappy overachievers. Like Ted Williams, Bear was a perfectionist who did not tolerate mistakes and had the ability to make kids believe in themselves. He was always on the defense against failure, and in the spirit of the Pre-Flighters, he believed that teams needed to keep from losing before they tried to win. Players knew he stood behind them as a coach. "Once you spilled your guts for the Bear, he never forgot you," stated a former player, benefiting from the motivational skills Bear perfected 50 years earlier in the Navy.[6]

In 2014, former University of Georgia football coach and athletic director Vince Dooley published the first academic article of his career in the *Georgia Historical Quarterly*. A large portion of the article was focused on the Georgia Pre-Flight's Sky Crackers football team, which was coached by Bear Bryant and which Dooley felt was just as good as his 1980 national championship team. As one of the most accomplished men of football, Dooley won 201 games, six SEC titles, and a national title on top of his success in building one of the nation's most accomplished athletic programs. Dooley spent years tracking down and interviewing surviving members of the 1942 team, including players like Noah Langdale, starting tackle for Alabama's Cotton Bowl championship team in 1941 before he got a law degree from Harvard and served as president of Georgia State University for 31 years. He was also able to trace Pre-Flight's legacy to present-day teams and techniques, such as the Split-T option offense, invented in 1941 by Lieutenant Don Faurot, who coached football at the Iowa Pre-Flight School.[7]

Lieutenant Commander Whitey Fuller, who recruited many of the Cloudbusters stars, spent time in the Arctic and the Panama Canal

---

[6] William F. Reed, *Sports Illustrated*, September 19. 1994, p. 108.

[7] Lee Shearer, *Athens Banner Herald*, January 5, 2015.

during the war, where he was responsible for the flow of operations against enemy submarines. He earned a degree from the Naval War College and returned to Dartmouth with his wife and son, Robert, at the end of the war, to head up the athletic publicity department.[8]

Of all of the players I researched, Buddy Hassett was the one who grabbed my heart. He was cute, with an underbite. Buddy was drawn to the most dangerous weapons in the military, yet he could sing like a lark. Though he was known to keep his chin up as captain of the Cloudbuster Nine, Buddy had some of the worst luck of his teammates later in life.

Forty years after the war ended, at age 83, Buddy got up in the morning to go to work at Metropolitan Trucking Company in Northern New Jersey because he needed money to make ends meet. Buddy was one of the players who never received a pension from playing major-league baseball. After three years of military service, the first baseman was cut by the Yankees—one year before the pension was established for major-league players. Walking with a cane, Buddy spoke up on behalf of the others like him—former players who needed that money much more than he did. Buddy was not bitter, claiming that he was richer for the memories. As a former plumber who held a number-two card for the plumbers and steamfitters union, he was proud of the generation of players he represented, reminding fans of the days when athletes did not play for the money or the fame—they played for the pure love of the game.[9]

By 1946, all of the Cloudbusters returned to professional ball in different ways: as players, coaches, or managers. At age 27, Ted returned to the Red Sox and some of his brothers from the clubhouse, but he wasn't through fighting for Uncle Sam.

In May 1952, Ted's name was dusted off the reserves list, and he was called back to duty as a Marine pilot. He was 33 years old and married, with a daughter. Korea was not the kind of war that cap-

---

[8] *Portsmouth Herald*, October 4, 1945, p. 8.

[9] John Harper, "Hassett Keeps on Truckin' Pre-Pension Yank Labors Away at 83," *New York Daily News*, February 6, 1995.

tured the admiration of the public like World War II. It was a cold, dreary, dark place during a dark time in history. While Ted complained bitterly about the call-up, he packed his bags and headed to Korea to serve his country.

It is impossible to determine how many home runs Ted may have hit during the seasons he missed. Though he formed lifelong bonds with airmen like John Glenn, his wingman on half of his missions in Korea, Ted returned to a younger league of players, not nearly as talented or experienced as his former teammates. They were certainly not players who had served in two wars, so once again, like Huck Finn, he set out alone to reinvent himself.[10]

In 1952, Austen Lake, a *Boston Evening American* reporter, sat down with Ted's best friend, Johnny Pesky, to examine the slugger's trajectory in and out of the service. At the beginning of his piece, Austen posed this question to his readers: "For the mills of our military sometimes grind weird figures. They defer, discharge, or exempt large numbers of eligible young athletes, both college and pros, for minor defects like leaky eardrums (Mickey McDermott), winter asthma (Chuck Stobbs), porous bones (Mickey Mantle) . . . to mention only a few. So now they grab Ted Williams who is 34, married, a parent and after serving more than three years in WWII. How can such contradiction be reconciled?"

For years, Lake tried to dig under Ted's crusty shell to see if he could find a charitable and gentle man. It took a friend who knew Ted's inner geography to paint a picture of the lonely, neglected boy from San Diego who practiced his swings alone, in the moonlight, in the tiny backyard behind his parents' bungalow. Johnny walked Austen back to the very beginning when they enlisted in the service, focusing on those long months at Amherst and Chapel Hill, where Ted showed a new side in the classroom as a 3.85-grade-point-average student. Chapel Hill was the place where his most generous attributes emerged. Johnny spoke of "classes til your brain reeled, sports,

---

[10] David Halberstam, *The Teammates: A Portrait of a Friendship*, Hyperion, 2003, p. 174.

hikes, inspections," and Ted never got the featherbed treatment. He said, "A lot of guys, knowing Ted's reputation as a pop-off, waited for him to explode. But he never blew any fuses or got a single bad behavior demerit. If anything, he took a little stiffer than the others, sort of stuff like, 'O so you're the great Ted Williams, huh? Okay Mister!'" Ted took it all, even if he was a loner then, as now. Johnny swore that, from the very beginning, all Ted wanted was his wings, and he vowed that he'd work "ten years for them" if that's what it took to earn them.

Johnny went on to talk about the month when they separated, where Ted's reputation as a natural flyer with finger-tip balance followed him. In Pensacola, he put in training with night flying, loops, snap rolls, and acrobatics like the Immelmann dogfight turn at advanced Marine training. "They said his reflexes, coordination, and visual-reaction made him a built-in part of the machine."

Johnny described Ted's gunnery skills—the combat pilot's payoff test where he would shoot from wingovers, barrel rolls, and zooms, tearing the sleeve to ribbons after a few passes. Then, he broke the all-time record for "hits"—playing its six pianos (machine guns) like a symphony orchestra.[11]

Though Ted never had an opportunity to become a Boy Scout, he lived by the code of honor. As a top student, he became an instructor at Bronson Field in Pensacola, where he flew the propeller-driven, single-engine, single-seat Vought F4U Corsair, a favorite mount of Marine aces in the South Pacific.

When the Navy insisted that he flunk the lower two-thirds of the class, because they had too many pilots, he refused. A true believer in meritocracy, Ted stood by his decision to pass every pilot who qualified for the job.[12] In 2002, John Harris of Andover, Massachusetts, recalled how he and his classmates were being chewed out by a check pilot for a routine formation exercise. Before they saw the man coming into the hangar, they heard a booming voice bellowing, "Leave

---

[11] Austen Lake, *Boston Evening American*, January 11, 1952, p. 46.

[12] Ed Linn, *Hitter*, p. 247.

them alone and get out of here. I'm taking over now, and they will do it right." By the time their session was over, the pilots were calling Williams "Granddaddy," a nickname reserved for the most ethical instructors who had the best interests of their trainees at heart.[13]

Ted stayed in touch with his roommates from Everett Dorm for the rest of his years. Don Pletts went on to pilot an Avenger, flying combat missions in Japan. After the war, he visited Ted regularly and was part of a joke played on Joe Cronin in 1946. Though Don did not play for the Cloudbusters, he was a decent ballplayer. According to Pletts's daughter Sarah, one afternoon Ted told Joe Cronin he had a friend he needed to look at for the team. Don came out to Fenway Park, warming up by knocking out a few respectable hits. Needing to get on his way, Cronin was polite, making no promises but saying, "We might be able to find him a spot on a minor-league team."

When the players started to laugh, Ted said, "Ha, the joke's on you," to Cronin. "Don is an old Navy buddy from Chapel Hill. He lives in Boston and sells insurance."

Years later, Don and his wife became good friends with Ted and his first wife, Doris. They moved to Florida because of Ted's friendship, and he loaned them $5,000 for their first house. Their daughters also became friends.

That loyalty was cemented on the day they met on the grass in front of Alexander Dormitory. Don's daughter was troubled by the violence of the war and wished she could have known her father when he slung his arm around Ted and welcomed his new roommate. She said her father was a resolute, firm man but was capable of having fun, despite the horrors he witnessed in Japan. She recorded 30 hours of his life story before he died, with long passages about his former roommate who was a fishing buddy, and a true friend.[14]

---

[13] John Vellante, *Boston Globe*, July 28, 2002, p. 9.
[14] Interview with Sarah Pletts, January 6, 2017.

## Presidential Pre-Flight Officers

Three future U.S. presidents had an appreciation for the Chapel Hill Pre-Flight school and its sports teams. Ronald Reagan met Gerald Ford when he performed at Memorial Hall in the fall of 1942, just 16 days after George Bush shipped off base. Reagan had gained acclaim with his play-by-play broadcasts of Chicago Cubs games he'd never seen, using telegraph reports inside a studio. He earned five dollars announcing a homecoming game for the University of Iowa versus Minnesota, earning a full-time position as a sports announcer for WHO radio. In 1940, Reagan broke into the movies as the halfback George Gipp in *Knute Rockne, All-American*. Later, he played pitcher Grover Cleveland Alexander in 1952's *The Winning Team*, but it was his role as Gipp that solidified Reagan's connection with sports. In the movie, it was Gipp who, on his deathbed, implored Coach Rockne to have the boys "win one for the Gipper," a phrase associated with Reagan for the rest of his life.

Gerald Ford is remembered as an athletics coach and for surviving two plane crashes during his Pre-Flight training as a pilot and a passenger at Horace Williams Field. In the first crash, Ford crash-landed a Piper Cub, tearing the wing off. The second accident occurred on a rainy evening in a twin-engine prop plane carrying Ford, an admiral, and three other men. When the plane landed at the wrong angle and veered into a ditch, it exploded and burned five minutes after Ford and the other passengers disembarked.[15]

What mattered most to Ford were the friendships he forged during his Pre-Flight training in Chapel Hill. He visited Salisbury, North Carolina, four times to campaign for the Honorable Earl B. Ruth, one of his roommates in the cabin near campus, whom President Ford appointed as governor of Samoa after Ruth served two terms as a U.S. Congressman.[16] Unbeknownst to his staff at the

---

[15] *Alumni Review*, December 29, 2006. Ford studied for a summer at UNC-CH Law School in 1938 and November 5, 1974, replies to alumni questionnaire.

[16] Congressman Gerald R. Ford Jr., press release issued September 23, 1968, and Mark Wineka, *The Salisbury Post*, May 18, 2015.

White House, Ford drafted countless handwritten letters to old Navy buddies like my grandfather and Donald Kepler, with whom he reunited 30 years later at Penn State. In a portrait titled "Donald Kepler and Friend," the former Pre-Flight coaches were photographed on the steps of a red brick building—both men balding, with broad smiles and hard-earned wrinkles.[17]

George H. W. Bush left Pre-Flight School more than six months before Ted arrived. Though Bush never saw Williams pound a line drive over the hedges at Emerson Field, he knew that one of his favorite baseball stars was reporting to base the following spring.

Bush has always stayed close the game, keeping an oiled first baseman's mitt from Yale in his drawer when he was president.[18] He understood the connection between baseball and aviation that was taught at Pre-Flight and knew the secret to Ted's success as a pilot. In an interview, he explained that coordination is the most important aspect of flying—"You have to get the feel of the airplane," and Ted "had that down cold."[19]

Bush said that Ted electrified everything he did, and years later, they fished together in the Florida Keys. Ted campaigned for the former first basemen during his 1988 presidential campaign in New Hampshire. In 1991, Bush hung a Presidential Medal of Freedom around his friend's neck, honoring a war hero and a fellow ballplayer.

---

[17] Kepler family picture shared with author.

[18] Thomas Boswell, "A President's Passion for Baseball," *Washington Post*, March 31, 1989, p. B1.

[19] HBO: Legends and Legacies: Ted Williams interview with George H. W. Bush, July 15, 2009.

# Chapter 25

# EXTRA INNINGS

During World War II, an estimated 1,400 major-league players, umpires, managers, and coaches served in the armed forces.[1]

It is impossible to estimate the number of ticket vendors, groundskeepers, clubhouse managers, custodial staff, ushers, and batboys who served in military uniforms.

By 1946, major-league baseball attendance shot up 71 percent. Warnings of air raids and rationing drives were no longer printed in game programs, the propaganda posters came down, and giant war bond billboards were dismantled at ballparks.

The names of military teams like the Cloudbusters disappeared from headlines as civilian teams returned. Thousands of generic NAVY baseball jerseys were recycled into rags, donated, or sold to recreation parks as major-league players and coaches suited back up in familiar team jerseys, coming back stronger than ever.

When baseball came home, so did the dreams of millions of kids who thought that one day they might follow in the footsteps of the

---

[1] "Memories and Dreams," *Baseball Hall of Fame* magazine, Spring 2017, p. 40.

diamond heroes who survived the most sweeping war of a generation as they served Uncle Sam.

Emerson Field became a symbol of the times. In the late 1940s and 1950s, baseball players were happy to find a room under the stands of the ballpark when they could not afford housing anywhere else on campus. Residents even had a famous rat named "Napoleon" who lived under the cement stands at the stadium as it slowly crumbled into disrepair. In the late 1960s, "Get Lost" was crudely scrawled on the ceiling above the stairwell as beer bottles, crumpled newspapers, and egg shells covered its grounds. In its final days, a message reading, "Free love Free speech Free university," was drawn on the ballpark's boarded-up windows of storage rooms junked up with lawnmowers and tractors used to maintain other parts of the campus.[2]

When the ballpark was torn down by the wrecking ball in the early 1970s, it was said that no one ever broke Ted's long-distance batting records.

Billy Carmichael, one of the original "Mad Men" of advertising, knew that sports was the glue that cemented relationships between the university and alumni. Billy employed his brilliant vision to restyle the university's image as a big-time sports school, where a tailback from Asheville, North Carolina, Charlie "Choo-Choo" Justice led Carolina to two conference championships and a No. 1 ranking. When Carmichael helped turn on the spigot for funding, the university was transformed by the postwar gifts from philanthropists such as John Motley Morehead III, a Union Carbide Corporation founder, who endowed millions for scholarships and landmarks such as the Morehead Planetarium.[3] As a scientist, Morehead hoped to open the minds of young North Carolinians to the wonders of astronomy, and former Pre-Flight alums such as Mercury Seven astronauts John Glenn and Scott Carpenter, who won the regimental

---

[2] Bonnie Schultz, *Daily Tar Heel*, October 13, 1967, p. 3

[3] Kenneth Joel Zogry, *Print News and Raise Hell: The Daily Tar Heel and the Evolution of a Modern University*, University of North Carolina Press, 2018, pp. 148–150.

Pre-Flight wrestling championship, trained for space missions in the Morehead simulator.[4]

With the help of the Federal GI Bill, student enrollment skyrocketed from a low of 1,788 in 1942 to 7,603 in the fall of 1948.

Orville Campbell stayed in touch with his good friend Ted Williams for the rest of his life. After the war, Orville hit his stride as a legendary newsman, founding Colonial Records and Colonial Press. In 1949, he co-wrote the song "All The Way Choo Choo," honoring UNC football great Charlie Justice, selling 32,000 copies of his record across North Carolina. His record company cut many discs, two of which launched superstar careers. Campbell recorded Andy Griffith's legendary "What It Was, Was Football" and George Hamilton IV's breakout hit "A Rose and a Baby Ruth." Orville's newspaper, the *Chapel Hill Weekly*, won many national awards, grooming the future Pulitzer Prize-winning cartoonist Jeff MacNelly.

## The Formula for V-5 Cadets

The sports-for-war training experiment proved to be one of the most successful training programs in military history, with millions of miles marched; tens of thousands of matches, meets, and games played; and hundreds of thousands of miles swum at the five Pre-Flight school bases.[5]

The Pre-Flight training formula, electrified by sporting competition, exulted by wartime staples like Wheaties, and demonstrated to the world on baseball fields like Yankee Stadium, really did produce Supermen.

"After V-5 training, I thought I could do anything," said Ray Marrs, who was raised on a dairy farm in Kansas. In 2004, Marrs authored the only known memoir about day-to-day Pre-Flight training, *I Was There When the World Stood Still*, shedding light on how the experience shaped him for the rest of his life. Ray felt like he might

---

[4] Scott Carpenter wrestling reference from his website, *Mercury Astronaut*, ScottCarpenter.com; Teresa Leonard, *Raleigh News & Observer*, April 6, 2017.

[5] St. Mary's Yearbook 1945, Swimming, p. 40.

never come home from the war, so he sold his car to his brother. He cried himself to sleep on the night before he left the farm, with a paper sack holding all of his personal belongings next to his bed. Coming in as a skinny farmboy, Ray was transformed by Pre-Flight training, gaining 29 pounds of muscle by graduation day. In his spiffy blue uniform with shiny brass buttons, he boarded the big Blue Bird bus to leave the school with "low black clouds that did not do justice to the beautiful spring day." Ray had only been off campus twice during hikes in remote areas with no homes or traffic. In 90 days, he saw no one except his troops and was glad to be set free as a creature transformed with a new identity and an indomitable attitude that would carry him through the skies.[6]

Other cadets wrote about the camaraderie that transformed them, becoming teary during interviews 70 years later. After telling a story about the day he broke his first five-minute mile with a two-inch splinter in his leg, Elger Berkley's voice broke, and he stated that Pre-Flight was absolutely the turning point in his life.[7]

Jimmie Doole, a member of the 1943 baseball team, wrote a soul-baring letter from Peru, Indiana, to Coach Kepler. Doole had played varsity baseball at Dartmouth before he enlisted in the Navy, and his letter was so eloquent that it was published in the *Cloudbuster*:

> When I left college I'd just about given up the thought of playing baseball . . . and certainly I had no intentions of playing ball with Ted, Johnny, Mr. Hassett etc. but when you called out the candidates from the "27th," I thought I might as well give it a try. All I know is in those few weeks I had more fun and picked up more tips than I ever could have in a whole season anywhere else. Actually, pitching for such a club was far beyond my dreams. That trip to New York was really the climax of the whole season for me. Just throwing batting practice at Yankee Stadium is enough to give any kid a thrill. When

---

[6] K. Ray Marrs, *I Was There When The World Stood Still*, pp. 17–40.

[7] Veterans History Project, Elger August Berkley, July 8, 2005.

guys like Mr. Hassett, Mr. Craft, Johnny, Ted and the others treat you like any other ball player and try to help you—well it gives you a fine impression of big-league ball players.

It wasn't all baseball—I enjoyed every day of my training. I know you hear lots of griping about the beating we get but every cadet who goes through Chapel Hill learns plenty that will help him for the rest of his life. The one real reason for this lies in the terrific staff of officers, athletes, platoons. It's hard for an outsider to realize the fine training each cadet receives but when you think that every great athlete is there to help you—well you dig in and get an even bigger kick out of it.[8]

## Ted's Legacy

Seventy-nine years after Williams batted .406, no major-leaguer has reached that level. During the war, Ted's fate could have changed in a millisecond by a training accident or enemy fire, but instead he lived large to become the ultimate major-league fighter pilot, symbolizing the type of hero people yearn for.

One of the men he credited for saving his life was the pilot who touched the stars, John Glenn. When Ted's F-9 Panther was hit by anti-aircraft fire in Korea, Glenn flew next to his wing, signaling with his hands to climb to higher, thinner air to extinguish the flames streaming from his jet. That split-second instinct honed on Pre-Flight sports fields led Ted Williams home. When Glenn soared far above the clouds to orbit the Earth, Ted wrote a tribute about his "fearless friend" in the *Boston Globe,* saying, "This was a man destined for something great; it was an intuitive feeling I had. John always had exceptional self-control and was one of the calmest men I have ever met, no matter how perilous the situation."[9]

---

[8] *Cloudbuster,* September 11, 1943, p. 3.

[9] Ted Williams, *Boston Globe,* June 17, 1962, p. 1. Alternative references exist concerning how other pilots, such as Larry Hawkins, also used hand signals to help Williams land safely.

This book goes beyond black-and-white pictures and film clips to capture the grit of a short-lived team and players like Ted Williams who boosted morale as they trained their hearts out to become pilots.

Never again would the nation see such an outpouring of sacrifice from thousands of professional athletes who forfeited the best years of their careers to serve their country.

It would be a quarter of a century before another professional athlete, Buffalo Bills football player Bob Kalsu, a husband and a father, died in Vietnam in 1970. More than 30 years later, NFL star Pat Tillman left a multimillion-dollar contract with the Arizona Cardinals to serve as a U.S. Army Ranger. He was killed in action in Afghanistan in 2004.

This book barely scrapes the surface of all the men and women who trained and worked at the five U.S. Navy Pre-Flight bases. By and large, they were unselfish patriots shaped by the Great Depression who did not dwell on their troubles, and they were always open to learning. Some Pre-Flight cadets and officers reconnected at reunions. Others never saw one another again, but they were all bound by this extraordinary experience that tested their will and harnessed every ounce of their physical capabilities.

Was there a secret formula to success?

The answer came from Johnny Pesky as he approached age 90 when he was interviewed by the National World War II Museum. When asked what advice he might give kids 50 years into the future, he chuckled and said, "The strength within yourself is what you gotta have—find it, and you will succeed."

Pesky laughed at himself, for tripping through the interview "like a baby robin." He recalled the jabs the Navy baseball players got from people who thought they got preferential treatment. He said it hurt like hell when he lost good friends in the war and remembered the injured servicemen in rehab at the games who poked fun at his players from the stands, yelling, "Get out there and play, you Dunkies!"

For the ballplayers of the future, he encouraged kids to put cotton in their ears if there is criticism from the stands. "Do the extra work," he said, "be on time . . . stragglers drive coaches crazy and they eliminate themselves." He said, with regard to injuries, "a good black and blue will disappear after a while," and above all, he encouraged kids to stay close to players who are better. "Watch and learn from those players," and like a Pre-Flighter who kept trying and striving for perfection, he said, "admire those players" because there is always something to learn.

Johnny hoped baseball would stay just the same with the same rules and regulations. "You'll get good players, mediocre players, bad players, and if you are a good player and get hurt you gotta find something else to do, especially if you are a family guy. That's just the way it works." For players like my dad who do not stay in the game, he encouraged them to stay involved in baseball: sell tickets, be a groundkeeper, be a coach, find a way to share the passion of baseball.[10]

In my book of heroes, humble men like Ivan Fleser, who have lived quiet impactful lives in small postage-stamp towns, are at the top of the list. After Ivan's Privateer crashed into the Pacific in January 1945, his crew jumped right back into duty, flying patrol missions over the Pacific. He never saw a Japanese airman—or a submarine, not even a periscope—and he never had any hatred in his heart for them, just compassion. Ivan was in Guam when he heard the war ended over the radio. On his way back to the homeland, he listened to the World Series between the Detroit Tigers and the Chicago Cubs over the radio, which made him feel at home.

When Ivan got out of the service, he had accrued 1,400 hours in flying time and needed 2,000 hours to become a commercial pilot. Instead of becoming a pilot for Eastern Airlines, like his co-pilot during the war, Ivan came home and finished his senior year at Western Michigan State. The following year, he became a teacher and an assistant baseball coach at Albion High School. He worked for four decades at Marshall High School, also serving as a guidance counselor, helping several generations of students to find their inner compass and secure the means to attend college.

---

[10] Johnny Pesky Oral History interview, National World War II Museum, New Orleans, November 8, 2007.

I asked Ivan to share advice he would give to the next generation of Pre-Flight cadets on how to live a long and productive life. He offered this guidance:

- Love your neighbors as yourself.
- Expect failure, life is not a bed of roses; there is always something that comes along that tests our mettle.
- Have no self-pity, don't let physical problems hold you back.
- Comportment, nice manners, and pleasant language is very important—No world leader should use foul language.
- Polish your shoes.
- Try to be upbeat—"The Lord has blessed me thus far, and he will take me to the end."

# Part VIII

# ALWAYS A
# BASEBALL PLAYER

# Chapter 26

## THE LOVE OF THE GAME

My husband took me to my first major-league game when I was in my late 40s. It was a day game at Wrigley Field between the Chicago Cubs and the San Diego Padres, perfect fall weather with the sun bearing down on our backs and a steady breeze pushing in from Lake Michigan. During the game, I spotted a sea of men who reminded me of my father. The old-timers jumped up and pumped their fists when they disagreed with the umpire's call; their eyes lit up with powerful hits and strikes. They may have struggled to come up with the money to buy that ticket, their health may have been failing, and they may have been widowed, but somewhere, someplace long ago, they knew what it felt like to stand on that electric-green stage. And that feeling took them home.

Over the years, I saw Dad light up when high school pitchers came by the house for Saturday morning pep talks. He never told us they were coming, I would just see a muddy souped-up truck in the driveway. For hours, his recruits would sit on the flowered couch in the living room clouded with a fog of cigarette smoke with iced teas sweating on the glass table. Dad looked like he was perched in the dugout with his legs splayed open when he mentored those players;

there was intensity and life restored to his eyes, and a precise rhythm to the way his cigarette moved when he described pitching techniques from the 1950s. If I walked in the room, neither of them acknowledged me—the kid usually came from one of the county high schools I'd never been to. Over the years, there were a few stocky little guys, not much bigger than me, hiding under ball caps with willowy moustaches. I remember one massive fellow, a Madison Bumgarner–type, with black hair falling down to his shoulders. He wore a Members Only jacket and white high-tops with black laces that contrasted against my father's V-neck sweater and loafers. Turns out they were exactly alike at the core, because the only thing that mattered was baseball. And I knew my father would have traded places with him in a second.

As I immersed myself into the world of baseball, touring the rooms of bronze plaques at the Hall of Fame in Cooperstown, taking a behind-the-scenes tour of the Green Monster and snapping a photo of the school-bus-yellow Pesky Pole in right field at Fenway Park, I began to understand the nation's fascination with baseball. I did not spend my money on souvenir trading cards with autopen signatures or shiny key chains with team logos. Rather, I was drawn to the dirt and the grit of the sport back in 1943, when players painted houses and sold cars in the off-season and Cloudbusters like Ray Scarborough peddled pickles to keep their lights turned on.

It was in Sutton's Drugstore on Franklin Street, having breakfast with a few retired Chapel Hillians, when I was enlightened to a longing for the no-frills, old-fashioned sports hero. Amidst the sounds of spatulas scrambling eggs on the flattop grill and chatter from the sheriffs at the next table, these locals explained the eternal fascination with Ted Williams and the world he represented. When I pulled out a Fleer aviation training baseball card, with Ted sitting tall in the cockpit of a Piper Cub in 1942, one of the men gasped. He described him as godlike. "Look at his teeth and his eyes, he radiates," he said, almost teary. Then he proclaimed, "He is divine."

Then, the most vocal of the three enlightened me to the aching truth of his generation. "We have lost our heroes," he said, "because our heroes drive Mercedes and tell cops to go fuck themselves." As I flipped through my scrapbook of black-and-white pictures of Ted and the Nine, one of the men put his head in his hands and said, "God damn it . . . we'll never see this again, fighter pilots and major-league baseball players rolled into one . . . Chapel Hill was crawling with them during the war, and we didn't even know it."[1]

## The Broken Ballplayer

For better or worse, I observed what happens to a man when his teammates realize their dreams and leave him behind.

It was July 1980. The sun was setting behind the mountains and the sky was the color of marigolds when my father had what we politely called his "pitching arm accident." That evening, my father stumbled into the kitchen with a white terry cloth towel from the garage wrapped around his right hand. Blood was running down his legs and splattering on the floor like the first drops of heavy rain.

From across the room, I recognized his signature yardwork scent of vodka melded with fresh-cut grass and the smell of sweat baked into the fibers of his dark-blue Penguin golf shirt. Dad was wearing black leather baseball cleats with metal spikes that clattered across the kitchen floor. The toes of his cleats were covered in soggy clots of grass, pine needles, and blood.

My father was about 45 years old that summer. The sloppy, avoidable accidents were occurring more frequently and more violently, leaving behind gashes, wide blue bruises, and burns that were getting difficult to sew up and hide.

I was almost 16, and perceptive enough to know that I was looking at a lost, middle-aged man whose heart had been broken by something I did not understand.

The accident happened when he stuck his hand under the carriage of a running Toro mower to remove a tree branch. Once again, he was lucky. The blade, rusted and coated with wet grass, only cut through flesh and nails, sparing the bones of his fingers. Luckily, a

---

[1] Conversation with Ted Williams admirers.

retired MASH surgeon lived next door. When I told him about the accident, he didn't bother to examine my father's hand, he just told me to meet him at his clinic downtown.

As a new driver trying to focus on the road, I remember how my father looked out the window, without saying a word, as blood cradled in his lap from the towel wrapped around his hand.

While Dad was being stitched up, I sat in the corner doing puzzles in a *Holiday* magazine, just as I did at the pediatrician's office. Two hours and about 30 stitches later, he bounced toward the car as if nothing had happened, swinging a hand that resembled a baseball seamed with black rows of thread.

## The Beginning of the End

Before Neil Armstrong walked on the moon, before the surgeon general announced that tobacco caused cancer, before hippies took over San Francisco, my father pitched in the Detroit Tigers system. When his baseball career came to an abrupt end for reasons he never disclosed, he traded his Spalding mitt for a leather attaché case and went to work hitting 20 states a year as a salesman peddling clotheslines.

The rest was history—for as long as I remember he was the father who walked into the kitchen in the morning with circles under his eyes, saying little as we ate our cereal. One snapshot taken in 1968 tells our entire family story. I am standing in the front yard in a snowsuit, waving for his attention. He is frowning and smoking a cigarette as he walks toward his car with a briefcase. That routine defined his life.

There were and still are millions of broken ballplayers just like him. The baseball uniform was replaced with a loud-colored sports jacket with a madras tie; instead of grabbing a baseball mitt, he walked out the door with a briefcase, and that was the man he became.

To outsiders, Dad seemed like a preppy, golly-gee-whiz kind of guy. He was a scratch golfer with true stories about his real-life encounters with the immortals of baseball, which made him different. In smoky bars and country clubs, he took clients back in time, placing them on the diamond at spring training when he struck out Mickey Mantle, who punched his arm in the locker room and harrumphed, *"Scared were you, rookie?"*

In the 1970s and '80s, the stories and the punch lines to his jokes remained the same as his collection of plastic swizzle sticks grew by the hundreds. By the 1990s, cocktail hour got earlier and the liquor got cheaper. Fancy glass bottles of premium liquor were replaced by plastic handles of Aristocrat from the below-the-knee shelf at the local ABC store. From five o'clock onward, a stiff cocktail, a pack of Kents, and a series of rescue mutts who did not pass judgment became his lifelong companions.

Dad was not a violent person; rather, he swallowed up the rage and turned on himself. Sometimes the frustration spilled out in the backyard, where he disappeared for hours for yardwork during weekends. As a kid, I saw him crack tree branches on his bare shins, splitting the skin wide open. Sometimes my sister and I found him spread-eagle and unresponsive near the creekbanks, covered in grass, staring at the sky. Most nights, he did not rouse to the table for dinner. Instead, he ate a carton of fudge ripple ice milk from the basement freezer and dissolved into a world of sports.

For years, he drank from the same plastic Harvest Gold colored tumbler from the 1970s imprinted with a smiley face and the slogan "Have a Happy Day." With the tumbler in his hand, I knew he wanted to forget another unhappy day, dreading the days ahead. I knew he felt like he'd let down a wide circle of people, but I could not figure out why he could not forgive the one person he hurt most of all—himself.

During baseball season, he sprinted into the house after work to change into Bermuda shorts and a golf shirt. I can see him now, in that dark-paneled basement, leaning back in a red plaid recliner from the days of the Lyndon Johnson administration with his feet resting on a battered vinyl hassock. For hours, he chain-smoked and imbibed below ground, taking in games, from side-by-side televisions, rabbit-eared with tin-foiled antennas. With a sharpened No. 2 pencil, he took copious notes on his favorite players on scrap paper, which we find in cushions and drawers to this day.

My father was not a betting man, but he had a photographic

memory for statistics and could have made a fortune with his spot-on predictions. My father never once relied on a computer, and he consistently picked teams that won the World Series.

Mother always claimed that the cocktails and the maudlin moods could be traced back to the season his arm gave out. Because I did not know him in the glory days, it was a loss that I could not fathom.

Before my father foreclosed on his identity, scrapbooks around the house told a bittersweet story about his baseball career that pulsed like a supernova, then collapsed like a dying star.

Dad was the product of the very proper Haverford Boys School on the leafy Main Line of Philadelphia. His star rose at Haverford, where he was president of his class four years in a row, captaining the baseball, football, and basketball teams. Though he could have attended Princeton, he returned to Chapel Hill for college, where that dream ignited at Emerson Field became eerily real.

Dad started out on the football team as an end and a punter, averaging 41 yards a boot. He eventually switched to baseball and became the Tar Heels' first All-American pitcher. What I did not know—evidenced by a crumpled feature story in the trunk—was that my father had been approached with major-league offers his sophomore year. At his parents' request, Dad ignored the calls, promising to stay in school until he graduated in 1957.

Of UNC's seven conference wins, five belonged to my father, who co-captained the team. One of the men watching him closely in the stands was Rick Ferrell, a former major-league catcher turned Detroit Tigers scout from Greensboro, North Carolina, who signed him the week of graduation. He received offers from four other teams, including Cleveland, Pittsburgh, Brooklyn, and the Chicago Cubs, but he settled on Detroit because he felt it was a young organization and building for the future.

In his final interview, he thanked his coach, Walter Rabb, and all of the reporters who were so nice to him at Carolina, saying that he hoped he could live up to their expectations in the future.[2]

---

[2] Jack Horner, "Former Ace Turns Pro," *Durham Herald*, " June 15, 1957.

Dad debuted as a rookie pitcher in June of 1957 with the Durham Bulls, a Class B Tigers farm club, using a big chunk of his $500 signing bonus to buy Mother an engagement ring. The manager of the Durham Bulls, Bobby Mavis, said he liked Raugh. "You know why I like him? He's got it here," pointing to his heart.[3]

My father always claimed that he received a contract with Durham because the team thought that his history as a graduate of UNC might draw in fans. "They didn't care if they won or lost as long as they filled the stands," he said. And he joked about the way players of my generation spent more on one dinner than he made in a year.

The first game he pitched was against the Wilson Tobs. On the night of his debut, he threw 87 pitches with 53 strikes in nine innings, beating them, 2–0, in just an hour and 23 minutes. When he left the Bulls after the season with a 6–4 record to move up to Double-A ball, the press called him "Smiling Raugh."

In 1958, he headed to Lakeland, Florida, for his first season of spring training. "Tigertown" was a virtual kingdom unto itself with about 250 players and 60 managers, scouts, and coaches who lived and breathed, ate and slept baseball. The temperature was in the high 30s under clear blue skies when Dad marched out onto the field, watched closely by a coach from the Pre-Flight School. After Pearl Harbor, Charles Gehringer, nicknamed "The Mechanical Man," was pushing 40. Too long in the tooth to fly, he became a V-5 athletic coach and went through indoctrination training in Chapel Hill in early 1943. For the remainder of the war, he was the head baseball coach at the St. Mary's Pre-Flight campus.

When Gehringer became vice president of the Tigers organization in the 1950s, he was one of the men who razed the training camp on the site of an Air Force fighter base in the northern edge of Lakeland. Several tons of dirt and topsoil were shipped in, and grass was planted. The old control tower stood in the middle of four bright-green diamonds, where coaches and the powers of baseball observed players for ten weeks, making and breaking futures.

---

[3] Jack Horner Sports Corner, *Durham Herald,* June 16, 1957.

That year, my father became what was known as an "iron man," pitching with a wad of chaw in his mouth for Detroit's Southern Association ballclub, the Birmingham Barons. It was in Birmingham where my father roomed with players who would step up to the big leagues, including Joe Grzenda, a coal miner's son who borrowed my father's car for dates. Phil Regan was another Birmingham team-mate who achieved big-league honors.

They started out in a little two-story brick house, where the room-mates regularly entertained neighborhood kids, tossing balls on the lawn. It was a good year, and he earned a key to the city of Birming-ham, a steel town where his father did business.

My father never knew why a reporter took it upon himself to write a story, labeling him as "No Bonus Jim," the rich kid whose steel executive father could buy all of the clubs in the Southern league.[4] Mother told me that he was deeply embarrassed—even scarred by the story written by Zipp Newman of the *Birmingham News* because it had no basis. From that day on, he distanced himself further from his family, stuffing the monogramed Oxfords and neckties in a bag under his bed, as he yearned to fit in as one of the boys on the bus.

## Life on the Road

My parents wed before spring training in 1959, and baseball drove the narrative of their marriage. Mother was just 23 years old and dreamed of attending law school, while my father talked baseball nonstop. She was lukewarm about being a player's wife. While the wives roasted in the sun in the bleachers, carrying on about "havin' babies," she curled up with novels and chain-smoked, wondering how she was going to get through the next few years.

While he traveled with the Barons, having the time of his life, Mother was left behind in Bessemer, Alabama, as racial tensions escalated. Having been raised by an African American housekeeper she loved dearly, she was haunted by the poverty she witnessed as a child. In insufferable heat, she closed the windows and locked herself

---

[4] Zipp Newman, sports editor, *Birmingham News, 1959.*

in an apartment, alone without air conditioning, wishing she could stand up for the people who had suffered for so long. As a player's wife, it was in that furnace of an apartment in Bessemer that she decided to do what every well-heeled Southern girl did for the sake of her family: stay married, keep her mouth shut about civil rights, and put her dreams of attending law school in a box.

A year earlier, the Barons won the Southern Association championship as Dad went 8–3 with an ERA of 3.21. At training camp in Lakeland, he pitched against some greats: Hank Aaron and Joe Torre with the Braves, and Yankees superstar Mickey Mantle. He told his story about the Mick a million times—"The bases were full, there were two outs when Mantle stepped in as a pinch-hitter," he said. "Mantle had a wad of tobacco in his mouth that day and of course he was wearing his number 7 jersey." When the Mick cracked his bat on one of my Dad's fastballs, he tossed it on the ground to grab another. About a minute later, he struck Mantle out—a scene my father lived off for the rest of his life.

In March of 1959, things looked up when my father won the Wish Egan award for the most improved Tigers minor-leaguer. His next stop was West Virginia with the Triple-A Charleston Senators. Then, like his pal Joe Grzenda, he got sent back down to Birmingham, where he tried to work his way back up.

In the spring of 1960, he pitched for the Victoria Rosebuds of the Double-A Texas League.

In Victoria, my father had his best season ever when he was managed by his childhood idol, Mr. Red Sox himself, Johnny Pesky. Mother said she still owns recipe cards handed down from Ruthie Pesky, who was very kind to players' wives, and she never forgot the pink-and-blue stadium. "It looked like a birthday cake . . . who in the hell could ever forget that?" she exclaimed. There was the oil man who owned the team, who landed his helicopter on the diamond to dry the field after a rain, and then there was the weekend at the King Ranch. Mother had grown up on a cotton farm with cowboy boots in the closet and a shotgun under her bed in the western part of North Carolina. As a player's wife, she was viewed as a funny green-eyed blonde with her nose buried in a book, but that weekend, she gained a reputation as a marksman when she beat all of the players and a few ranchers in a skeet-shooting contest.

That season, my father was mixed in with half a dozen pitchers who had played for major-league teams, some of whom would be called back to the bigs. There was Bob Humphreys (1964 World Series with St. Louis), Jim Brady (Detroit, 1956), Chuck Daniel (Detroit, 1957), Jerry Davie (Detroit, 1959), Bill Graham (Detroit, 1966; New York Mets, 1967), Joe Grzenda (five major-league teams between 1961 and 1972), Cuban Manny Montejo (Detroit, 1961), and Jim Proctor (Detroit, 1959).

Sitting in the office in the blue-and-pink ballpark, Johnny Pesky remembered him as a scruffy little kid perched on his knee at the Navy base in a grass-stained uniform, when he sat Dad down and talked to him like he was a cadet. Johnny told him that he had to gut up his courage and work harder than ever if he wanted to make it to the major-leagues. There would be long after-hours training, running up and down stadium steps to improve his legs and his lungs; there would be nights alone, pitching on the mound to strengthen his fastball. When the pain came, his advice was simple: he had to find a way to find his power and push himself through it.

Going back to that Pre-Flight mind-set, where "second place doesn't count" in a life-and-death situation, Johnny helped my father do what those fighter pilots did best—expect failure and find a way to outsmart the pain that was lingering in his arm. He said Johnny would carry on and lose his temper when he made mistakes. Five minutes later, he'd be laughing and patting him on the back, and those tender bursts of confidence were assurances he did not feel at home.

Decades later, my father told me that he never worked harder in his life, running stadium steps and bases alone until he crumpled into a heap from the Texas heat; he threw pitches alone in the dark until his elbow was numb. When the pain came, he prayed, hoping to find his power.

Johnny's Pre-Flight pep talk worked like a charm, and Dad was the team's best pitcher: 11–4, 3.33 ERA.[5]

In Austin that season, a reporter called him the "bellwether of the Victoria pitching staff" when he pitched the Rosebuds out of a four-game losing streak with a seven-hitter that subdued Austin, 5–0. Then, he pitched his third complete game with a win against Monterrey, tying the Rosebuds for second place in the Texas League.

In August 1960, he was awarded minor-league "Player of the Month" honors by Topps chewing gum. That fall, the bubblegum empire gave him a golden Bulova watch, adding his name on the ballot for the National Association of Baseball Writers, who selected the Topps Player of the Year.

That December, my father was one of only four players invited to Panama to play with the Panama League's Azucareros Sugar Kings. My parents lived near the Canal Zone in an apartment above a furniture store. That winter, he played for the Sugar Kings, training with a cadre of major-league players. It was a wild time in a wild place. Instead of "Little Johnny" Roventini in his red bellhop suit, a carnival of performers traipsed onto the field on stilts, throwing packs of Cigarvillos Royal into the stands to the sounds of rolling drums.

But in the wilderness of that season, something had definitely changed. In scrapbook portraits, I could see my father's smile stiffen, and he looked frightened. Perhaps it was the unraveling of his arm; perhaps he felt like he had let Johnny Pesky down; perhaps it was the promise he had made to his parents that he would abandon baseball and go to business school if he did not get an invitation to a big-league team.

Life doles out its surprises and disappointments. Dad was no exception. Later that season, the rest of the pages in the scrapbook went blank, and he joined a population of baseball fans sitting in the stands of life.

In his era, major-leaguers played 154 games a year. It was common for pitchers to throw 200 pitches in a single game—double the amount managers allow them to throw today. Arms were ruined like

---

[5] Bill Nowlin, *Mr. Red Sox,* p. 185.

stripped gears on an overworked Bobcat tractor.[6] Steroids were a thing of the future. Miracle procedures like Tommy John surgery did not exist—not even for the supposed rich boys like No Bonus Jim. Suffering was a badge of honor that bonded players, and my father smiled when he described the old days on the team bus, thundering down back roads with a swollen elbow swimming in a bucket of ice. Someone always had a tin of Atomic Balm for aching muscles, and there were homemade remedies such as the trainer's concoction of Epsom salts and egg whites that did not make a dent in the pain. To reduce swelling, players wrapped their arms in old inner tubes from car tires. Frozen milk cartons were always around the park, another homemade trick that would lead to arthritis. Recalling all of the failed treatments, my father proclaimed Novocain as the salve that masked his tears, allowing him to swagger back to the mound to pitch another game.

Though my father was young and at the top of his game, his body had other ideas. Decades later, he told me that his arm felt as if it were on fire in Panama City, throbbing from his elbow to the bend in his wrist. The diagnosis was medial epicondylitis, otherwise known as pitcher's elbow, the death knell that "drops a diamond star toward the horizon."[7] My father always said that he could tolerate the pain— no problem, but the swelling fouled his range of motion. Wild, career-ruining pitches followed. From a distant memory, one story he told long ago came back to me after he died.

Like his personal shot heard 'round the world, he said the end of his career had a sound. He described a "noise like crunching rocks" coming from his shoulder when he threw his weight into a fastball that was never fast enough for the majors.

In Panama City, my father was pulled into the office one afternoon for a one-on-one meeting with his manager. Five minutes later,

---

[6] Author's father's insights on playing and pitching more games in minors than college and overuse of arm in the days before Tommy John surgery.

[7] Charles Emmett Van Loan (compiled by Trey Strecker), *The Collected Baseball Stories*, "The Good Old Wagon," McFarland and Company, 2004, p. 199.

he was sent back down to the minors yet again, and in his mind, he knew his career was over.

At the end of May, *The Sporting News* reported that the Birmingham team got some bad news on May 18: Jim Raugh notified the club that he had decided to quit the game. He told General Manager Eddie Glennon that he decided to quit because he failed to make the majors within the five-year limit he set for himself.[8]

Mother said he plummeted into a permanent depression soon after he was sent back to Birmingham after failing to stick with Triple-A Syracuse.

She told me that his parents had such high expectations for him. "Oh, they thought your father was going to become president of General Motors," she said, with a laugh. "After he quit baseball, they mailed him the *Wall Street Journal* for years. He never cracked that paper open once," she said, "But we had some high-grade kindling."

In the fall of 1961, Dad was pictured in his small-town newspaper in North Carolina with 15 coworkers from Pittsburgh Plate Glass after the company softball championship. He did not look anguished or broken, but those days were around the corner.

Over the years, reporters with the *Shelby Star* sought his insights during big events like the World Series, where he remembered Tigers stars such as Mickey Lolich, who was a "high school greenhorn" pitcher when he trained at Lakeland. In one story from 1968, the year Lolich won three games in the Tigers' World Series win over the St. Louis Cardinals, my father's last name is misspelled as "Rough." He is pictured behind a metal desk in an Oxford shirt, looking miserable, with a rotary telephone pressed to his ear. The sunburn is gone, his cheeks are white, his blond sun-streaked hair is shaven into a dark military-style buzz. It is as if the life has been sucked out of him. The newspaper feature, squeezed in between ads for hunting boots and car washes, reads like an obituary when he talks about former teammates who left him behind. In the last paragraph, he offers advice to young players, telling them to "run and keep those

---

[8] *The Sporting News*, May 31, 1961, p. 33.

legs in shape. Regardless of what position you play your legs are the most important thing. It is a struggle to make it to pro ball. You have to be dedicated and educated. The competition is unbelievable."[9]

---

[9] *Shelby Daily Star,* "Former Tiger Hurler," October 16, 1968, p. 25.

# Chapter 27

# LONGING FOR THE OLD LEAGUER

To understand how a trade in a back office smelling of sweat and stale cigarettes can break a player's spirit, I reached out to some of the highest men in baseball.

In addition to Dr. Bobby Brown, I had an opportunity to speak with another major-league World War II veteran from Texas.

In 1942, Eddie Robinson was a first baseman for the Cleveland Indians when he joined the Navy, where he was stationed at Norfolk Naval Station. In Norfolk, he played for the Navy team known as the Bluejackets, practicing on McClure Field, the second-oldest brick ballpark in the country behind Chicago's Wrigley Field.

At age 96, Eddie was the last living major-league veteran who had played against the Cloudbuster Nine. As handsome and strong as ever, "The Big Easy," as he was known because of his smile, remembered those wartime games vividly.

In interviews reflecting on WWII baseball, Eddie described the electronic bell mounted on the edge of the dugout at McClure Field. He described the nightly blackouts on the Seaboard base and recalled the packed grandstands at those Norfolk games where service members cranked up that old Navy spirit. Growing up in Paris,

Texas, picking cotton before school to put food on the table, Eddie had certainly seen his share of hard times, and he was honored to play a little baseball for his country during the war.[1] In fact, it was a joy he would not trade for the world.

From his ranch in the Texas Hill Country, he reflected on his journey into the service, when Gene Tunney recruited him to join the Navy on December 15, 1942. Eddie was 22 years old when he reported to Norfolk Naval Station to serve as a chief petty officer with 60 top athletic coaches from around the country. In Norfolk, baseball was serious business, and Eddie knew Coach Gary Bodie would ship him out to the South Pacific if he fouled up, so he did his best to compete and to boost morale. It was no secret that Bodie and McClure aimed to have the best teams in the service. To make sure his players got the message, the quote above the exit door of the baseball locker room read, ORDERS FOR THE DAY: WIN. That edict not only scared the pants off his team, it inspired an extraordinary camaraderie that helped to win the war.[2]

After the service, the rugged and humble Texan became a four-time American League All-Star. He was the first baseman for the Cleveland Indians when the Tribe won the 1948 World Series and played in the 1955 Series for the New York Yankees. When Eddie hung up his spikes, he lived on the road, working as a scout and a front office executive. Through the years, he witnessed integration and the organization of the players' union, the steroid era and the explosion of players' salaries.

After 65 years in baseball, he told me that one of the toughest things he ever did in his life had nothing to do with the war or the scandals that plagued the sport. His hardest days were those face-to-face meetings with players as a farm director, when he was the bearer of bad news. Eddie said that releasing minor-league players during spring training was one of the saddest, most difficult decisions he

---

[1] Brock Vergakis, *The Virginia Pilot,* June 30, 2017, p. 1.

[2] *The Sporting News* "In the Service" column reported how many men were taken and rejected from service every week, March 19, 1942, p. 12.

ever had to make. "If players don't have the talent, and you know they are not going to make the big league . . . you just have to do it," he said. Sitting on a rocking chair on the porch of his ranch, overlooking rolling acreage and a river, Eddie still carries their pain, holding deep respect for every ballplayer who trained their hearts out to achieve a dream.

## Vintage Portraits

Seventy-five years after Bunn Hearn coached baseball at the University of North Carolina, a former Tar Heel second baseman from Asheville, North Carolina, fills his shoes and makes a point to remember the men who came before him. Mike Fox has taken the Diamond Heels to the College World Series six times, establishing a legacy as one of the winningest coaches in the history of college baseball. When we met in his office at Boshamer Baseball Stadium, overlooking an ocean of summer campers, Fox cut to the chase, asking me if my father was good enough to make it to the big leagues. "Did he have 'it'?" he asked, referring to the raw talent, before he invested a minute of his time on a history lesson about Pre-Flight baseball.

That day, I learned that there was a yearning to hold onto the spirit of the Old Leaguer, the naturally talented, unentitled kid who played baseball because he loved the game. Before social media and multimillion-dollar contracts, people admired major-league players who painted houses in the off-season and teams that hit the road on cramped trains and broken-down buses. They also longed for the pure days of baseball when players like Ted Williams could wind through the stands, signing scraps of paper and baseballs; and in Mike's own way, he has kept that spirit alive at the park.

At the beginning of his coaching career at UNC, Fox discovered a storage room at the ballpark, jammed with so many boxes that the door would barely open. Inside mildewed boxes were vintage images of some of the greatest coaches and players in the history of the Heels. Mike and his wife stayed up late into the night, sitting on the floor and spreading out the images they could save. Some of the best

pictures of UNC baseball legends were destroyed by mold and mois-
ture. Digging into his own pocket, Mike salvaged portraits of the
Old Leaguers he deeply respected but never knew. Today, images of
some of the most storied coaches and ballplayers of Carolina's past,
dating back to the late 1800s, are framed on back stairwells and hall-
ways of the stadium. Mike preserved iconic black-and-white and
color portraits of Carolina's 1960 and 1966 teams—the first teams to
make it to the World Series—and very few people know the secret
history about the young couple who mounted those images on the
walls of the stadium. As luck would have it, the camera was pointed
at my father in one of Fox's best-preserved pictures. In his 1957
All-American portrait, my father has a steel toe plate attached to his
cleat. As he winds up for a pitch, there is a glint in his eye, and one
can see that his dream was very much alive.[3]

Wondering if my father had "it," I turned to Don Saine, a right-
handed pitcher from Gastonia and a former teammate at Carolina.
Saine channeled his passion as a high school coach and an athletic
director, helping hundreds if not thousands of players take their
game to a higher level, earning a well-deserved spot in the North
Carolina Hall of Fame. Don told me that players must have three
things to be successful: talent, luck, and a manager who will stand
behind them. Going back to Emerson Field, Don said that my father
worked harder than many of his teammates. He said he definitely
had the fire in his belly and the talent. He said he had a lot of good
people supporting him, such as longtime UNC coach Walter Rabb,
a legend in his own right. But when he got hurt, his luck ran out.[4]

## Shaky Joe—Mr. America

Ted Williams nicknamed another Old Leaguer I interviewed "Mr.
America." One of the players he managed with the Senators was
"Shaky Joe" Grzenda, a skinny side-armed pitcher from Scranton,
Pennsylvania. Joe grew up poor, admitting in an interview that his

---

[3] Interview with Mike Fox, July 18, 2017.
[4] Phone interview with Don Saine, April 26, 2017.

father whipped him so liberally with a belt that his daddy would not just be in jail, "he'd be under it." When we spoke on the telephone, the coal miner's son remembered my father as a "big guy who laughed all of the time." He had a "good mouth on him—the kind of guy who would make a great coach," he said. Joe told me that my father threw an 86- to 89-mile-per-hour fastball, then he took a few seconds to settle on an 87-mile-per-hour speed with certainty. The players lived in a backhouse apartment in Birmingham with two other players, including Phil Regan, who earned a call-up with the Detroit Tigers midway through 1960 and spent 13 seasons in the majors.[5] Their landlord was an older gentleman named Mr. McClusky, a nice man who liked to hang out with the players when he came to collect the rent each month.

Shaky Joe's nickname came from his two-pot-a-day coffee and three-pack-a-day Lucky Strike habits, which gave him the shakes. He was known to leave a cigarette burning on the end of the bench while he pitched, racing back to the dugout to take a few more drags before it burned out. Over his 20-season career, including eight seasons with major-league teams, Joe was sent back to Birmingham five times. When he made his major-league debut in April 1961, his arm ached constantly. Years later, the left-hander pointed to his elbow, telling a reporter the "ache" is where he "learned to pitch" instead of throwing.

When I spoke with Joe one summer evening, he had just returned from a walk near his home out in the country in Covington Township, Pennsylvania. He quit smoking in the early 1990s, when his doctor gave him an ultimatum to choose between cigarettes or his life. On the afternoon he put down his smokes, Joe started walking three and a half miles a day and has never stopped. When Joe signed with the Tigers, there were only 600 major-league players in the country. He told me that to this day he is still amazed by the magnitude of the accomplishment that no one could ever take away from

---

[5] Phil Regan has been associated with baseball for over 60 years and is currently a minor-league pitching instructor for the New York Mets.

him. Each month, he receives five to ten letters from kids seeking autographs. "I sign every one of them, never taking a penny from a kid before I drop the letters in the mail," he said.

Standing 6-foot-3, with crystal-clear blue eyes, Grzenda had a wicked 90-plus-mile-an-hour fastball he called the "whip" and one of the sharpest curves in the Southern League when he joined the Birmingham Barons in 1958. In Birmingham, Grzenda played through the "Checkers Rule," a law preventing blacks from playing sports with whites, even at a game of checkers. He pitched the Barons' first season with an integrated roster and went on to become one of the most popular players in the history of the franchise.

After bouncing between the minors and majors like a pinball, Joe was traded to the Senators in 1970. Williams called him "Mr. America" because Joe insisted on taking his family with him on the road, never leaving them behind. At the time, Ted had a young son, and Joe said, "If Ted was hollering at you, you had to find a way to talk about John Henry. He really loved that little boy."

As the season wore on, Ted knew how worried Joe was about earning his five-year pension. On the day he met that goal, Ted tapped him on the shoulder in the locker room and asked in that booming voice, "How do you feel today?"

That gesture changed everything.

"My attitude, my personality, I was not afraid to lose no more. If it was not for Ted having faith and believing in me, this would never have happened. Ted was the most intelligent man I'd ever been around. He was loud, but he was a real leader," he said.

He also told me that Ted never talked about the war.

"Though he was one of the best, he never talked about being a pilot, either," he said, explaining that evidence of his knowledge about the aerodynamic Theory of Flight was everywhere in his office, where Ted had diagrams of home plate, curveballs, and so forth. As Joe spoke about the aerodynamics of baseball, I recalled that Ted was fascinated by classes taught by Pre-Flight professors who described the how and why of flight—how a plane moves through the air, what to expect when a plane hits the ground. And I realized that it was in classrooms of buildings like Caldwell and Manning Halls where that understanding of pilots being one with the plane was no doubt seared into his mind, and he used those analogies to explain the science of hitting.[6] Joe recalled how Ted described a curveball when it left the pitcher's hand as a wing on one of his jets, describing how a ball moves through the air, how it spins, and why it breaks. Ted's instruction made perfect sense to a boy with a high school education from a Pennsylvania mining town, and Joe never forgot the analogy.

In 1971, Williams relied on Joe with even greater confidence. "It wasn't a winning club, but I got to pitch more," he said. "I could make something more of myself, which I did. I had the opportunity, and I think Ted Williams had a lot to do with it because he respected the older ballplayer."

After spending years on broken-down buses, for the first time in Joe's life, he had some security, and the next year he posted a sparkling 1.92 ERA in 46 relief appearances. With newfound confidence, he enlightened reporters with humor about the unglamorous life of a major-leaguer, telling *The Sporting News,* "I'd like to stay in baseball long enough to buy a bus . . . then set fire to it."

By the end of the 1972 season, which he spent with the St. Louis Cardinals, Joe was 35 years old. Though he loved the game, his body felt like a bag full of nuts and bolts, and he earned $22,000 a year. He was contemplating retirement because, in his words, "It was a matter of making enough money to survive. That was the reason I got out. I couldn't afford to play."[7]

Joe was on the precipice of the big-money era, as the Old Leaguers were being replaced by a generation of new players. He passed on an offer to become a minor-league pitching coach for the Yankees in

---

[6] Comptroller's Papers 1941–1945, Box 6, Pre-Flight correspondence; *Navyator,* May 22, 1943, p. 2, Science and Theory of Flight curriculum and images of cadets in class.

[7] William Gildea, "The Ultimate Closer," *Washington Post,* October 25, 2004, p. D01.

West Haven, Connecticut, because the cost of living was too steep. Having pitched in 219 major-league games, Joe moved his family back home to northeastern Pennsylvania, near Moosic High School, where he got his start. Initially he took a job as a security guard at a vacant building. When an auto battery manufacturer moved into the building, he went to work for the company, earning four dollars an hour. For the next 25 years, Mr. America worked on an assembly line at Gould Battery Company, as he drifted into the fringes of the baseball world. There were moments when he stepped back into the major-league spotlight. When the Washington Nationals brought baseball back to RFK Stadium in 2005, Grzenda returned to hand President George W. Bush the original ball that he would have pitched at the end of the 1971 season. The Spalding American League baseball (from the last game the Senators played, which they forfeited to the Yankees 34 years earlier after the Washington fans rushed the field before he could record the final out) had been in his drawer in a wrinkled manila envelope. Bush used that ball for the ceremonial first pitch: "I handed it to him," he said in an emotional interview with the *New York Times*. "It was like a dream."[8]

Though Ted Williams struggled to hold his own family together, he let Mr. America bring his son, Joe Jr., into the clubhouse at almost every home game. The boy had a small cut-down Senators uniform, and he scampered out on the field with the players before games. Williams even showed junior how to throw a curveball, offering intelligence that was no doubt inspired in those classrooms when he trained to become a pilot.[9]

---

[8] Richard Sandomir, *New York Times*, "Yankees' Last Trip to R.F.K. Ended with Fan Rampage," June 16, 2006, p. D5.

[9] Telephone interview with Joe Grzenda, July 11, 2017.

# Epilogue

## FOREVER A BATBOY

During the war, kids across America listened to Jack Armstrong on the tabletop radio, following the Wheaties' All-American Boy who promoted the habits of Navy flyers and Pre-Flight Training Kits. While most kids collected the wooden baseball pencils Wheaties promoted in 1943 and mailed box tops to win flying lessons and a genuine Piper Cub airplane, my father got to experience the real thing, and nothing was ever as grand.

Jimmy Raugh, one-time mascot and batboy for baseball's greatest stars, was not a total dreamer. Sixty years after he left Chapel Hill, he was inducted into The Haverford School's Athletic Hall of Fame. When he returned to his alma mater to pick up his blanket with a crimson-and-gold H and the obligatory acrylic plaque, Dad stared back at the camera lens from a table filled with old classmates. All night, the ex-athletes were called to the podium to share their stories about how sports primed them for success later in life, while he was harnessed to an oxygen tank strapped to a bag under his chair. The reunion of old-timers seemed like a happy one, but it was my father's stunned, complete lack of expression that made his pain stand out.

At his lowest points, my father claimed that his father never approved of him. My grandfather may have been a stoic, hardened man with high standards, but he took care of his family and served his country in two wars. Perhaps he provided materially what he could not provide emotionally, evidenced by a picture of my father on his 16th birthday, hugging the roof of a brand-new Chevrolet he received as a gift, with the keys in his hand.

There is one story that I do believe, and perhaps it offers a note of redemption that is supposed to conclude every book.

Before my father died, he claimed that when he was at a crossroads, trying to decide if he should stay in baseball, he went to his father for advice. The perennial five-year limit had expired, and they both knew it. Sitting in the living room of the apartment overlooking Michigan Avenue in Chicago where his parents lived in 1961, my grandfather most assuredly had a cigarette in one hand and a drink in another. That evening, he told my father that, in his opinion, perhaps he was "not good enough for the majors—never was, never would be. Maybe it was time to grow up."

And that statement—which went against everything my father heard as a kid on that ragged baseball field in Chapel Hill—absolutely broke his heart.

My father never became president of General Motors or any other conglomerate. For two decades, he drove a dented Carolina-blue Mustang with a souvenir baseball bat in the backseat signed by Mickey Mantle, after he cracked it on one of Dad's pitches at spring training. When race riots ravaged the South, a police officer pulled my father over for speeding and took possession of the bat, claiming that it could be considered a weapon. Today, that bat may be displayed in some stranger's trophy case, where no one will ever realize that it is a symbol of Jimmy's shattered but star-kissed life.

His death at least ended in a bit of a providential note. I was told that nurse Vickie from hospice was the only person who ever properly answered his riddle, *"What are the nine ways a player gets on base?"*

I knew their conversation took them both back to a better place—back to the days when her son first played the game in a park that smelled like fresh-cut grass, back to the days of old wooden bleachers that sent spectators home with splinters, back to Emerson Field when a temporary baseball team took the world's mind off of a world war.

To this day, I cannot begin to answer that brain teaser, but we all agreed that after the riddle was solved, my father was ready to die in peace.

# AFTERWORD

If this environment were to be duplicated in modern times, a Pre-Flight base might see Michael Phelps on the pool deck with Justin Leonard on a driving range and Bode Miller on the field to teach conditioning; Tim Duncan might be stationed on the basketball court with Carl Lewis kicking around Fetzer Field. It would not be a stretch of the imagination to put Tom Brady and Mike Tomlin on the gridiron at Kenan Stadium with a string of All-American players from high schools and colleges wearing the Pre-Flight jersey.

There were countless stories that I was unable to include in this work, and many more that I will discover. One story honored the short life of the base artist in Chapel Hill, who immortalized the Pre-Flight cadet on canvas. Ensign Eugene Aiello grew up in the Flatlands area of Brooklyn. With one year of college under his belt, Gene was a self-taught artist when he went to work in Hollywood as an art director at Paramount's advertising department, where he painted the likes of Lucille Ball, Vivien Leigh, and Douglas Fairbanks, and he had connections to starlets such as Paulette Goddard and Susan Hayward. After drilling all day and ranking in the top ten percent of his class in Chapel Hill, Gene smoked cigarettes as he painted portraits of officers and brought cadets to life with cartoons.[1]

---

[1] *Cloudbuster,* January 1, 1943, pp. 2–6.

In January 1943, Gene put the finishing touches on a mural of a Navy flier in dress blues before he shipped out to another base in Hollywood, Florida. The mural was likely a self-portrait of a dark-haired cadet in a Navy-blue uniform, looking indomitable. As the cadet stepped across a patchy field resembling Emerson's war-torn diamond, airplanes soared in the background. He was flanked by trainees wearing uniforms for football, baseball, track, gunnery, and boxing, symbolizing the sports-for-war training experiment that was turning the tide on the war.[2]

Two weeks before Ted Williams and the trainees from Amherst arrived on campus, Gene was sent out on a routine nighttime aviation training exercise. His plane went down for unknown reasons about 12 miles off the coast of Miami, Florida, on April 24. The instructor and all five crew members died in the accident. After a three-day search-and-rescue effort, Gene's remains were never recovered; only an aviation life jacket with an attached navigator's watch belonging to one of the men was found.[3]

When Gene's family received the telegram, his father was 82 years old. His mother was an invalid.[4] For months, his brother Vincent wrote to and telegraphed the Navy to determine the cause of the wreck, which remained a mystery. Six months after Gene perished, an Italian tailor who had sewn his size 41 forest-green military uniform wrote to the Navy, trying to dispose of the uniform that was never fully paid for or picked up. Seventy-five years after Gene died, it was his self-portrait that immortalizes the Pre-Flight cadet to this day.

When my father talked about Pre-Flight cadets on television we laughed at him, but it turns out he was telling the truth about the personalities who trained at Pre-Flight bases.

Dennis Weaver, who portrayed Deputy Chester Goode in the classic TV western *Gunsmoke* and Sam McCloud, the rangy New Mexico

---

[2] *Cloudbuster,* May 1, 1943, p. 1.

[3] Death certificate for Eugene Victor Louis Aiello, April 24, 1943.

[4] Letter from Frank Aiello to Casualty Branch of the Adjunct General's Office, Munitions Building, Washington, D.C., October 10, 1945.

deputy who galloped through the streets of New York to solve crime in *McCloud,* trained at St. Mary's; and he proved to be quite the athlete, qualifying as a decathlon finalist in the 1948 U.S. Olympic trials.[5] Johnny Carson's sidekick, Ed McMahon, trained to become a fighter pilot on the Georgia Pre-Flight campus. In typical comedic form, McMahon affirmed the priceless value of this program when he said, "I would not go through Pre-Flight School again for a million dollars, but I would not trade the experience for ten million." Another notable St. Mary's cadet was 20-year-old William Clay Ford, son of Edsel Ford and grandson of Henry T. Ford, who was pictured swabbing the deck with a mop and playing soccer.[6]

Kidd Brewer mentioned little about his years in the Pre-Flight public affairs office, focusing instead on his role as an aide to several senators from North Carolina and his run for lieutenant governor in 1956. The charismatic dealmaker made headlines again in 1962 when he attempted suicide in a barn behind his house. At age 54, Kidd stuffed himself with pills and slashed his wrists with razors when he was charged with bid rigging and tax evasion. When sentenced to 18 months in jail, Kidd told the newspaper he was going to throw one of the biggest "going-in" galas Raleigh had ever seen at his mansion on Kidd's Hill. Never shy about his intentions, Kidd got out of jail four months later. When media asked the natural-born spin master about his future plans, he replied, "I'm going to peddle influence," which is what he did at Pre-Flight to boost morale.

Surprisingly few people knew much about Brewer, or they shied away from talking about him. I did gain an interesting insight on him from one of the most highly regarded legal figures in North Carolina. The Honorable Burley B. Mitchell is a former chief justice for the state supreme court. He is also a U.S. Navy veteran and is widely known as a fair man who sees the value in people giving back.

---

[5] *Kokomo Tribune,* June 26, 1948, p. 7; *Miami Daily News-Record*, Miami, Oklahoma, April 8, 1948, p. 5.

[6] Associated Press, April 23, 1945.

Burley grew up in Raleigh and was a young boy when the war broke out. He recalled that the little kids always had a sense of insecurity about growing up in the war and remembered sitting on a man's shoulders and watching a ship burn after it had been bombed by a German sub about ten miles off the coast of Carolina Beach. Burley used to hang out at Hayes Barton Firehouse after supper, listening to World War II veterans talking after they came home from the war. "They were proud, quiet men," he said over the telephone. "There was no air conditioning or televisions at the station, but they had each other." He agreed that people long for patriots; they yearn for the way we were, holding nostalgia for the generation of veterans who are fading away by the day.

Burley remembered Kidd at church when he was older, looking beaten down and sad. His wife had died, and he lost his son, Kidd Jr., a master diver who inherited his fair share of his father's exhibitionism and who starred in James Cameron's film, *The Abyss*.

Kidd's daughter, Linney, who struggled with her own issues, watched her family fall from the bulwarks of the community to the depths. They were indeed a storied family with theatrical blood, as Brewer's second wife was a Linney, related to playwright Romulus Linney and his daughter, actress Laura Linney.

Burley said, "I felt badly for him and the way people were so cool to him." He described Kidd as a Greek tragedy kind of guy with a flaw of perhaps going to the trough too many times. "But he was a kind and genuine man who cared about people."

We laughed about what Kidd would have done if Twitter was around in his day. But because of his bold, devil-may-care style and liberal use of cameras, the sporty Pre-Flight story is artfully preserved.[7]

When I began to search for Kidd Brewer's descendants, I located a nephew with the same name of Benjamin Kidd Brewer who lives in suburb of Salt Lake City, Utah. I was surprised by how little he knew about his uncle's service in the Navy. The only thing he asked me to

---

[7] Telephone conversation with Burley B. Mitchell, July 23, 2017.

do was defend his namesake's good name through this work. As I wrote this book, I often felt Kidd's presence, and his famous campaign slogan, "You'll be glad you did," stayed with me, guiding me to reach out to complete strangers and the most highly respected baseball people with obsessive abandon to return to that glorious season of 1943.

As I worked my way through Pre-Flight baseball, I was struck by the story of a scientist and a Red Sox fan who may very well have established the basis for Ted's formula for hitting, which he passed down to millions of players.

Like Ted Williams, Harold Irving "Doc" Ewen was a thinker and doer. Doc and his wife, Mary Ann, had eight children, and they were the kind of close-knit family that Ted Williams admired. Doc pursued undergraduate studies in mathematics and astronomy at Amherst College, working nights and weekends to tackle graduate studies at Harvard University in physics. While at Harvard, Doc detected interstellar hydrogen (the 21-centimeter line), thereby launching the field of radio astronomy. Working in the Cyclotron Lab at Harvard, his efforts led to the development of the first external beam, an achievement that was ultimately adapted for the treatment of brain tumors.

Doc served as second lieutenant in the Navy during World War II. He taught celestial navigation for a pilot training program at Amherst College where Ted was one of his most curious students. Doc later served as co-director of the Harvard Radio Astronomy Program and as CEO of Ewen Knight and Ewen Dae Corporations. But at his core the brilliant and approachable Doc Ewen was just a kid who loved baseball, and his passion for the game inspired him to build a ballfield in the backyard, where he played ball with his children.

Long after the war, a tall and lanky guy would show up at the front desk of the Lyman Lab to say hello to his former professor from Amherst.[8]

I cannot speak for Ted Williams, but I believe that Doc possessed the traits that he admired most—brains, a humble spirit, and strong

---

[8] Memories by Doc Ewen, 2003. http://www.nrao.edu/archives/Ewen/ewen.

family values. Some might say they were more evolved than the average man, but they related to all sorts of people, and Doc remained active until his death on October 8, 2015, at the age of 93.[9]

One of my best discoveries is saved for last. When I located Sarah Pletts, the daughter of Ted's roommate at Everett Dormitory in Chapel Hill, she expressed an insight about these old friends. "They were the first to tell you that they were 'ordinary guys,'" she said, but they were doers, not men who watched life from the stands. The two reminded her of bucks, circling, and charging at one another. She remembers them laughing in a boat, and carousing on the ballfield; she can still see Ted, tying flies for hours in the basement while parties were going on upstairs, or sitting behind the wheel of a shiny black Cadillac, going somewhere, to do something productive.

"He never assumed star status," she said. "Ted got up every day, thinking, *it's a new day*, and I've got to pay attention."

---

[9] Harold Irving "Doc" Ewen obituary, *Boston Globe*, October 22, 2015.

# Appendix

## MAJOR-LEAGUE PLAYERS WHO TRAINED AT CHAPEL HILL DURING WORLD WAR II

**Lt. Pete "Jabby" Appleton, Cincinnati Reds, Cleveland Indians, Boston Red Sox, New York Yankees, Washington Senators, Chicago White Sox, St. Louis Browns—** Pete had a 14-year major-league career starting in 1926 with the Cincinnati Reds. He pitched his final major-league game with the Washington Senators as a 41-year-old in September 1945. After playing  a few more seasons of minor-league ball, Appleton played in his last professional baseball game in 1951 with the Erie Sailors in the Middle Atlantic League. He spent more than 20 years as a scout and manager in the minors, before serving as a full-time scout and pitching instructor for the Washington Senators and Minnesota Twins. By the time of his death on January 18, 1974, in Trenton, New Jersey, Appleton had spent 47 years associated with professional baseball.

He shipped into Pre-Flight in early December 1942 for indoctrination training and was designated as assistant baseball coach on March 17, 1943. He reported to to Quonset Naval Air Station, Rhode Island, in June 1943, where he coached and pitched for the baseball team. He likely lived at the Carolina Inn or Carr Dormitory in Chapel Hill.

**Lt. Henry Victor "Vic" Bradford, New York Giants**—A native of Tennessee, Vic worked as a laborer in steel mills, earning accolades for his Superman physique. His most noteworthy athletic achievements were rooted on the football field as a quarterback for the University of Alabama, where he appeared in the 1938 Rose Bowl. In 1943, he appeared in six games as an outfielder and pinch-runner for the New York Giants. In June of that year, he participated in the 11th V-5 officer training course in Chapel Hill, completed training, and detached afterward to Iowa City. He died in Paris, Kentucky, on June 10, 1994, at age 79. Vic likely lived at Carr Dormitory in Chapel Hill.

**Cadet Joe Coleman, Philadelphia Athletics, Baltimore Orioles, Detroit Tigers**—Following his war years, Joe returned to the Philadelphia Athletics in 1946, where he played for several more years before moving on to the Baltimore Orioles and ending his career in 1955 with the Detroit Tigers. In 1948, Coleman was named to the American League All-Star Team. His son, Joe Coleman, pitched for 15 seasons; and his grandson, Casey Coleman, reached the majors in 2010. Coleman died in Fort Myers, Florida, at the age of 74 on April 9, 1997. He shipped into Pre-Flight on May 6, 1943, and left on July 24, 1943. He was assigned to the 25th Battalion, Company B-2, and lived in Room 218 in Everett Dormitory in Chapel Hill.

**Lt. Allen "Dusty" Cooke, New York Yankees, Boston Red Sox, Cincinnati Reds**—After his Pre-Flight training, Cooke was shipped to the Pacific and fought in Okinawa. After the war, he became the athletic trainer for the Philadelphia Phillies. Two years later, in 1948, he joined the team's coaching staff, where he was a mainstay for several years, including service on the 1950  "Whiz Kids" team that won the National League pennant. In July of 1948, he was the Phillies' interim manager, where he posted a 6–6 record before handing over the reins to Eddie Sawyer. Cooke died on November 21, 1987, in Raleigh, North Carolina, at age 80. He shipped into Pre-Flight by March 1943 with the 11th Battalion training class and transferred to San Bruno, California, the week of August 12, 1944. One of the longest onsite residents of Pre-Flight, he likely lived at Carr Dormitory in Chapel Hill.

**Lt. Harry Craft, Cincinnati Reds**—Craft's best year as a major-league ballplayer came in 1938, his rookie season. In June of that season, he caught the ninth-inning pop fly for the final out of the historic game that gave Johnny Vander Meer his second consecutive no-hitter, a feat that hasn't been equaled to this day. After the war, Craft had a long career as a manager, first in the minors, where he managed a young Mickey Mantle in 1949. He would later manage Roger Maris in 1958–59 with the Kansas City Athletics and was the first manager for the Houston Colt .45s (now Astros) in 1962. Craft later served as a scout for several major-league teams before retiring in 1991. He died on August 3, 1995, in Conroe, Texas, at age 80. Harry shipped into Pre-Flight in June 1943 and shipped out to the Del Monte Pre-Flight base on August 9, 1943. He likely lived at Carr Dormitory in Chapel Hill.

**Lt. Charles Gehringer, Detroit Tigers**—Known as "The Mechanical Man" because of his endurance and consistently strong hitting and fielding, Gehringer played his entire 19-year big-league career with the Detroit Tigers from 1924 to 1942. A six-time All-Star, he batted above .300 in 13 full seasons, had more than 200 hits seven times, drove in more than 100 runs seven times, and won the 1937 American League MVP and batting title. He was elected to the

Hall of Fame by the Baseball Writers Association of America in 1949. After the war, Gehringer considered a comeback but decided to pursue a career in business instead, and he served as the Tigers' general manager and in the team's front office through the mid-1950s. He passed away on January 21, 1993, in Bloomfield Hills, Michigan, at age 89. He shipped into Pre-Flight in February 1942 for indoctrination training, leaving in the spring to serve as the head baseball coach at St. Mary's. He likely lived in Carr Dormitory or the Carolina Inn while he trained in Chapel Hill.

**Lt. Charles Gelbert, St. Louis Cardinals, Cincinnati Reds, Detroit Tigers, Washington Senators, Boston Red Sox**—Former infielder for the St. Louis Cardinals between 1929 and 1936, playing in back-to-back World Series (winning in 1931). Gelbert also played for the Reds, the Detroit Tigers, the Washington Senators, and the Boston Red Sox primarily as a shortstop. Gelbert was featured in *Ripley's*

*Believe It or Not!* in 1941, after he played 239 major-league games after he lost part of his left leg to a shotgun blast during an off-season hunting trip. Ten years after the accident, he reported to Chapel Hill on August 27, 1942, for indoctrination training, finishing his course on September 26. He later detached and was ultimately promoted to lieutenant commander at Norman Naval Air Station in Oklahoma, where he coached a baseball team. He died of a heart attack in Scranton, Pennsylvania, 13 days before his 61st birthday on January 13, 1967. He likely lived at Carr Dormitory in Chapel Hill.

**Lt. Joe Gonzales, Boston Red Sox**—Gonzales pitched briefly in the majors in 1937 and appeared as a pitcher and outfielder for a total of 11 minor-league teams, making his last playing appearances while managing the Porterville (California) Packers in the Sunset League in 1950. After retiring from baseball, Gonzales was a field judge in the National

Football League for 21 seasons and officiated in Super Bowl III. He also served as a teacher and baseball coach at Westchester High

School and as baseball coach at Loyola University. Gonzales died in Torrance, California, at age 81 on November 16, 1996. He shipped into Pre-Flight in March 1943, with the ninth indoctrination class, playing in the first games of the season, shipping off base to St. Mary's in April. He likely lived at Carr Dormitory in Chapel Hill.

**Cadet Lewis "Buddy" Gremp, Boston Braves**—Gremp played infield for several years in the minors before earning a September call-up by the Boston Braves in 1940, where he would remain as a backup first baseman. He played 72 games for the Braves before attending naval training at Amherst College. In May 1943, he and Johnny Sain, Johnny Pesky, Ted Williams, and Joe Coleman were sent to Chapel Hill, North Carolina. Like Williams, Gremp entered Chapel Hill with a severe knee injury. As one of the most popular cadets at the school, Buddy was elected as commander of the 25th Battalion, taking leave for four months to recover from knee surgery. He reentered Pre-Flight with the 39th Battalion in December. His next stations were Whiting Field at Pensacola NATB in 1944 and USNAAS Saufley Field, Florida, in 1945, where he played baseball with service teams. Gremp returned to the Braves organization in 1946 and was assigned to Hartford of the Eastern League, where the 26-year-old batted .281, his last season in organized baseball. He passed away on January 30, 1995, at the age of 75 in Manteca, California. He shipped into Pre-Flight on May 6, 1943, and was assigned to Company A-2. He lived in Room 207, Everett Dormitory in Chapel Hill.

Courtesy of the Boston Public Library, Leslie Jones Collection.

**Lt. John Aloysius "Buddy" Hassett, Yankees, Brooklyn Dodgers, Boston Braves. New York Yankees**–After several years in the minor leagues, Hassett broke into the major-leagues as a first baseman and outfielder for the Brooklyn Dodgers in 1936. He also played for the Boston Braves (1938–41) before joining the New York Yankees in 1942. In 1943, he served as a player-manager for the Cloudbusters team before being assigned as athletic director aboard the new aircraft carrier USS *Bennington*, bound for

the Pacific theater. After the war, Hassett played minor-league ball for a few years and also managed the Yankees' farm team in Newark, New Jersey. He died on August 23, 1997, shortly before his 86th birthday, in Westwood, New Jersey. He shipped into Pre-Flight on December 29, 1942, for indoctrination training, shipping out in the spring of 1944. He lived at 1-C Graham Court Apartments in Chapel Hill.

**Lt. Ed Moriarty, Boston Braves/ Bees**—A second baseman, Moriarty played a total of 14 major-league games in 1935–36. Born in Holyoke, Massachusetts, the Irish Catholic from Holy Cross contemplated studying for the priesthood in 1935 before opting for baseball. Moriarty had a 44 year career as an educator in the Holyoke, Massachusetts, public schools as a teacher,

Courtesy of the Boston Public Library, Leslie Jones Collection.

department head, principal, and, finally, superintendent of schools. He died at age 78 on September 29, 1991, in Holyoke, Massachusetts. Moriarty shipped into Pre-Flight on March 25, 1943, and likely departed in the summer of 1943, assuming a position as head baseball and soccer coach for the Norman naval base in Oklahoma in 1944. He lived at 205 North Boundary Street in Chapel Hill.

**Lt. Al Niemiec, Boston Red Sox, Philadelphia Athletics**—Niemiec had brief stints in the majors during the 1934 and 1936 seasons for the Boston Red Sox and Philadelphia Athletics after a long and noteworthy career as a minor-league infielder. A native of Meriden, Connecticut, he will forever be linked to two experiences that distinguished his career in baseball: in 1937, he was traded for the Splendid Splinter himself, Ted Williams; and, following his military service, he successfully fought for  returning veterans to be rehired as ballplayers. In 1942, Niemiec was assigned to the Navy's Pre-Flight training program at St. Mary's College in Moraga, California, where he played third base under Charlie Gehringer. After his discharge in 1946, he was hired as the general manager of the Great Falls, Montana, team in the Pioneer League, a farm club of the Seattle Rainiers, the team he had sued for violating the spirt of the GI Bill. Niemiec eventually became a golf pro before retiring in the 1970s. He died in Kirkland, Washington, on October 29, 1995, at the age of 84. He likely shipped into Pre-Flight in the fall of 1942 for indoctrination training and transferred to St. Mary's by May 1943, where he coached swimming and played third base for the Air Devils. He likely lived in Carr Dormitory in Chapel Hill.

**Cadet Johnny Pesky, Boston Red Sox**—"Mr. Red Sox" began his 60-plus year major-league career with a bang, hitting .331 for the team with which he would always be associated. He is a charter member of

the team's Hall of Fame. To this
day, the right-field foul pole at Fenway Park, named the "Pesky Pole,"
honors the singles-hitting infielder,
who hit only 17 round-trippers in
his 4,745 at-bats in the majors. He
batted .331 and led the league in
hits as a rookie in 1942. After his
three years in the service, Pesky
picked up where he left off, again
leading the American League in

hits, batting .335, finishing fourth in MVP voting, and making his
only All-Star team. He was traded to the Detroit Tigers in 1952 and
ended his major-league career with the Washington Senators in
1954. Pesky went on to manage the Red Sox from 1963 to 1964 before
spending several years in the Pittsburgh Pirates organization. He
would return to the Red Sox as a coach and was a familiar sight in
the team's dugout and in stands, joyfully signing autographs, for the
rest of his life. Pesky died on August 13, 2012, at age 93, in Danvers,
Massachusetts. He shipped into Pre-Flight on May 6, 1943, and left
on August 9, 1943, shipping into Bunker Hill Naval Air Station in
Peru, Indiana, with Ted Williams. He lived in Room 206 in Everett
Dormitory in Chapel Hill.

**Ensign Antone James "Andy" Pil-
ney, Boston Bees**—Pilney began
his professional baseball career in
1936 as an outfielder. While he
spent most of the season with the
minor-league Syracuse Chiefs, he
played three games with the Boston Bees in June, appearing twice
as a pinch-hitter and once as a
pinch-runner, but did not play the
field. He continued to play in the

minors until 1939. Pilney played football as a halfback at Notre Dame. In 1935, he led the Irish to a come-from-behind win against top-ranked Ohio State in a contest considered to be an early "Game of the Century." Pilney was selected by the Detroit Lions in the third round (26th overall pick) of the 1936 NFL Draft. He served as the head football coach at Tulane University from 1954 to 1961, compiling a record of 25–49–6. Pilney died on September 15, 1996, at age 83 in Kenner, Louisiana. Pilney shipped into Pre-Flight in the summer of 1943, where he coached and played on the baseball team. Pilney likely lived in Carr Dormitory in Chapel Hill.

**Lt. Alex Sabo, Washington Senators**—A native of New Brunswick, New Jersey, Sabo played a total of five major-league games as a catcher for the Washington Senators, in 1936 and 1937. He played college baseball and football at Fordham University in New York City. He was later an assistant football coach at Rutgers University. Sabo died in Tuckerton, New Jersey, on January 3, 2001, at the age of 90. Lieutenant D-V (S) Sabo shipped into Pre-Flight on July 21,1942 and transferred to the St. Mary's base, where he served as a coach for the baseball team until 1946. During his stint in Chapel Hill, he lived at 407 East Rosemary Street.

**Cadet Johnny Sain, Boston Braves, New York Yankees, Kansas City Athletics**—A right-handed hurler forever linked with lefty Warren Spahn as half of one of baseball's immortal pitching duos, Sain pitched for 11 years, winning 139 games while losing 116, with a career-earned run average of 3.49. Though he later pitched in relief for the New York Yankees, it was during his run with the National League's Boston Braves teams from 1946 to 1951 that Sain gained his fame. He was the runner-up for the National League's Most Valuable

Player Award in the Braves' pen-
nant-winning season of 1948 after
leading the National League in
wins, complete games, and
innings pitched. He later became
well known as one of the top
pitching coaches in the majors.
Sain also had the distinction of
being the last pitcher to face Babe
Ruth, in July of 1943 during an
exhibition game, as well as the

first major-leaguer to throw a pitch against Jackie Robinson in 1947.
Sain died at age 89 in Downers Grove, Illinois, on November 7, 2006.
He shipped into Pre-Flight on May 6, 1943, and departed in August.
Sain was amongst the Cloudbusters' most skilled pilots and best stu-
dents, earning high marks for intelligence, loyalty, and cooperation
at advanced training at Corpus Christi Naval Air Training Center in
1944. He remained in the Naval Reserves until 1951. Sain lived in
Room 301 in Everett Dormitory in Chapel Hill.

**Lt. Ray Scarborough, Washington
Senators, Chicago White Sox, Boston Red Sox, New York Yankees,
Detroit Tigers**—A native of Mount
Gilead, North Carolina, he had a
ten-year major-league career. After
spending two years in the U.S.
Navy, he developed into a reliable
starting pitcher with a sizzling fastball. His most productive season

came in 1948, when he had a 15–8 mark and recorded a 2.82 earned
run average. The next season, Scarborough achieved his biggest
claim to fame, when, on September 28, 1949, he ended Ted Williams's streak of most consecutive games reaching base safely at 84
games. Scarborough often received attention from the press in New

York and Boston for his off-season work as a pickle salesman for the Mt. Olive Pickle Company in North Carolina, where he became known as the "pickle peddler." After his playing days, Scarborough returned to the Tar Heel state to open an oil and supply company. He later scouted for the Baltimore Orioles, California Angels, and Milwaukee Brewers organizations and also helped establish a baseball program at Mount Olive College. Scarborough died in Mount Olive, North Carolina, in 1982 at the age of 64. He shipped into Pre-Flight in August 1943, transferring to St. Mary's Pre-Flight, where he played on the baseball team. He likely lived at Carr Dormitory in Chapel Hill.

**Lt. Hal Schumacher, New York Giants**—"Prince Hal" Schumacher was the right-handed complement to the New York Giants' star lefty Carl Hubbell during the 1930s. His career record of 158–121 included a stretch of three strong seasons from 1933 to 1935 when he went 19–12, 23–10, and 19–9. He was selected for the 1933 and 1935 All-Star

Games and pitched in the 1933, 1936, and 1937 World Series. In the fifth game of the 1936 Series, he beat the New York Yankees in a ten-inning complete game, 5–4, with ten strikeouts,. Schumacher was a good-hitting pitcher, hitting 15 home runs lifetime, including six in 1934. He served in the U.S. Navy from 1942 to 1945 before returning to baseball briefly in 1946. He died in 1993 at age 82. He completed Pre-Flight indoctrination training in Chapel Hill on February 6, 1943, detaching to Memphis Training Station. He likely lived at Carr Dormitory in Chapel Hill.

**Lt. Fred Sington, Washington Senators, Brooklyn Dodgers**—Sington was a prominent tackle for Wallace Wade's Alabama Crimson Tide football teams, becoming an All-American the year Alabama won the

national championship in 1930. He
would also play major-league baseball as an outfielder with the Washington Senators (1934–37) and
Brooklyn Dodgers (1938–39). Sington was an accomplished saxophon-
ist and Rudy Vallée wrote a song
about Sington titled "Football Fred-
die" that would go on to become a
nationwide hit. Sington died on
August 20, 1998, at age 88 in Bir-

mingham, Alabama. Fred shipped in with the 12th Battalion at Chapel
Hill Pre-Flight from Decatur, Georgia, in late July 1943 to March 1944,
detaching to CAA WTS at Central Michigan College. Sington's
address in Chapel Hill is unknown.

**Lt. Ray Stoviak, Philadelphia Phil-**
**lies**—In 1938, Stoviak played ten
games as an outfielder for the Philadelphia Phillies, his one and only
season in major-league baseball.
He graduated from Villanova College (now Villanova University) in
1938, where he quarterbacked the
Wildcats for three years and helped
compile a record of 22–4–2. During
World War II, Stoviak was a first

lieutenant in the Navy stationed at Chapel Hill, North Carolina, and
Pensacola, Florida, where he coached baseball with Bob Kennedy
and Ted Williams. After his service, he was a math teacher and foot-
ball coach at Meriden High School in Connecticut and later served
as assistant football coach at Yale University. Stoviak died in Nicoya,
Costa Rica, on February 23, 1998, at age 82. Stoviak shipped into
Pre-Flight on February 16, 1943, and lived at 4 Oakwood Drive in
Chapel Hill.

**Lt. Robert Fulton "Ace" Williams, Boston Bees/Braves**—Ace was 23 years old when he broke into the big leagues on July 15, 1940, as a pitcher with the Boston Bees before the team's name was changed back to the Braves. At Pre-Flight School, he served under Lieutenant Gerald Ford as an assistant battalion officer in the 17th Battalion. After his military service, Williams got one  last shot in the big leagues, giving up a hit and a walk to the only batters he faced in his last appearance. Williams died on September 16, 1999, in Fort Myers, Florida, at age 82. He shipped into Pre-Flight on October 17, 1942, and transferred to Naval Flight Preparatory School in Hamilton, New York, the week of March 11, 1944. He lived at 308 McCauley Street in Chapel Hill.

**Cadet Ted Williams, Boston Red Sox**—Theodore Samuel Williams didn't aspire to much—just to be recognized as "the greatest hitter that ever lived." In the eyes of many, the Marine earned that accolade, though he ranked fellow Hall of Famers Babe Ruth, Lou Gehrig, Jimmie Foxx, Rogers Hornsby, and Joe DiMaggio as the top five hitters of all time. (He chose not to include himself in his rankings.) Williams  played his entire career with the Red Sox, from 1939 to 1960, a span interrupted by two stints in the military, during World War II and the Korean War. Over his illustrious career, which included two American League MVP awards, six batting titles, and two Triple Crowns, he also earned his share of nicknames—"The Splendid

Splinter," "The Kid," and "Teddy Ballgame," to name a few. He was inducted into the Hall of Fame in 1966 in his first year of eligibility. After his playing days were over, the San Diego native went on to manage the Washington Senators/Texas Rangers before retiring to pursue his other love: fishing. He died on July 5, 2002, in Inverness, Florida, at the age of 83. He shipped into Pre-Flight on May 6, 1943, and left on August 9, 1943, transferring to Bunker Hill Naval Air Station in Peru, Indiana, with Johnny Pesky. He lived in Room 315 in Everett Dormitory in Chapel Hill.

## Cloudbuster Baseball Coaches at Pre-Flight

**Coach Lt. George Donald Kepler—** Pre-Flight baseball coach in that storied season of 1943. Kepler played nine seasons of minor-league baseball. He returned to Pine Grove Mills, Pennsylvania, after the war to became a farmer, refining his survival skills and running Kepler Sporting Goods. He taught health and physical education at Pennsylvania State University from 1960 to 1975,

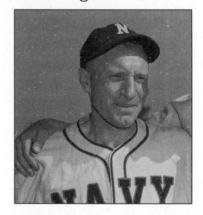

developing the first university-level survival course. Kepler also trained the nation's first class of Peace Corps volunteers in the 1960s and 1970s in his backyard camp at Stone Valley. Kepler never strayed far from baseball, serving as Penn State's freshman baseball coach and assistant varsity coach for many years. In addition to co-authoring *How to Survive on Land and Sea*, he founded a production company with videos offering instruction on outdoor survival. After he retired, Kepler returned to his roots as a kid with the Civil War veterans, bottling free three-ounce containers of his "Old-Timers First Aid Kit" bear grease to anyone who requested the treatment with a letter, telling locals, "the letters are worth more than the money I could charge." Kepler made baseball history as the first man to pitch a night game on a lighted baseball diamond in July 1930 in Indianapolis and the last man to manage against Babe Ruth. While playing minor-league baseball in Wilson, North Carolina, in 1938, he married Betsy Heyward, a former cheerleader from the University of North Carolina at Greensboro. The beloved mentor, coach, and survivalist died of natural causes at his home on the ridge of Tussey Mountain on May 31, 1988, at age 79. He lived at 218 Vance Street in Chapel Hill.

**Coach Lt. William Glenn Killinger**—Head coach of the 1942 and 1944 Cloudbusters baseball team and head of the football training course, Killinger was an American football, basketball, and baseball player, coach, and college athletics administrator. He lettered in three sports at Pennsylvania State University, where he was an All-American in football in 1921. After trying out for the Yankees, he had a successful run as a minor-league baseball player from 1922 until 1932. During that time, he played for the Jersey City Skeeters (1922), Atlanta Crackers (1923), Harrisburg Senators (1924, 1927–1928), Shamokin Indians (1926), and Williamsport Grays (1929–1932). He also served as a minor-league manager.

A multi-sport phenom, Killinger also played in the National Football League for the Canton Bulldogs and the New York Giants, as well as for the Philadelphia Quakers of the first American Football League in 1926. Killinger served as the head football coach at Dickinson College in 1922, Rensselaer Polytechnic Institute (1927–1931), Moravian College in 1933, and West Chester University of Pennsylvania (1934–1941, 1945–1959), compiling a career college football record of 176–72–16. He was inducted into the College Football Hall of Fame as a player in 1971.

As the Cloudbuster Eleven football coach, Killinger's team upset the heavily favored Naval Academy in 1944, going on to rank among the best grid teams in the country. Under Killinger's leadership, the 1944 Cloudbusters baseball team captured the Ration-League title for the first and only time. Killinger's son, Will Jr., was a Cloudbusters batboy who grew up to play baseball for a St. Louis Cardinals minor-league team. Killinger left Chapel Hill and detached for duty at a naval air station in Florida in February 1945. He was replaced by Lieutenant Bear Bryant, who took command of the Cloudbusters football program until the end of the war. Killinger died on July 25, 1988, at age 89 in Stanton, Delaware. It is not known where Killinger lived in Chapel Hill.

**Coach Lt. Edward Wesley "Wes" Schulmerich**—Born to German immigrants in Hillsboro, Oregon, on August 21, 1901, Schulmerich earned the nickname of "Iron-horse" on the football field, playing fullback on offense, linebacker on defense, and on special teams as the placekicker. On the track team, he ran the 100-yard dash at a clip of 10.5 seconds. Schulmerich  graduated with a bachelor's degree in business in 1927 from Oregon State, making his major-league debut with the Boston Braves in 1931. He was the first person from Oregon State University to play in the major-leagues. In 1933, he batted .247 in 29 games before he was traded to the Philadelphia Phillies, where he hit .334 in 97 games. He split 1934 between the Phillies and Cincinnati Reds, hitting .261 in 74 games. After leaving baseball, he worked for Shell Oil until joining the U.S. Navy during World War II. He began his Pre-Flight training career at Iowa Station, transferring to the Chapel Hill base in November 1944. He was named head coach of the Cloudbusters

Pre-Flight baseball team in 1945. He lived at 411 McCauley Street in Chapel Hill.

Schulmerich was inducted into the inaugural class of the Oregon Sports Hall of Fame in 1980, followed in 1991 by induction into Oregon State University's Sports Hall of Fame. He died in Corvallis, Oregon, on June 26, 1985, at the age of 83 and was buried in his hometown of Hillsboro at the Valley Memorial Mausoleum.

**Note sources for addresses:**
James E. Wadsworth Papers, 1942–1976 (University Archives, Collection Number 05075, Box 1: Folder 3 [1943]), Chapel Hill telephone directory (1942–1944 issues), and word of mouth from memory based on family stories and cadet interviews.

V-5 Indoctrination Reporting and Departure, Detachment of Stationed Officers: *The Cloudbuster* (U.S. Navy Pre-Flight School, published in Chapel Hill 1942–1945. In the North Carolina Collection, Call Number: FFC378 UXC1).

Cadet addresses, reporting and departure dates: United States Navy Pre-Flight School, research materials (compiled and created by William L. Pendergraph, published 2004. In the North Carolina Collection, Call Number: FFVC378 UZu).

Additional information on players provided by Gary Bedingfield (Baseball in Wartime) and the Society for American Baseball Research (SABR).

# ACKNOWLEDGMENTS

Early on, my agent, Jim Hornfischer, told me that a naval historian could easily pen a history of the V-5 program. A baseball scribe could write a respectable book about this team, but it was my father's story, about a fragile man broken by baseball, that humanized this account. As I journeyed into baseball's past, my father's story moved grown men to tears for different reasons: injuries that derailed careers and memories of players who stole their hearts, like Ted Williams and his monstrous home runs. People remember the factory workers and shipbuilders cheering on the Cloudbusters from wooden stands, and they long for the days when families gathered around tabletop radios, listening to ballgames. Most of all, people yearn for the major-league players with spot-on nicknames who painted houses in the off-season—those guys in baggy grass-stained uniforms who fought in a war to preserve the traditions we enjoy today—especially America's game of baseball.

Scores of people and institutions rallied to help me tell this story about an extraordinary, generation-shaping training school for pilots. I would like to thank my agent, a naval historian, author, and lifelong Red Sox fan, for making it possible to share this narrative with the world. My editor, Ken Samelson, a former editor of *The Baseball Encyclopedia*, not only helped me reconstruct the Cloudbusters' season of 1943, he encouraged me to shine a light on Ted Williams during this little-explored period of his life—a decision that proved to be revelatory.

Ted Williams's daughter, Claudia Williams, encouraged me in her father's commanding voice to "think big" and to be bold with my words; David and Alison Pesky shared private family scrapbooks featuring rare photographs of Johnny and the Cloudbusters as fledgling pilots before they shipped into Chapel Hill. The Kepler children, Richard, Rob, Vicky and Don Jr., shared private soulful stories to honor the legacy of their father, an amazing human being who passed on the ancient wisdom of Native Americans and Civil War veterans to thousands of pilots. Members of the Craighead wilderness dynasty shared images of the twins, John and Frank, and John's son shared papers from his father's service in Chapel Hill, just months before he passed away at age 100. Much appreciation goes to Bill Hamilton, Rear Admiral Tom Hamilton's son, and to his cousin Betty Hamilton Buscy, who invited me to her beautiful estate in Virginia, where we reminisced for hours during a thunderstorm about Chapel Hill and her father's invaluable contributions to naval aviation. These conversations inspired a succession of miracles, resurrecting a fraternity of cadets and baseball players who stayed in touch long after the war. One of those discoveries was Sarah Pletts, daughter of Ted Williams's roommate at Everett Dormitory, who shared a *LIFE* magazine image of the former cadets having lunch in 1952, illustrating the most enduring vestige of Pre-Flight training—friendship.

Gratitude is due to my dear friend Ivan Fleser, who put me on that rambling old bus with his teammates as it crisscrossed North Carolina backroads in a heat wave with players sleeping and singing and cramming for exams. As a former baseball coach, a community volunteer, and a teacher and counselor who helped many students blaze a better path in life, Ivan is a person that every kid in America should know. Also, a thank you to his daughter Debbie, who offered her prayers and support in my journey to capture her father's rare story in Chapel Hill.

When I finished this book, there were only 45 living major-league veterans who served in World War II. Two human landmarks of baseball reside in Texas. Eddie Robinson's memories not only placed me back in Chapel Hill and McClure Field, where he trained at Naval Station Norfolk, he explained how a trade in a manager's office can fulfill a dream or break a player's heart for life. I am also extremely grateful to Dr. Bobby Brown, who spent half a day with me at his home in Fort Worth, casually sharing stories about Cloudbusters legends like Ted Williams, Johnny Sain, and Buddy Hassett, who were his good friends.

There were people who pulled back the veil to the world of Pre-Flight, when so much of this history has been scattered over the past 75 years. Rear Admiral Jerry Holland reflected back to the Iowa Pre-Flight base, when he was recruited by aviation cadet John Glenn to be the base's mascot and batboy for the baseball team. A special thank you goes to Betty Brewer Pettersen, Kidd Brewer's daughter, who rode a pony around Chapel Hill during the war. Betty entrusted me with a precious box of materials from her father's estate that unveiled some of his most redeeming work. Knowing that 90 percent of America's professional baseball players served in this war in some capacity, the psychology of this story is significant. Family members of players, such as Harry "Wildfire" Craft's niece, Addie Beth Craft Denton, a Dallas psychologist, helped me understand the mindset of these players who surrendered their best playing years to the war, and how future generations have been shaped by that sacrifice.

I was fortunate to interview former players from different eras who changed the sport for a new generation including Joe Grzenda, Don Saine, and the University of North Carolina at Chapel Hill's coach Mike Fox, a modern coach with an old soul who helped me rekindle that lost spirit of the Old Leaguer.

There were the people who trained on other Pre-Flight bases or attended school in Chapel Hill during the war. Frank Selwyn Johnson, who trained at St. Mary's, rides his motorcycle in his 90s; Ernest Frankel, a Marine Corps Colonel who became a well-known television producer, described Eleanor Roosevelt when she ambled down the stairs at University President Graham's house in 1942; and my friends at Carolina Meadows, Charles Kahn, Joseph Mengel, and the late Bruce Martindale, took me back to the campus at the height of the war when moonshiners lurked in the woods.

From early drafts, many people helped me find my voice, including Gary Rasp, a talented Austin scribe with a deep knowledge of baseball who gave me the courage and counsel to find the words to tell my father's story. Bill Nowlin, one of Ted's most trusted biographers, met with me in Cambridge, Massachusetts, and encouraged me to follow my instincts to capture Ted and the team, just as I saw them.

On that journey, I met many people who opened the doors to baseball history: Chris Holaday, Lee Pace, Lee Gliarmis, Todd Mealy, Wilbur Jones, Jim Bayless, Jack Hilliard, Jack Betts, Janis Carter, Robert Epting, Donald Rominger, C. Paul Rogers, William Holloway, Michael Gelfand, the late Dave Rosenfield, Calvin Morrow, and Ann Trevor and her colleagues at NARA. Archivists shared Pre-Flight materials from the Iowa, St. Mary's, Del Monte, and Georgia bases; and Lori Miller pulled players' files from National Personnel Records Center in St. Louis, shaking out medical charts, flight test scores, and records that evaluated these players when they learned new sports like football, boxing, and swimming. In Chapel Hill, my friend Clark Smith helped me locate the gatekeepers of university athletics including a host of coaches and baseball fans who saw the Cloudbusters play. Members of the staff at the university's alumni affairs office were also extremely generous with their resources, including Paul Gardner and David Brown, who piqued curiosities with his sweeping account of the Navy Pre-Flight School in 1995.

Key to this work is the brilliant Tommy Lasater, who helped me turn the archives upside down at Wilson Library, locating major-league players and their former addresses through handwritten logs, telephone books, and housing records in Chapel Hill. What began as nine major-league Cloudbusters mushroomed into roughly 25 professional players who trained at Chapel Hill. The staff at Wilson Library show why the university is one of the top institutions of higher learning and research in the nation, helping me locate rare images and papers when I was unable to travel from Texas. They include Stephen Fletcher, Patrick Cullom, Keith Longiotti, Jason Tomberlin, Jennifer Coggins, Sarah Carrier, and many others who have meticulously preserved thousands of Pre-Flight documents at the library. What a treasure you have preserved. Also, I am indebted to "Val" Lauder, the feature-writing teacher and former reporter at the *Chicago Daily News*, who inspired me to put my words on paper as a journalism student at Howell Hall. I also appreciate the insights of Dr. Ken Zogry, PhD, author and university historian, who helped me gain a perspective on the campus during the war years.

The staff of dozens of museums and archives around the country brought this material to my fingertips, including The Chapel Hill Historical Society, volunteer archivists at the Pensacola Naval Museum, and archivists at the United States Naval Academy. Toni Kiser, from the New Orleans World War II History Museum, provided Johnny Pesky's humorous oral history interview about his days in the Navy; and Sarah Coffin, curator for the Red Sox museum at Fenway Park, where Ted's V-5 aviation wings are held, shared rare images of Williams from his early Navy days. People associated with the National Baseball Hall of Fame and Museum in Cooperstown were instrumental in the development of this narrative including my go-to archivist Matt Rothenberg, manager of the Giamatti Research Center at the Hall of Fame; the museum's former curator, Ted "Williams" Spencer; and the Hall of Fame's former president, Dale Petroskey, who explained the gravity of what it takes to become a major-leaguer. If you want to hear my father tell this story in his own colorful words on audio, Dr. Jorge Iber and Monte Monroe, chief archivists with the Southwest Collection at Texas Tech University, interviewed him six months before he died to capture the Cloudbusters' tale on tape at the National College Baseball Hall of Fame. As his lungs were failing, they were worried that my father would not be able to speak and had to cut him off after the one-and-one-half-hour interview.

There are important sidebar stories to the Chapel Hill Pre-Flight base that deserve historic notice. Alex Albright is a passionate historian who wrote the only account of the B-1 Cloudbusters Band, a moving account about the African American musicians who broke the color barrier in the Navy. Thanks to Alex and other North Carolina historians, the band's legacy is honored with an historic marker located near their dormitory at the intersection of West Franklin and Roberson Streets in Chapel Hill.

On a personal note, thank you to family, friends, and the good people of my hometown of Hickory, North Carolina, who rallied around my father in those final years when he ached to relive the old days of baseball including Bill Seitz, Jack MacMillan, Nate Bachman, his nurses, former baseball players, coaches, and people at the Hickory Crawdads minor-league ballpark; friends he encountered at banks, the club, the YMCA, grocery stores, dry cleaners, and restaurants; our long-time neighbors; and a special thank you to the strangers who put shiny pennies on his grave.

Last, thank you to my family, who supported me on this long journey, including my husband, Russell, a voracious reader and amateur historian, my sister Carson, and my mother, Marianna, the funniest, most courageous woman I have ever known. And of course, a note of gratitude goes to my faithful tribe of friends who lifted my spirits and encouraged me to keep writing when I lost faith and had to feel my way through the dark to capture this story.

This is a generational story. When my grandfather, James P. Raugh Sr., a Naval Academy graduate and businessman, re-enlisted in the Navy after two rejections, he unwittingly exposed his son to one of the most impactful athletic training programs of all time. Though I scarcely remember my grandfather, I was fortunate to inherit the privilege of telling the story about his service and commitment to country that began on the morning that Pearl Harbor was bombed.

My late father, Jim Raugh, is an example of an innocent kid who experienced something truly extraordinary, and I hope there is something to be learned from his bittersweet journey. As an end note, I'd like to recognize the millions of people who are doing their part to keep the pastime of baseball alive—ticket sellers, groundskeepers, concessionaires, umpires, and the coaches and volunteers who put a bat in kids' hands and send them to the plate to see if they might be the next Ted Williams. Ted took up baseball as a lonely latchkey kid who practiced his swing in the moonlight, aiming to become the greatest hitter who ever lived. Through this portrait of Ted as a rookie Pre-Flight cadet, I hope that readers will recognize how his curious mind and his work ethic helped him prove that the impossible is indeed possible.

# BIBLIOGRAPHY

## Books

Albright, Alex. *The Forgotten First: B-1 and the Integration of the Modern Navy*. Fountain, NC: R. A. Fountain, 2013.

Appel, Marty. *Pinstripe Empire: The New York Yankees from Before Babe to After the Boss*. New York: Bloomsbury USA, 2012.

Benjey, Tom. *Glorious Times: Adventures of the Craighead Naturalists*. Missoula: The University of Montana Press, 2016.

Bradlee, Ben Jr. *The Kid: The Immortal Life of Ted Williams*. New York: Little, Brown and Company, 2013.

Carmichael, William Jr., Covington, Howard E., and Ellis, Marion A. *The North Carolina Century, Tar Heels Who Made a Difference, 1900–2000*. Chapel Hill: University of North Carolina Press, 2002.

Craighead, Frank, and Craighead, John. *Hawks in the Hand: Adventures in Photography and Falconry, Lyons and Buford*. Boston: Houghton Mifflin, 1997.

Crissey, Harrington E. Jr. *Athletes Away: A Selective Look at Professional Baseball Players in the Navy During World War II*. Philadelphia: Self-Published, 1984.

Davis, Seth. *Wooden: A Coach's Life*. New York: Times Books, 2014.

Ehle, John. *Dr. Frank: Life with Frank Porter Graham*. Chapel Hill: Franklin Street Books, 1993.

Fountain, Charles. *Sportswriter: The Life and Times of Grantland Rice.* New York: Oxford University Press, 1993.

Gelfand, Michael. *Tomorrow We Fly: A History of the United States Navy Pre-Flight School on the Campus of the University of Georgia.* Athens: University of Georgia, 1994.

Gilbert, Brother. *Young Babe Ruth: His Early Life and Baseball Career, from the Memoirs of Xavierian Brother.* Jefferson, NC: McFarland, 1999.

Halberstam, David. *The Teammates: A Portrait of a Friendship.* New York: Hyperion, 2003.

Holland, W. J. Jr. *The Navy.* Washington Yard: Hugh Lauter Levin, 2000.

Hurt, H. H. *Aerodynamics for Naval Aviators.* Los Angeles: NAVAIR, 1965.

Hyams, Joe. *Flight of the Avenger: George Bush at War.* San Diego, New York, London: Harcourt Brace, 1991.

Krammer, Arnold. *Nazi Prisoners of War in America.* New York: Stein & Day, 1979.

Linn, Ed. *Hitter: The Life and Turmoils of Ted Williams.* San Diego, New York, London: Harcourt, 1993.

Macht, Norman. *The Grand Old Man of Baseball: Connie Mack in His Final Years, 1932–1956.* Lincoln: University of Nebraska Press, 2015.

Marrs, K. Ray. *I Was There When the Earth Stood Still,* Bloomington, IN: 1st Book Library, 2003.

Miller, Stuart. *Good Wood: The Story of the Baseball Bat.* Chicago: ACTA Publications, 2011.

Montville, Leigh. *Ted Williams: The Biography of an American Hero.* New York: Doubleday, 2004.

Newton, Wesley Phillips, and Rea, Robert R. *Wings of Gold: An Account of Naval Aviation Training in World War II, The Correspondence of Aviation Cadet/Ensign Robert R. Rea.* Tuscaloosa: University of Alabama Press, 1987.

Nowlin, Bill. *Mr. Red Sox: The Johnny Pesky Story.* Cambridge: Rounder Books, 2004.

_____. *Ted Williams: A Tribute.* Indianapolis: Masters Press, 1997.

_____. *Ted Williams at War*. Burlington, MA: Rounder Books, 1997.

Nowlin, Bill, and Prime, Jim. *Ted Williams: The Pursuit of Perfection*. Champaign, IL: Sports Publishing, 2002.

Ogburn, William Fielding. *American Society in Wartime*. Chicago: University of Chicago Press, 1943.

Patterson, Ted. *Football in Baltimore: History and Memorabilia from Colts to Ravens*. Baltimore: Johns Hopkins University Press.

Rogers, Paul, and Robinson, Eddie. *Lucky Me*. Dallas: Southern Methodist University Press, 2011.

Scott, James. *The War Below: The Story of Three Submarines That Battled Japan*. New York: Simon & Schuster, 2014.

Shampoe, Clay, and Garrett, Thomas R. *Baseball in Norfolk*. Virginia: Arcadia, 2003.

Smelser, Marshall. *The Life That Ruth Built: A Biography*. Lincoln: University of Nebraska Press, 1975.

The United States Naval Institute. *The Physics of Aviation*. Annapolis, MD: The United States Naval Institute, 1942.

Tunney, Gene. *How I Became Naval Air Training Director of Physical Fitness*. Pittsburgh: Pittsburgh Press, 1942.

Van Loan, Charles Emmett. "The Good Old Wagon." In *The Collected Baseball Stories*, compiled by Trey Strecker, 199. Jefferson, NC: McFarland and Company, 2004.

Williams, Ted. *My Turn at Bat: The Story of My Life*. New York: Simon & Shuster, 1988.

Zogry, Kenneth Joel. *Print News and Raise Hell: The Daily Tar Heel and the Evolution of a Modern University*. Chapel Hill: University of North Carolina Press, 2018.

_____. *The University's Living Room: A History of the Carolina Inn*. Chapel Hill: University of North Carolina Press, 1999.

## Periodicals

*Alumni Review Magazine*
    December 29, 2006.
    May 1942.

*Asheville Citizen-Times*
 August 8, 1943.
 May 13, 1943.
 May 24, 1942.
Associated Press
 January 18, 1935.
 December 31, 1941.
 July 13, 1943.
 May 25, 1943.
 May 28, 1943.
 July 24, 1943.
 July 29, 1943.
 October 31, 1934.
Associated Press in *Altoona Tribune,* July 11, 1947.
Associated Press in *Asheville Citizen-Times,* May 13, 1943.
Associated Press in *Philadelphia Inquirer,* May 9, 1943.
*Baltimore Sun*
 June 6, 1943.
 May 9, 1943.
*Bremen Enquirer,* March 27, 1930.
*Call-Leader,* June 2, 1943.
*Carolina Alumni Review,* January 1974.
*Chapel Hill Weekly*
 June 30, 1944.
 November 13, 1942.
 November 2, 1945.
*Chicago Tribune*
 July 24, 1929.
 February 3, 1942.
*Cloudbuster*
 September 19, 1942.
 October 10, 1942.
 October 24, 1942.
 November 28, 1942.
 December 19, 1942.

January 1, 1943.

January 23, 1943.

March 13, 1943.

April 3, 1943.

May 1, 1943.

May 22, 1943.

May 29, 1943.

June 26, 1943.

June 5, 1943.

September 11, 1943.

February 2, 1945.

February 23, 1945.

July 27, 1945.

August 24, 1945.

October 3, 1945.

*Corsicana Daily Sun,* April 6, 1951.

*Daily Press, The,* May 16, 1943.

*Daily Tar Heel, The*

December 9, 1941.

January 14, 1942.

January 17, 1942.

January 21, 1942.

January 22, 1942.

February 28, 1942.

February 3, 1942.

March 26, 1942.

January 14, 1943.

July 1, 1943.

October 9, 1943.

April 11, 1944.

August 1, 1944.

*Daily Times-News,* June 1, 1943.

*Des Moines Register,* October 11, 1942.

*Des Moines Tribune,* July 19, 1943.

*Elmira Star Gazette,* September 21, 1958.

*Esquire*
   July, 1942.
   December, 1, 1942.
   September 1, 1943.
*Evening Capital, The,* May 6, 1943.
*Greensboro Daily News*
   April 2, 1916.
   August 16, 1943.
   July 17, 1943.
   July 16, 1943.
   August 2, 1943.
*Harris Telegraph,* July 20, 1943.
*Indianapolis Star,* February 1, 1942.
*Kokomo Tribune,* June 26, 1948.
*Lansing Journal,* February 2, 1942.
*Lansing State Journal,* May 24, 1953.
*Memories and Dreams,* Spring 2017.
*Miami Daily News-Record,* April 8, 1948.
*Morning Call,* June 7, 1942.
*Navyator,* May 22, 1943.
*News-Press Fort Myers,* May 10, 1995.
*New York Times, The*
   August 20, 1942.
   July 25, 1943.
   May 31, 1943.
*Our State Magazine,* April, 2015.
*Pittsburgh Post-Gazette*
   April 6, 1951.
   September 15, 1943.
*Portsmouth Herald*
   October 4, 1945.
   September 12, 1942.
*Raleigh News & Observer*
   April 1, 1943.
   July 11, 1943.

July 15, 1943.

June 27, 1943.

May 16, 1943.

May 23, 1943.

May 6, 1943.

*San Bernardino Sun,* December 5, 1942.

*Saturday Evening Post, The* May 29, 1943.

*Sporting News, The*

July 22, 1943.

June 10, 1943.

May 31, 1961.

*St. Cloud Times,* August 27, 1942.

*St. Louis Times,* December 30, 1941.

*Stars and Stripes (Middle East Cairo Edition),* August 6, 1943.

*State Magazine,* Spring 1942.

*Sunday Mirror,* September 30, 1973.

*The Michigan Alumnus,* November 7, 1942.

*The State Magazine*

February 27, 1943.

September 29, 1945.

*Valley Morning Star,* December 10, 1942.

*World War II Magazine,* May 2007.


## Articles

Abrahamson, Jesse. *New York Herald Tribune,* July 28, 1943.

Barrier, Smith. *Greensboro Daily Record,* August 2, 1943.

_____. *Greensboro Daily Record,* July 16, 1943.

_____. *Greensboro Daily Record,* July 19, 1943.

Barry, Fred. "Balata ball." *Boston Globe,* July 12, 1943.

_____. "Babe in locker room." *Boston Globe,* July 13, 1943.

Boney, F. N., and Doster, Gary L. "A University Goes to War: The Navy at the University of Georgia During World War II" *Georgia Historical Quarterly* LXXVI, no. 1 (Spring 1993).

Boswell, Thomas. "A President's Passion for Baseball." *Washington Post,* March 31, 1989.

Brown, David E. "The War Years." *Carolina Alumni Review,* September/October 1995.

Cantaneo, David. *Boston Herald,* April 14, 1986.

Carlton, Mike. *Philadelphia Inquirer,* December 2, 1973.

Chesworth, Jo. "A Quest for Survival." *Penn State Magazine.*

Croke, Vicki Constantine. *Washington Post,* November 11, 2007.

Daley, Arthur. "The Babe Comes Home." *New York Times,* July 28, 1943.

Daniel, Daniel M. *Baseball Magazine,* June 1945.

Danzig, Allison. "Greatest football pageant." *New York Times,* November 26, 1936.

Dawson, James P. "The Indians and Boudreau." *New York Times,* July 29, 1943.

Decker, James H. "They Have to be Tough to Win." *Athletic Journal* 23, 1943.

Devlin, Sherry. "Think like mountain." *Missoulian,* September 17, 1988.

Egan, Dave. "Longest, hardest homerun of Ted's career." *Boston Record,* May 23, 1942.

Fraley, Gerry. "Ward and Knute Rockne." *Dallas Morning News,* May 10, 1995.

Frankel, Ernie. "The Finest College Airport in the Nation." *Daily Tar Heel,* May 10, 1942.

Fullerton, Hugh. "Norfolk recruiting machine." *Associated Press,* February 8, 1943.

Gildea, William. "The Ultimate Closer." *Washington Post,* October 25, 2004.

Goldwater, Bob. "Ration-League and rain at May 11th game." *Daily Tar Heel,* May 12, 1943.

Graffis, Herb. "The Sports Scene." *Esquire,* August 1942.

Hamilton, T. "Football in the Navy." *The Official NCAA 1942 Football Guide,* 1942.

Harper, John. "Hassett Keeps on Truckin' Pre-Pension Yank Labors Away at 83." *New York Daily News,* February 6, 1995.

Holaday, Chris., *Baseball in North Carolina's Piedmont,* Acadia, 2003, p. 33.

Hawes, Gayle. "Titanic battle of stars." *Honolulu Advertiser*, September 25, 1945.

Horner, Jack. "Former Ace Turns Pro." *Durham Herald*, June 15, 1957.

———. "Sports Corner." *Durham Herald*, June 16, 1957.

Jordan, Pat. "In a World of Windmills, John Sain." *Sports Illustrated*, May 8, 1972.

Joyce, Nick. "Spotting the Enemy." *American Psychological Association Monitor on Psychology* 41, Number 3 (2010), 24.

Komisaruk, Paul. "Airport." *Daily Tar Heel*, March 9, 1941.

Lake, Austen. "Pesky's analysis of Ted." *Boston Evening American*, January 11, 1952.

Laurence, Charles. "San Jacinto and Bush." *The Telegraph*, February 6, 2017.

Lenger, John. "Conquests of the Air." *Harvard Magazine*, May–June 2003.

Leonard, Teresa. "John Glenn and Morehead." *Raleigh News & Observer*, April 6, 2017.

Malaney, Jack. "Ted's performance." *Boston Post*, July 31, 1943.

Marsico, Joe, and Maurer, Joe. "Stirnweiss's death." *Journal News*, September 19, 1958.

Muir, Malcolm Jr. "The Human Tradition in the WWII Era." *Scholarly Resources Books*, no. 8 (2001).

Nelson, Gordon. "Air show." *Quincy Historic Society* Volume, no. 4 (Spring 1981).

Newman, Zipp. "No Bonus Raugh." *Birmingham News*, [Illegible], 1959.

O'Gara, Frank. "Pre-Flight miracle." *Philadelphia Inquirer*, November 6, 1942.

O'Leary, Josh. "Seahawks and Bierman." *The University of Iowa Alumni Magazine*, November 2017.

Papalus, Anthony. "Lil' Rastus Cobb's Good Luck Charm." *Baseball Research Journal*.

Pleasants, Julian M. "A Question of Loyalty: Frank Porter Graham and the Atomic Energy Commission." *The North Carolina Historical Review* 69, no. 4 (1992).

Radford, Rich. "Norfolk players." *Virginia Pilot,* July 24, 2011.

Rawlings, Wade. "Kidd and high school education." *Raleigh News & Observer,* November 26, 1991.

Reed, William F. "Bear standing behind players." *Sports Illustrated,* September 19, 1994.

Reichler, Joe. "Ruth retires jersey." Associated Press story in *Burlington Free Press,* June 14, 1948.

Rennie, Rud. "Yanklands." *New York Herald,* July 29, 1943.

Rice, Grantland. "Pre-Flight training miracle." *North American Newspaper Alliance,* December 6, 1942.

Rominger, Donald. "From Playing Field to Battleground." *Journal of Sports History,* no. 3 (1985), 256.

Royal, Chip. "Tries His Hand at Managing." Associated Press, July 29, 1943.

Sandomir, Richard. "Yankees' Last Trip to R.F.K. Ended with Fan Rampage." *New York Times,* June 16, 2006.

Schmidt, Ray. "The Greatest Army–Navy." *College Football Historical Society Newsletter,* February 2004.

Schudel, Matt. "Machiavellian approach and Sain." *Washington Post,* November 9, 2006.

Schultz, Bonnie. "Emerson Field." *Daily Tar Heel,* October 13, 1967.

Segar, Charles. "Yanks Bow to Tribe; Ruth Bats in Fund Tilt." *New York Daily Mirror,* July 29, 1943.

Shearer, Lee. "Dooley and Split-T." *Athens Banner Herald,* January 5, 2015.

Stafford, Dale. "Pre-Flight training." *Detroit Free Press,* November 8, 1942.

Stancill, Jane. "It Was Wartime." *Carolina Alumni Review,* Fall 1987.

Sullivan, William. "Eckersall." *Daily Tar Heel,* May 28, 1942.

Sullivan, William H. Jr. "The Naval Aviation Physical Training Program." *The Journal of Health and Physical Education* 14, no. 1 (1943), 3, 6–7, 54, 56.

Taylor, Larry. "Ted Williams." *The Retired Officer Magazine,* November 1999.

Thompson, Wright. "The Greatest Hitter Who Ever Lived On." *ESPN The Magazine,* May 5, 2015.

United Press. "Yanklands players." July 17, 1943.

United Press. "Johnny Pesky Still Playing Ball, But B'lieve Me, Mister, That Ain't All." *Akron Beacon Journal,* June 27, 1943.

Vellante, John. "Ted refuses to flunk pilots." *Boston Globe,* July 28, 2002.

Vergakis, Brock. "Norfolk and Robinson." *Virginia Pilot,* June 30, 2017.

Ward, Arch. "V-5 success." *Chicago Tribune,* March 29, 1942.

Webb, Chet. "In the Realm of Sports." *Call-Leader* (Elwood, Indiana), April 6, 1942, p. 2.

Wellman, Paul I. "Combat Without Weapons." *Athletic Journal,* June 27, 1942.

Williams, Ted. "John Glenn tribute." *Boston Globe,* June 17, 1962.

Wineka, Mark. "Ford and Ruth, roommate at Pre-Flight." *Salisbury Post,* May 18, 2015.

Wittels, David G. "You Are Not as Smart as You Can Be." *Saturday Evening Post,* April 17, 1948.

Woolner, Frank. "Hunter Orange: Your Shield for Safety." *Field & Stream,* October 1960.

## Op-eds

"Analysis of Ted Williams baseball activity and games played during WWII and Korea, with most significant play in Chapel Hill." Zwald, Duff. SABR research of *Honolulu Star Bulletin* and *Honolulu Advertiser* for Bill Nowlin.

"Babe Tires Fast." Associated Press, July 29, 1943.

"Basil Lamar Sherrill Obituary." *News & Observer,* March 25, 2017.

*Boston Daily Record, Boston Globe,* and *Boston Traveler,* July 13, 1943, and poet laureate Dick Flavin's article, "The Day Ted and Babe Squared Off" that ran in Red Sox program in the summer of 2000.

"Defense, Alumni—and the University." *Carolina Alumni Review, Mid-summer,* July 1941.

"Former Tiger Hurler." *Shelby Daily Star,* October 16, 1968.

"Gets a Headache." Associated Press, July 29, 1943.

"Harold Irving 'Doc' Ewen Obituary." *Boston Globe.* October 22, 2015.

"In the Service." *The Sporting News,* February 18, 1943.

"In the Service." *The Sporting News,* March 19, 1942, p. 12.

"Naval Flying Cadets Will Work Victory Garden on 35-Acre-Plot." *Athens Banner Herald,* June 11, 1943.

"Naval Pre-Flight School." *News and Observer,* May 18, 1952.

"Pre-Flight Cadets Learn to Swim in War Conditions." *Athens Banner-Herald,* July 4, 1943.

"Reference to student Lou Finger," Finnegan, Herb. *Boston Sunday Advertiser* and *Boston American,* no date available.

"Roly Poly Pilot." *The Sporting News,* August 5, 1943.

"Shortwaves." *St. Louis Post-Dispatch,* July 24, 1943.

"The 'Gray Ladies.'" *Chapel Hill Weekly,* May 14, 1943.

"The Surrender." 1945 *Daily Tar Heel* story.

"War Relief Society Meeting." *Chapel Hill Weekly,* May 7, 1943.

"What good is them one base knockers? Three of them guys have got to hit safe to get one run. Give me the guy that can slap the ball against them outfield walls." Salsiger, Harry. *Detroit News* story in *Stars and Stripes,* February 17, 1943.

## Additional Sources

BUPERS telegram from Chief of Navy Personal to Lieutenant Commander C. S. Appleby, Aide to BUPERS, Chapel Hill, 1943.

Chapel Hill Naval Aviation Physical Training Record Card. According to Williams medical records, he received a smallpox vaccination on May 15, 1943.

*Chapel Hill Telephone Directory.* 1942–1944.

*Charter of Incorporation.* Oakridge Institute of Nuclear Studies, President's Office Records.

Collectables: Yanklands scorecard with handwritten number lists Ted as number 39.

Colt Stadium press release. Harry Craft and Cincinnati Reds. 1962.

Comptroller's Papers 1941–1945, Box 6, Pre-Flight correspondence.

Congressman Gerald R. Ford Jr., press release, 1968.

Conversations with Ted Williams admirers. Interviewed by Anne R. Keene.

Correspondence, June 5, 1942, recommendation letter for USN Aviation Training Selection Board.

Correspondence, June 9, 1942, Hoover High letter of recommendation.

Death records. Ancestry.com.

DeWitt Diary, "Diary, I'm Doing Graduate Work in the Navy," by Lieutenant (j.g.) DeWitt A. Portal, USNR. p. 7.

Dick Hamilton's family records and short story shared with author, 2017.

Don Freeman Official Website. https://donfreeman.info.

Donald Kepler's personal speech titled "Survival," from daughter's files. No date. Original speech.

Draft Pre-Flight Training plan delivered in December 1941.

Engraved advertisement certificate 1930 of Bromo Building in downtown Baltimore.

Family letters, written memorial honoring Pierce Oliver Brewer by sister Faith Brewer Laursen, November 28, 1991. Materials provided by Brewer's daughter, Betty Brewer Pettersen.

Flight grading report, Naval Aviation records, from as noted from September 11, 1943 through late October. "Naval Aviation Records." United States Navy. September–October 1943.

Hamilton, Emmie. "Second Fiddle to a Pigskin." *Family Scrapbook*. February 1984.

Head of Physical Training Department to Director of Aviation Training, n.d. Memo, Chapel Hill player records.

History.com.

June Friest, 1943 letters.

Kepler copy of Donald Kepler's stump speech delivered to survival training students, Kepler family records. Didato, Victoria. "Survival Training." Undated.

Kepler family picture shared with author. Kepler Family Collection.

Kidd Brewer's handwritten application to United States Naval Reserves. Tettenton family records, 1942.

Letter U.S. NAS Bunker Hill, Indiana, memo "Request to be dropped from Flight Training," signed by John M. Paveskovich, AvCad, V-5, USNR. December 4, 1943.

May 22, 1942, Naval Aviation Cadet Selection Board, Boston, Massachusetts. Report of Medical Examination.

Memories by Doc Ewen, 2003. http://www.nrao.edu/archives/Ewen /ewen.

NAS Atlanta, April 30, 1945 record rating by Commander Wm. H. White.

Naval Air Primary Training Command to C.E. Smith Bureau of Naval Personnel Papers. National Archives and Records Administration.

Naval Aviation Cadet Selection Board Senior Member, NACSB, The Chief of Naval Personnel to 1942. Memo. From National Archives.

Naval Aviation Cadet Training Transcript. 1944.

Naval Aviation Records–Grades for Amherst. From National Archives and Records Administration NARA.

NCpedia, https://www.ncpedia.org/biography/carmichael-william.

Notes, V-5 1943 vaccinations described by John Sain, applied to all cadets, including Williams, who had same vaccinations administered in stages.

*Office of the Vice President for Finance of the University of North Carolina (System) Records, 1923–1972, #40011.* University Archives.

Paramount newsreel made films of cadets in July, 1944.

*Physical Fitness Correspondence*, date illegible. NARA, Tunney File.

Physical Fitness Correspondence, Records Group 24, Command file, BuAero Folder.

Scott Carpenter wrestling reference from his website *Mercury Astronaut*, Scott Carpenter.com.

Sheet from Howard Hamilton's personal papers, with outline on notebook paper outlining staff, salary, structure for training.

State of Ohio death records, Hamilton, December 8, 1968.

Stories passed down from Raugh family history.

TedWilliams.com.

The Theory of Flight classes, notations from diaries, scrapbooks and images from Chapel Hill and St. Mary's.

The World Behind the Headlines, in *US Pre-Flight School Scrapbook*. U.S. Navy. 1942.

Thomas Hamilton oral history interview conducted by E. B. Kitchen, CDR., USN (Ret). April 21, 1978. From U.S. Naval Institute.

Tom Burlin Player Questionnaire Collection, Baseball Hall of Fame.

Tunney and remarks at Catholic Men's Luncheon Club of Birmingham, Alabama, February 17, 1942.

U.S. Navy Pre-Flight School hiking map and images of cadets in Carrboro.

U.S. Navy Press Release, date unavailable, 1942.

University Archives. *James E. Wadsworth Papers, 1942–1976*. Collection Number 05075, Box 1: Folder 3.

University of North Carolina Pre-Flight Photography archives.

University of South Carolina, FOX Movietone film archive.

V-5 Indoctrination Reporting and Departure, Detachment of Stationed Officers: The Cloudbuster (U.S. Navy Pre-Flight School, published in Chapel Hill 1942–1945. In the North Carolina Collection, Call Number: FFC378 UXC1).

Walt Harrington, George Bush, WWII Navy Pilot, www.History.net.

Weather according to the National Ocean and Atmospheric Association for week of May 6, 1943.

White House correspondence. Roosevelt, Franklin Delano. Franklin Delano Roosevelt to President Graham, Feb. 9, 1942. Letter from Wilson Library.

Williams's personnel file in Chapel Hill; his official V-5 service number recorded by the Naval Aviation Cadet Selection Board, Suffolk County, Boston, Massachusetts, on May 22, 1942, was 705-53-11.

World War II Distinguished Flying Cross database.

Yanklands game scorecard, handwritten notes with jersey numbers.

## Interviews

Aiello, Frank. Frank Aiello to Casualty Branch of the Adjunct General's Office, 1945.

Ayn Rand's 'The Fountainhead is Published.'" Jewish Women's Archive. May 6, 1943. Accessed https://jwa.org/thisweek/may/06/1943/ayn -rand.

Baker, Mary Lane. *"The Sky's the Limit, The University of North Carolina and the Chapel Hill Communities' Response to the Establishment of the United States Naval Pre-Flight School During World War II."* Master's thesis, University of North Carolina, 1976.

Billinger, Robert D. Jr. "Enemies and Friends," From the Tar Heel Junior Historian *Association*, NC Museum of History.

Brewer, Kidd. Family records and personal letters provided by Betty Brewer Tettenton.

Brown, Bobby. Interview by Anne R. Keene. January 11, 2016.

Bryan, G.N. G.N. Bryan to Naval Aviation Selection Board for John Sain. August 15, 1942.

BUPERS records, 1942–1945.

Busey, Betty Hamilton. Interview by Anne R. Keene. July 2017.

Busey, Betty Hamilton. Interview by Anne R. Keene. June 19, 2017.

*Camp Davis vs. North Carolina 1942 Pre-Flight Naval Aviation Program.* Athletic Associations of U.S. Navy Pre-Flight Schools. 1942.

*Camp Davis vs. Pre-Flight Football Program.* Athletic Associations of U.S. Navy Pre-Flight Schools. October 16, 1943.

*Camp Lejeune vs. Chapel Hill Pre-Flight Program.* Athletic Associations of U.S. Navy Pre-Flight Schools. 1945.

Carmichael, William D. Carmichael to Commander Tom Hamilton, 1942.

*Chapel Hill Pre-Flight Yearbook.* Merin-Baliban Studios, Philadelphia: United States Navy. 1942–1943.

"College Baseball Hall of Fame oral history interview with Jim Raugh conducted by professor Jorge Iber 2013-05-14." From Texas Tech University, *Southwest Collection General Oral Histories.*

Compton, Buford. Buford Compton to Naval Aviation Cadet Board, 1942. Johnny Sain letter. Of recommendation, August 18, 1942.

Craighead, John Jr. Interviewed by Anne R. Keene on multiple occasions. July–August 2016.

Daugherty, Pat. Interview by Anne R. Keene. June 18, 2017.

Death certificate for Eugene Victor Louis Aiello, April 24, 1943. U.S. Navy Hollywood, Florida, for Coral Gables Branch. Bureau of Naval Personnel. Copy in possession of St. Louis, Naval Archives.

Deezen, Eddie. "Babe Ruth's Final Years." Mental Floss. August 6, 2012. http://mentalfloss.com/article/31471/babe-ruths-final-years.

Didado, Victoria Kepler. Multiple interviews by Anne R. Keene and correspondence, 2017.

Edward Deutchman oral history interviewer conducted by Del Monte Pre-Flight History Project in Del Monte, CA, 2011-05-02.

Elger August Berkley oral history interview conducted by Del Monte Pre-Flight History Project, in Del Monte, CA, 2005-07-08. From *Veterans History Project Oral History*.

Fleser, Ivan. Interview by Anne R. Keene. April 11, 2016

Fleser, Ivan. Interview by Anne R. Keene. April 25, 2016.

Fox, Mike. Interview by Anne R. Keene. July 18, 2017.

Frankel, Ernest. Interview by Anne R. Keene. August 4, 2017.

Grzenda, Joe. Interview by Anne R. Keene. July 11, 2017.

Hamilton, Thomas. Thomas Hamilton to Captain Radford, 1942. From U.S. Department of the Navy, Navy Historical Center, Naval Archives, Washington, D.C.

Harkness, John R. John R. Harkness to—1942. Letter.

Holland, Jerry. Interview by Anne R. Keene. November 21, 2016.

Holloway, William. Unpublished manuscript.

Jeffries, Ray. Interview by Anne R. Keene. July 8, 2017.

Johnny Pesky oral history interview conducted on 2007-11-08, at National World War II Museum, New Orleans.

Johnson, Frank Selwyn. Interview by Anne R. Keene. September 17, 2015.

Kahn, Charles Howard, and Mengel, Joseph Warren. Interview by Anne R. Keene. July 20, 2017.

Kepler, George Don Jr. and family interviewed by Anne R. Keene. June 17, 2017.

Kepler, Richard. Interview by Anne R. Keene. December 6, 2017.

Kepler, Rob. Interview by Anne R. Keene. June and August 14, 2017.

Lee, Richard. "How Much Effect Does Temperature Have on Home Runs?" Diamond Kinetics. March 10, 2016. https://diamondkinetics .com/how-much-effect-does-temperature-have-on-home-runs.

"Legend and Lore." Fitchipedia. 2017. http://wiki.pygmyisland.net /fitchipedia.

*Legends and Legacies: Ted Williams.* HBO Sports, July 15, 2009.

Martindale, Bruce. Interview by Anne R. Keene. May 28, 2017.

Martindale, Bruce. Interview by Anne R. Keene. November 20, 2015

Mitchell, Burley B. "Kidd Brewer Query." Interview by Anne R. Keene. July 23, 2017.

Morris, Taylor. Interview by Michael H. Gelfand. Tomorrow We Fly. June 5, 1994.

Morrow, Calvin. Interview by Anne R. Keene. December 5, 2017.

*Navy Regulation Manual for Incoming Cadets.* 1942. From University of North Carolina at Chapel Hill. *Wilson Library Papers.*

O. J. Fergeson to Naval Aviation Selection Board, August 18, 1942. Letter of recommendation for John Sain.

Pesky, David, and Pesky, Alison. Interview by Anne R. Keene. June 14, 2017.

Petroskey, Dale, former Baseball Hall of Fame president, Dallas, Texas, June 2, 2017.

Pletts, Sarah. Interview by Anne R. Keene. January 6, 2018.

Pletts, Sarah. Interview by Anne R. Keene. January 8, 2018.

Raugh, James P. Sr. 1942–1945. Memo and personal letters.

Rea, Robert. Interview by Michael H. Gelfand. *Tomorrow We Fly.* June 21, 1994.

Records of the College for War Training, 1940–1945 (#40074) in the University Archives, University of North Carolina at Chapel Hill.

Records of the Dept. of Naval Science, 1940–1943; 1962–1997 (#40083) in the University Archives, University of North Carolina at Chapel Hill.

Robinson, Eddie. Telephone interview, May 15, 2017.

Rominger, Donald W. Jr. "The Impact of the United States Government's Sports and Physical Training Policy on Organized Athletics During World War II." PhD dissertation, Oklahoma State University, 1976.

Roosevelt, Franklin D. "Executive Order 8989 Establishing the Office of Defense Transportation." December 18, 1941.

Saine, Don. Interview by Anne R. Keene. April 26, 2017.

Sanders, John. "Del Monte Historian." Interview by Anne R. Keene. September 6, 2017.

Smallwood, Irwin. Interview by Anne R. Keene. June 26, 2017.

Spencer, Ted. Interview by Anne R. Keene. June 16, 2017.

*St. Mary's Yearbook 1945*, created by members of the committee in charge of the "History of the U.S. Navy Pre-Flight School."

*The Aviation Sports Program in the U.S. Navy Pre-Flight Training Schools.* 1944. From United States Navy Bureau of Aeronautics.

"The War at Home." PBS, September 2007. Accessed http://www.pbs .org/thewar/at_home.htm.

Thomas Hamilton oral history interview conducted by E. B. Kitchen, CDR., USN (Ret). April 21, 1978. From U.S. Naval Institute.

Thuot, Clifford. Interview by Michael H. Gelfand. *Tomorrow We Fly*, March 31, 1994.

Thurman, Abe. Interview by Anne R. Keene. April 23, 2016.

*U.S. Navy Pre-Flight Registration Log May 21, 1943.* Handwritten records. Wilson Library Holdings.

University correspondence, where a few officials loosely mention "keen competition from one or two Eastern universities" in papers, but no specific dates or documents identify specific universities.

*V-5 Association Constitution of Bylaws of the V-5 Association of America.* 1947. From U.S. Naval Academy.

Vautravers, James. "Rating Website Champions of 1926 Army-Navy Football Game." TipTop 25.com.

Williams, Claudia. Interview by Anne R. Keene. November 6, 2017.

Williams, Claudia. Interview by Anne R. Keene. December 6, 2017.

## Tours of Historic Sites

Auction houses and estate sales

Boston and Fenway Park

Burlington, North Carolina, ballparks, former sites of parks and mills to trace walking routes

Carrboro hiking trails and Chapel Hill, North Carolina

Cooperstown, New York, and the Hall of Fame Museum and Archives

Duke University Archives

Durham Bulls Park and Downtown Durham, train stations, bus depots

Gloucester, Massachusetts

Greensboro War Memorial Stadium

Haverford, Pennsylvania

Hickory, North Carolina, stadiums and ballparks and cemeteries

Horace Williams Airfield, Chapel Hill

Maritime Museum of San Diego

National Naval Aviation Museum, Pensacola, Florida

Naval Shipyard Washington, D.C.

Pearl Harbor, Hawaii

Penn State and State College, Pennsylvania

Pine Grove Mills, Tussey Mountain

The National Museum of the Pacific War, Fredericksburg, Texas

The University of North Carolina at Chapel Hill archives at The Louis Round Wilson Library

Wrigley Field

Yankee Stadium

# PHOTO CREDITS

# INDEX